WITHDRAWN
UTSA LIBRARIES

D0149632

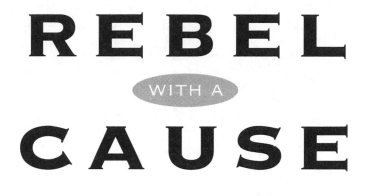

REBEL

WITH A

CAUSE

REBEL

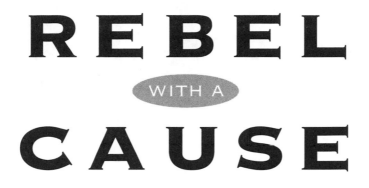

WITH A

CAUSE

THE ENTREPRENEUR WHO CREATED THE UNIVERSITY OF PHOENIX AND THE FOR-PROFIT REVOLUTION IN HIGHER EDUCATION

JOHN SPERLING

John Wiley & Sons, Inc.

New York • Chichester • Weinheim • Brisbane • Singapore • Toronto

Contents

1

Lessons

I have been successful in business—very successful. My essential metier, however, has been, and is, stimulating and enabling personal transformation and social reform. The reason for these interests will become evident as you read about my personal/company history. The typical American success story no longer begins with birth in a backwoods log cabin, but mine does. And that is only the first on a long list of anomalies in my life.

The money I've made notwithstanding, I am an unintentional entrepreneur and an accidental CEO. The company I founded in 1972 with $26,000 in hard-earned savings now has a market value close to $3 billion. This stroke of good fortune occurred after a largely misspent youth, dutiful but undistinguished military service, a graduate education that went on far too long simply because I had nothing better to do, and a lackluster academic career (except for the effectiveness of my teaching), that led me to delay finding my calling until the age of 39. Even then, the calling I found was not business—it was union organizing.

I did not become an entrepreneur until the age of 52. I created my first company with no thought for building a business, per se, but merely as a way to preserve an educational innovation from being destroyed by a small-minded bureaucracy. I had designed a program specifically for working adults that would allow them to earn a degree in the same amount of time it took full-time students on campus. Because this challenged many of the sacred tenets of academe, it was met with hostility bordering on rage.

The depth of opposition I encountered made it clear to me that creating a new, independent structure was necessary for the survival of my ideas, but even the decision to establish my new venture as for-profit—the ultimate apostasy in academe—still had nothing to do with business. In fact, as a left-leaning academic in a word culture, I was not only ignorant of business, I was hostile to it. I had recently been voted out of the presidency and control of a faculty union that I had built from almost nothing to one that was both important and prosperous. That experience cured me of my socialist sentiments in favor of nonprofits. I correctly perceived that the only sure way to maintain and enjoy the fruits of my labor was to create a venture I could control—it would be a for-profit corporation with majority control firmly in my hands.

This decision led me to found what would become the nation's largest and fastest-growing private university. It also gave me a fortune beyond my wildest imaginings. The company I began in 1972 became, in 1985, the Apollo Group, which went public in 1994 and now has operations in 35 states and, by distance education, all over the world. We have a total enrollment of over 120,000 students and an annual growth rate of 25 percent.

There is probably something to be learned from all this, but what I'm offering here is not a conventional how-to-succeed-in-business business biography. I have always found the lessons in such books rather tedious, and I have never taken one of them to heart. I have learned far more about how to conduct my business affairs from such novels as: *Tom Jones, Emma, Notes From the Underground, The Red and The Black, Death Comes to the Archbishop,* and *The Great Gatsby* than I ever have from reading a business book. So, if there are lessons to be learned from my life, I have left them simply embedded in the story. I trust the reader to have the good sense to find them and to choose from among them.

However, there is another, perhaps more important, reason for avoiding a didactic presentation of what life has taught me. A reader would be well advised to strenuously avoid most of the behaviors that made me successful. For example, if one chooses to "challenge authority," as I have done, but is not tough enough or shrewd enough to carry it off, he or she will be ill served by the advice. The same can be said for any number of my other characteristics—opportunism, indifference to the advice of experts, and lack of concern for what peers and authority figures think of me. Behaving this way in most companies would soon lead to a reputation as an unsavory character and, most likely, an invitation to work elsewhere.

The three behaviors that have served me best in my career as union organizer and entrepreneur are implacable opportunism, joy in conflict, and getting a thrill from taking risks—none of them a safe ride. Janis Joplin immortalized Kris Kristofferson's observation that "freedom's just another word for nothing left to lose," and that's the freedom that comes to those who, like me, embark on life with nowhere to go but up. Having nothing, and therefore nothing to lose, makes implacable opportunism a rational behavior, and, eventually, such behavior becomes habitual. It is also vastly easier to take risks when the upside is so much greater than the downside. And, if one is an opportunist who engages in risky behavior, conflict is inevitable, so you might as well enjoy it.

Even though I now have much to lose, I'm still an opportunist, still get into a lot of conflicts, and still find risky ventures exciting because they heighten my survival instincts, focus all my senses, and force me to perform at maximum effectiveness. It was this bet-the-farm behavior that helped to build the Apollo Group, but now that Apollo is a large organization with very effective controls, I have to exercise my penchant for risk elsewhere. Fortunately, because of Apollo's success, I can afford to.

I now invest my risk capital in ventures that truly interest me, but also ones that stand some chance of promoting positive social change. One of these is Seaphire International, an effort to expand the world's food supply by developing saltwater agriculture suitable for third-world countries. Another is the Kronos Group, Inc., a commercial venture into longevity research, linked with the delivery of age management therapy in a clinical setting. These are hardly areas free of controversy, but to truly indulge my passion for conflict, I've also adopted drug law reform as my political passion. Working with financier George Soros and insurance executive Peter Lewis, we have formed a troika dedicated to demilitarizing America's "War on Drugs," which, in a time of sharply declining crime rates, has filled our prisons to overflowing.

The final chapters of this book describe these current passions of my "golden years." The other chapters describe how I built the wealth that now allows me to invest in controversial socioeconomic and political ventures. Most of the people who read this book will never be in a position to create a company like Apollo, or have the resources to engage in the kind of activism I've undertaken. However, they might enjoy reading about how someone with a propensity to *bet the farm* managed to do so.

Obviously, my own success did not just happen suddenly at the age of 52. It did not begin with the formation of my original company, or with the academic research that was its intellectual foundation. It began at my birth and slowly took shape as my intelligence, personality, values, ideology, aesthetics, persona, and world view were shaped by the people, places, and experiences of a lifetime.

There is a Chinese proverb that states, "Pain teaches." The American variation offers, "That which does not kill us makes us stronger."

If these adages have any truth to them, then I was lucky, indeed, to be born into the Missouri Ozark hamlet of Freedom School House, in a cabin made of rough-cut logs, in the year of 1921. Or, as Roberto Benigni put it at the 1999 Academy Awards ceremony, my parents gave me the greatest gift of all—poverty.

Survival: Years 0 to 7

From birth to my 15th year was mostly a period of physical and psychic survival amid two quarreling parents, two quarreling brothers, and two long-suffering sisters—ideal preparation for the life of a contrarian and pioneer.

My first great physical trauma came at age four. The only source of heat in the house, other than a coal-burning kitchen stove, was a coal-burning potbellied stove that sat in the corner of the dining room and on this late afternoon, one of my older brothers was laying a fire. As I stood at his side watching, he opened the mica-windowed door, put in some crumpled up paper and then several scoops of coal from the coal scuttle. He had brought a small can of gasoline into the house when he brought in the coal and he now poured the gasoline over the coal. As he lit a match to throw into the stove, I looked directly into the stove to see the firelight. My next memory was lying on a narrow bed with my hands tied to either side. I lay there for nearly a month as my mother and sisters and brothers placed water-soaked cotton on the blisters that covered my face and hands. I remember hearing the doctor tell my mother something like, "Don't let him break the blisters. Keep them full of water by soaking them with wet cotton 24 hours a day. If you do this, the blisters will finally go down, the skin will reattach and he will have no scars." The doctor was right.

I had most of the childhood diseases—mumps, measles, whooping cough, chicken pox—but not scarlet fever. Sore throats were treated with cold cloths wrapped around my neck (I still use this remedy because it works); coughs were treated with spoons full of sugar dampened with kerosene; and croup was treated with a pot of hot water under a flannel blanket that was draped over a chair, with me kneeling on the floor and with my elbows on the chair. Constipation meant a dose of castor oil, and diarrhea was handled with tea and rice.

We always lived in tiny houses, the best having four original rooms—two bedrooms, a front room, a dining room, a built-on kitchen, and an outhouse—crowded with people, noise, and tensions. We ate mostly what came out of the garden, the henhouse, and two milk cows. Dinners included greens picked from dandelions and mustard added to the leaf lettuce and tomatoes from the garden, plus navy or lima beans cooked with salt pork. There was seldom any meat, but on most Sundays we had fried chicken.

In winter, the only greens were cabbage and brussels sprouts with potatoes and beans. As winter narrowed the available food, my mother's anxiety rose and her daily tirade against my feckless and almost always workless father was now punctuated with, "We're all going to starve to death; mark my words." It did not take too many "We're all going to starve," outbursts for fear to settle in. I didn't dare ask how the starvation would occur but, lying in bed at night, I ran through the scenarios of dwindling food and rising hunger. "Would I actually starve? No, I would beg for food from the neighbors, even strangers."

Perhaps in those moments an entrepreneur was born.

As the months passed with only minor diminution in the amount of food reaching the table, my fears subsided as my understanding of the hyperbole of marital warfare increased. Years later, I came to a better understanding of my mother's anxieties when she told me of

our family's departure when, in 1916, they abandoned their homestead in Cochise County, Arizona. The homestead was one of my
father's chronically unsuccessful initiatives in his attempts to provide
a better life for his family. The family had sold enough farm equipment to buy an old Model T, and loaded it with four children and
whatever else they could carry. As they were doing the final packing
for the trip back to Missouri from where they had come, a friendly
neighbor dropped by to wish them a safe trip together with a bit of
derived wisdom for my mother. Out of earshot of my father and the
children, he told her, "Mrs. Sperling, if these children are to be fed,
you are going to have to feed them."

Except for the blistered face, I do not recall any serious problems
with my health until my seventh year. Sometime in the late spring of
that year, I invaded a neighbor's cherry orchard and gorged myself on
half-ripe cherries. That evening, I became violently ill—vomiting and
diarrhea with a fever. I went to bed and stayed there until the following spring. No one could tell what role the cherries played, but the
fever was a symptom of pneumonia. Whether the cherry-induced
sickness lowered my immune response or whether I had contracted a
particularly virulent pneumococcus, I don't know. All I know for sure
is that it nearly killed me.

From that first day, the fever did not leave me for nearly a year. As
the weeks passed, I grew thinner and weaker and then, because of
lying in bed for so many weeks, my left lung filled with pus—a condition called empyema. The doctor who came to see me informed my
parents that if the other lung started to fill, I would die. Apparently, he
consulted some other physicians who said that the only hope was to
cut through the rib in my back—a procedure called a rib resection—
place a tube in my lung and drain the pus. Because I had only one
functioning lung, they could not give me a gas-based anesthetic—in
1928 there were no intravenous general anesthetics, so only a local
anaesthetic could be used.

The primary doctor told my parents that I was so weak, the operation would probably kill me but that it was my only hope. I have a vivid
memory of the operation. It was a small brick hospital and I was taken
into the operating room as soon as I arrived in my parent's Model T.
The preparations for the operation were done quickly. They placed me
on my stomach on the operating table. I felt the pricks of the needles as

they injected the anaesthetic. Then, while two doctors and two nurses held my arms and legs, the operation began. I felt the incision like a knife in my brain. As the surgeon began sawing a piece out of my rib, I screamed and struggled—according to my mother who was in the operating room, it took all the strength of the two doctors and two nurses to hold me down. My mother said that when it was over and as I lay moaning, I kept repeating, "Oh, please let me die."

I was only in the hospital for one day and then back to bed at home on my stomach and then slowly on my side until the lung was drained. After two weeks, the lung had drained and the fever ebbed away. Then I began to mend but I was so wasted and weak I could barely sit up. Slowly, I was able to stand, but it was a month before I could walk, and it took the summer for me to regain my health. By September, 18 months after eating the cherries, I was ready to return to school.

During the year in bed, I was too ill most of the time to perceive much of the world about me. My mother and sisters spoon-fed me at every meal, although I could eat very little and my appetite dwindled to only a couple of foods; it revived only after the rib resection. I spent that year in my parents' tiny bedroom. At night, I slept on a trundle bed that slid under their bed; in the morning, I was lifted into my parents' bed where I spent the day.

I am not fully aware of how that year in bed with its attendant pains, discomforts, frights, and boredom affected my soma or my psyche, much less my future business success. Before the sickness, I was the leader of the boys in my circle, prone to risky behavior and relatively indifferent to physical pain. After that, I ceased to lead and shied from pain. It was not until my late teens that my animal spirits revived, the fear of pain disappeared, and the thrill of risk returned. It was not until my late *thirties* that I again exercised leadership; however, when I did, it felt completely natural.

One thing that seemed to have sprung from that year in bed was my inability to tolerate boredom. Whenever it closes in, I take action. As my academic and business colleagues have often pointed out, I take action whether it is prudent or not even when doing nothing seems to be the wisest course. Fortunately, what appeared at the moment as unwise, has often proved to be very effective and, for this, my colleagues have accorded me the gift of insight and the power of vision.

Grade School

I went to two grade schools, one in the country south of Kansas City, Missouri, and one on the edge of the city. I started in the school in Kansas City, moved to the country, then back to Kansas City, but I can't remember which grades were which. I remember little of either school in years five and six, but I do remember that I found it difficult to learn to read. Although I was a very verbal child, I simply could not connect the words on the page to their meaning. Reading time was painful; I knew that I couldn't read, but neither my teacher nor my parents did anything about it. I suppose they figured I would learn eventually. I did finally learn simple sentences, but once I made them out, I memorized them so I could read them in class when my turn came. I have what some of my friends say is an exceptional memory and any natural ability was probably strengthened by that early exercise. After reading came writing and, here again, no matter how hard I tried, I could not do cursive. My writing book was a mess and the best I could manage was to print in large capitals. Although in my late teens I learned to read quite well, I have never been able to write a cursive script and, with the exception of my barely legible signature, I print everything I write.

After I returned to school from my year in bed, I do not remember anything about school that I enjoyed. I do not remember whether I was held back a grade or rejoined my class. I hardly remember school at all. Whether I was in the country or in Kansas City, I simply wasn't understanding much that was going on. In fact, I began to think of myself as rather dumb. The only powerful memory of the final years of grade school was having to fight many more times than I wanted to. On my way home each day, I passed the house of my main tormentor, Louie Adams, who was much stronger than I. Most days he presented me with a Hobson's choice: either absorb his taunts or else fight him and get knocked down. I usually absorbed the taunts because the fear of pain that followed my lung operation carried over into every aspect of my life. It made me less than a stellar performer in any childhood games that required physical contact, especially football, and I slowly but surely developed a reputation as a coward. That reputation became a barrier to participation in almost any activity with other children and I became a marginal.

High School

I don't remember finishing grade school, but I do remember going to high school because I had to ride the streetcar. Kansas City's Paseo High School was a prison set on a hill. It was concrete block with four stories, endless hallways, and what seemed to me to be hundreds of classrooms. I was a loner who wandered from class to class with little interest in what was going on. The only class that I remember doing well in was algebra, but I remember doing so poorly in Latin and geometry that I failed. Often times, I would become disoriented and have to go to the office for help in finding the classroom. Although school was bad, riding the streetcar was worse. The ride to school was okay because there were lots of people going to work as well as to school. However, most of the passengers going home in the afternoon were students from Paseo. I was the butt of jokes; my books were dropped down behind seats; and because I have kinky hair with a slightly brown complexion, I became "Nigger John." All of this probably built my character, but it didn't do my self-concept much good.

Mother

My mother was 36 when I was born, and my nearest sibling was five years older. Although I was the result of an unwanted pregnancy, my mother was possessively loving. However, she was not, as one finds in biographies of men with possessive mothers, a person who urged me to study hard and to do great things. Rather, I think I was a surrogate love for the one she did not have with her husband. She was very solicitous of my health, provided loving care during sickness, and shielded me from my father's anger, but she was largely indifferent to my psychic well-being or intellectual development.

My mother was a Macnama of Scotch-Irish lineage. They were a hard lot, and from what little contact I had with them, I can understand why the troubles in Northern Ireland have persisted for so long. Her forebears, so she claimed, had arrived in America in the early 1700s. If that was true, then the clan must have migrated down the Appalachian chain, down the Ohio valley, and across the Mississippi into southern Missouri. Her family considered themselves to be

Southerners and, as was the case with most yeomen farmers, they wanted nothing to do with Negroes.

My maternal grandfather was a prosperous farmer and cattle trader who, according to all accounts, was small, compact, and very tough both physically and mentally. He was domineering with his wife, his children, and his workers. He lived into his nineties and was gored to death by a bull. I think my mother must have taken after her father. Like him, she was small and tough as nails, and she dominated her husband, her children, and anyone else who happened to be around. When my big hulking brothers, who were quite violent with one another, would fight in the house, knocking over furniture, she would take a pan and whack their heads until they stopped. Then, when one of them would raise a hand as if to strike her, she would stand, arms akimbo, looking up at him and say, "You wouldn't dare strike your mother."

When I reflect on how family genes are distributed, it is clear that my brothers got the Sperling genes. They, like my father, were large and, like him, died of heart attacks in their mid-sixties. I got the Macnama genes—I'm small and alive and well at 79.

Not only was my mother domineering, she was also one of the nosiest persons I have ever known. She wanted to know about everything I did, where I was going, where I had been, with whom I had talked, what they said, and so on.

Over the years, I learned to combat this constant intrusion by lying. I simply related events and conversations as I knew she would want to hear them. She was not stupid and would immediately seize on any inconsistency in what I told her. As a consequence, I had to create a counterworld of people, places, and activities she found acceptable. Because lying was necessary to my psychic integrity, lying became my standard response to almost any question. I would simply give a plausible answer that gave me time to consider just how I wanted to respond. This was a difficult habit to break and I had to work very hard at it. When I finally figured out that lying was counterproductive, I learned to tell the truth by pausing before I answered a question and then making a conscious decision to answer accurately. Years later, Ray Shaffer, a board member of my holding company, the Apollo Group, gave me a simple prescription for veracity: "If you tell the truth, you never have to remember what you've said."

My mother was an incessant talker, an unflagging moralist, and a midwestern Mrs. Malaprop. "If you can't say something good about someone, then don't say anything," she would pontificate and then launch into a diatribe about some neighbor whom she would characterize as a "floor flusher." Her speech was constantly interspersed with quotations, usually incorrect, from the *Bible*. "Woeful waste makes willful want." "Blessed are the poor for they shall inherit the earth." She was also a vocal racist. There were "niggers in the woodpile," and if one of us had a persistent cold or pain, it was hanging on "like grim death to a sick nigger." She was no more charitable toward Catlikers, Sheenies, Wops, Dagos, Pollocks, or Spiks. The only group she did not criticize was the Jews. "Son, the Jews are God's chosen people, you leave them alone." If someone did something of which she approved, "that was mighty white of them," and if someone was "free, white, and twenty-one," they had all they needed for success. She was also a Calvinist, a fundamentalist Presbyterian when that denomination still preached John Knox's brand of Christianity. Her religion was about the only thing she was unable to impose on my father or brothers; they ignored the religion, but they adhered to her rules: no swearing, no liquor, and no smoking inside the house.

The local minister, Dr. Sutton, delivered fire-and-brimstone sermons every Sunday, and church was a must for me and my sisters. My one personal encounter with the good Doctor was one Sunday morning when we had gotten to church early and he interrogated me on my faith. My answers were not pleasing to him, and then he fixed me with his pale blue eyes and asked, "Son, are you saved?" I stammered that I didn't know, but I would search for a sign. At that point, he let me go. I knew that I wasn't saved, that I probably would never have a sign, and that I would die and go to hell.

The *Bible* and *Pilgrim's Progress* were the only books I remember my mother mentioning. When things were going wrong, she was in the "slough of despond"; when she thought I was too smart for my britches, I was "worldly wiseman." Whenever she spoke of her third-grade education, bitterness spilled out of her. Although I was a lackluster student with few things to brag about, I did not dare brag about them to my mother. If I did, her usual reply was, "I can do that too and all I have is a third-grade education."

Despite the need to develop very bad habits to protect myself from my mother's suffocating love and knowing that, compared with the mothers of my few friends, she was a very difficult person, my love for my mother was total. Ours would later become a love-hate relationship, and I was not free from what I considered her malign influence until long after her death.

It would be an understatement to say that my mother was and remains the most important influence in my life. Because of her, I have never again wanted to have anyone with a hold on me. At whatever cost, I try to stand alone rather than be beholden to someone to whom I must acknowledge superior status. No doubt, this sense of false pride has denied me the humility needed to curry favor with mentors who might have furthered my career. I often seek advice and profit greatly from it, but I have never been a client. Whenever I have asked for a recommendation or a loan, it was because I believed I deserved it. It has not been the most efficient way to go through life, but, at least, I am beholden to very few individuals.

Father

My father was a classic ne'er-do-well. In his later years, he became what today would be called a bagman, but there were no shopping carts back then; he carried most of the things he brought home in a gunny sack. He was some 50 years old when I was born, and the only job I knew him to have, other than his pathetic attempts at farming, was as a "butcher" who sold drinks and snacks on a train that ran between Kansas City and somewhere.

I do not know what education he had, but he could read and calculate and, in listening to him talk to others, he seemed intelligent and articulate. Over the years, I have wondered why someone who was reasonably good looking and intelligent could be so useless.

While I was very young and before my year-long illness, I was not aware that he was a bum, but by the time I was eight years old, that perception matured. Whether we lived in the country or on the outskirts of Kansas City, he was equally incompetent. When he farmed it was with one horse, a couple of cows, and a few goats, chickens, ducks, and rabbits. He was never able to produce enough to feed the family, and his efforts had always to be supplemented by what my mother and brothers could earn at outside jobs, always menial. I worked for him on the farm, but it was when we lived in Kansas City that my contempt for him changed to loathing. In the country, he was hidden from the neighbors and I had to feel little sense of shame when I went to the country school. In Kansas City, though, he was a very visible bum who ranged several miles from home doing what, I did not know or care. I only knew that when I was with schoolmates and he came into view, I would ignore him and, if possible, change direction and walk away. In school, when there was any discussion of parents, I never mentioned him and, because of the shame I felt at having a bum for a father, I never invited anyone to my house.

My father's workless life led me often to ponder how work was created. Why did most other fathers have jobs, why were they hired, who paid them, where did the people who paid them get the money to pay them, and how did the money spent in the grocery store get to the people who produced the food in the store, and on and on? In short, the workings of the economic system were a complete puzzle, but it was a puzzle I was too ashamed to ask my teachers to explain. Eventually, of course, that curiosity would lead me to become an economic historian—but that gets us ahead of our story.

One night when I was 10 and my mother was gone from the house, my father decided I needed a beating. This was not an uncommon occurrence: He would make me stand while he whipped me with a belt. This particular evening, however, I ran, and he followed me yelling what was going to happen to me when he caught me. I easily outran him and hid until it got very dark. When I went back to the house he was standing outside. I stopped far enough from him so that I could dart away if he lunged for me, and then I told him, "If you ever hit me again, I'll kill you in your sleep." He went back into the house, and he never hit me again.

By the time I was 15, it was pretty clear that my father's health was failing, and he spent most of his time in the house. Then, one day the miracle happened—he died in his sleep. In the morning when my mother told me my father was dead, I could hardly contain my joy. I raced outside, rolled in the grass squealing with delight. There I lay looking up into a clear blue sky, and I realized that this was the happiest day of my life. It still is. When I went back into the house I told my mother that I would find it difficult not to smile when I told anyone my father had died. She said she understood but that I should try to look somber.

Siblings

My parents had six children. Leon, the oldest, was lame; he was 17 years older than I. He had a short Achilles tendon and walked with a cane. Leon was another source of shame; to me he was proof that our family was congenitally twisted. I carried that sense into adulthood, and one of the reasons I have only one child is my fear that any child of mine would be born lame. Lewis, a year younger, was the next and he was normal. Both were broad shouldered and powerful, and both died in their early sixties of heart attacks. By the time I was old enough to really know them, Leon, who had apprenticed as a watch repairman, had married and moved into an apartment in Kansas City. When Leon died, he was still a watch repairman, although he owned a tiny jewelry store. Lewis worked as a draftsman and lived at home. He graduated from drafting to self-taught civil engineer, became a construction superintendent, started and failed in a building supply business, and died a bankrupt. Lewis was not the kindest brother one might imagine. For example, one day I was lying on our old couch on the porch when he came out of the house, lit a cigarette, and told me to get up because he wanted to lie down. I replied that I was there first and didn't have to move. He didn't say anything; rather, he simply took the cigarette he was smoking out of his mouth and began to shove it into the back of my hand. He only had to do that once.

The third child, whose name was never mentioned, died in infancy. Ruth was the fourth, eight years older than I. She was sweet and beautiful and the only sibling I loved, although she had little to do with me because she was very popular and had lots of boyfriends, all of whom wanted to marry her. Although Ruth wanted to marry a diaper wash driver, my mother persuaded her to continue her education. She went to live with my mother's only friend, a woman who had married a pharmacist and lived in Ashland, Oregon, where she attended a normal school. It was a good decision for Ruth. After two years, she got her teaching certificate, took a job in a small town in the ranching country of central Oregon, met and married a rich rancher, and was the only member of the family, other than myself, to achieve affluence, in her case through marriage.

Helen, the fifth, was five years older than I and the only sibling with whom I had an ongoing relationship, but it was not a good one.

Helen was plain and had a sour temper that never left her until the day she died. We did not like one another and quarreled regularly. A couple of times I challenged her physically and she promptly decked me. Helen followed Ruth to Ashland, also got her teaching certificate, took a job in a small town in the ranching country of central Oregon and married a ranch foreman. She did not achieve affluence and predeceased her husband.

As one might gather from the preceding, we were not a close-knit family, and I spent much of my life putting as much psychic and social distance as I could between my family and myself. During their lifetimes, except for Ruth, I saw them or their families as seldom as possible. I neither asked of them nor gave of myself.

Oregon

My father died in the spring of 1936. I finished my sophomore year at the Paseo High School "Prison," but I did not enroll the following September. Late in the fall, my mother and I left Kansas City for Oregon. I don't remember where she got the money for the trip; she must have sold the house, but I do not know how or when. I do remember that my brother Lewis had just bought a new Ford sedan and that we drove with him to Albuquerque, New Mexico. In Albuquerque, we stayed for a few days with my mother's oldest brother, who had become a modestly successful businessman. I also met one of her other brothers, two sisters, and three cousins. We stayed about a month and then left by train for Oregon.

We were met at the Klamath Falls station by Ruth and her intended husband. Ruth had rented a small house across the road from her school that was some 25 miles west of Lakeview. It was mid-November when we arrived; it was cold with snow cover and I had no overcoat. Fortunately, the car was warm and the drive over the mountains to Lakeview was exciting; the arrival was not.

The school was located at the crossing of two country roads, and the hamlet consisted of a tiny store, a post office, a creamery, and the school. It took us several days to get settled, and then my mother and sister addressed the issue of my returning to high school in Lakeview. I flatly refused. Not only would I have to ride the bus for 25 miles twice a day, I had no winter clothes I considered decent enough to wear to school. That was the excuse, but mostly I feared being friend-less. In my view, there was nothing that would recommend me to any potential friend—I would be a marginal student, I was small with no athletic abilities and, worse still, no social abilities. I wouldn't go to school and there was no work for either my mother or myself, so we spent the days sitting around the house, talking about how we were going to get out of the situation, and taking long walks while we dis-cussed the same subject.

In early spring, I was offered a job as a farm laborer by a wheat farmer whose wife had become friends with Ruth. Ruth bought me some work shoes, a heavy work jacket, gloves, and a stocking cap, and I took up residence as the sole occupant of a bunkhouse at the farm. I had done farm work before, but not on a large commercial farm; this was real work. My first task was the plowing on the night shift that lasted from 6 P.M. until 6 A.M. I had never driven a tractor before; there I was on a large diesel cat pulling a gangplow all night long. It was cold and lonely, especially when I pulled up to a shed out of the wind to eat my lunch and drink a cup of coffee. Sometimes, I would go to sleep, but fortunately I never fell off or I would surely have killed myself. Once the plowing was done and the wheat was sowed, things improved somewhat. I worked days as a sort of jack-of-all-trades doing the hundred things serious farming requires. I worked there until my sister's school was out.

My sister then married and moved to her husband's ranch. My mother and I moved to Ashland where my sisters had attended nor-mal school. There we hoped my mother's friend, who had befriended my sisters, would befriend us. We stayed with her and her husband for a couple of weeks until we could find more permanent quarters. We finally found a partially furnished cottage, but work was harder to find. My mother took in washing and ironing, and I worked as a day laborer in the orchards that dotted the valley. It soon became apparent that we had no future in Ashland and, with the last of whatever sav-ings we had, we took the train to Portland.

High School: Round II

We arrived in Portland in late August and moved into a small apart-ment. My mother got a job sewing sacks in a burlap bag factory and

I got a job as a busboy. In September I was persuaded to return to school. We had enough money to buy some decent clothes for myself, and by working two jobs, delivering papers in the morning and bussing dishes at night, I even had a bit of pocket money. I was no better a student at Portland's Washington High School than I had been at the "Prison," but Washington was much more on a human scale and I formed my first important friendship.

I suppose it was formed in an odd way, like many friendships. In this case, it was in some math class where I managed to do fairly well. It was during one of the multiple-choice tests when the boy behind me who was quite large reached up and pushed me aside so that he could read my test paper. I tried to push back but he whispered that if I didn't cooperate he would make certain that I would be sorry. That was enough for me, so not only did I cooperate then, but cooperation with Jack O'Keefe became my way of life. After that, we slowly became friends and, for the first time in years, I had someone to pal around with. Jack was not only large, he was a good athlete and just right for me as a friend. I did not have to worry about having to fight anyone, because he made it clear that anyone who messed with me would have to mess with him but, more important, he was popular and I was happy to be a hanger-on.

During my two years at Washington High, I slowly became partially socialized in the sense that I managed to make a few more friends and even took girls out on dates. About the only indelible thing that happened to me in those years was my final break with my mother's religion. I was dating a girl and I knew that I wanted to have sex with her, but I also realized that it would be a sin. One afternoon while walking home from school on a day that I was to have a date with the girl, I decided that I would try to seduce her. I now had to face the fact that I truly believed that if I carried out my intention, I would be a lost sinner and go to hell. I also knew that I was firm in my decision that I would try to seduce her. Not wanting to spend a lifetime waiting for hell, I stopped, looked up, and said, "God, I am going to sin, if you have the power, strike me dead now." When nothing happened, I looked up again and said, "I reject you forever." I walked on free from God and free from my fear of hell, and free from my mother's religion.

As far as school was concerned, my poor reading ability and

almost total lack of intellectual interest in my classes meant that I continued to receive low grades, but not so low that I flunked out. When graduation came, I did not go to any prom or to the graduation ceremony, I just left.

A Dead End

Once graduated, I lost my best friend. Jack left shortly after graduation to attend the maritime academy and without him as an intercessor, I soon dropped the other friends I had made and reverted to my loner behavior. Nineteen thirty-nine was not a good year for a high school graduate with no skills to find a job. I read the help-wanted ads, went to the federal department of employment; however, it was some time before I finally landed a job as a stock boy at a local department store. Although I thought that I was a pretty good worker, I was not fast enough for the supervisor and he sacked me after two weeks. That was the last job I had in Portland for some time.

In 1939, my prospects were bleak. There was still a depression, I was unemployed and, even though I had graduated from high school, I was semiliterate and fit only for common labor. Worse still was my utter lack of confidence or sense of self-worth. I considered myself to be quite unintelligent, physically unattractive, without any family support, and with no prospects of things getting any better. I wonder sometimes why I did not become a bum like my father; it must have been my mother's nature and nurture that prevailed. The Macnama genes are tough, as was my mother's nurture, and, just when matters looked really hopeless, good fortune sent me on the first positive path I had trod since the age of seven.

2

The Education
of John Sperling

Part I—1939 to 1954
A Sea Change

Melville's Ishmael described the whaling ship as his Harvard College. For me, it was the merchant marine that provided my first real education and two of the most important years of my life.

One day while aimlessly looking for work, it dawned on me that Portland was a seaport; Jack O'Keefe had gone to the Maritime Academy; maybe I could go to sea. However, that would mean joining a union. Even though I had no experience with unions or any understanding of how unions functioned, my basically rural family was Republican and fervently antiunion. Still, I was in no position to let that deter me, so the next day I took up residence in the hiring hall of the maritime unions—the Sailors' Union of the Pacific and Marine Firemen, Oilers, and Watertenders. The cooks and stewards were all Black and they had their own hall.

There were two ways one could begin a seagoing trade: as an apprentice sailor or as a wiper in the Black gang (i.e., the part of the crew that ran the engine room). I would have much preferred the job of sailor, but I was in no position to be picky; so, after sitting in the union hall every day for three weeks, I took the first position offered, that of wiper on a Matson line freighter sailing for Hawaii the next day. I went home, gathered a few clothes in a bag and came back to go to work.

The ship was berthed at a lumber loading dock on the lower Columbia River, so at the hiring hall they gave me a ticket for the bus that traveled between Portland and Astoria with instructions to the driver of where to drop me off.

Only a couple of hours after I boarded, the ship left the dock and within a few minutes was passing over the bar at the mouth of the Columbia. Once at sea, our routine was to work eight hours and sleep no more than another eight, which left eight hours to talk, play cards, and read. It was at sea that I not only learned to read well, but, more important, to love to read. I also, for the first time, had workmates that I got to know well. In 1939, there were many men working in the merchant marine who would not have been there had there not been a depression. Not only did some of them read from the well-stocked libraries they brought aboard, some of them wrote; one ship even had a poet. I was introduced into a reading culture that was also a highly articulate ideological culture—a culture of the left. Most of the men were socialists plus a sprinkling of communists, and various members of any crew I sailed with claimed allegiance to the Democratic Socialists, the Socialist Workers, the Trotskyites, the Stalinists, and even the Wobblies.

There was a sufficient leaven to ensure constant debate on economics, politics, and philosophy. All of this was *terra incognita* to me; it opened up a new world of ideas and, of special importance, history. Even though it was history as seen through the eyes of the seafaring proletariat and dealt primarily with the internecine struggles of the left, still it ranged over the history of Europe and America from the formation of the first socialist parties in nineteenth-century Germany down to current battles between the Trotskys and the Stalinists. I had only a vague idea of fascism and the evils of Hitler, but every member of every crew was an ardent antifascist. Even after two years, I had not gained enough understanding of economics or politics to adopt a specific ideology, but I became a convert to radical democracy and socialist economics. Since then, I have drifted somewhat toward the center in politics. My socialism has been replaced by an allegiance to free markets with the caveat, as anyone familiar with Marx and Schumpeter understands, that the power of markets to disrupt fragile social orders must be restrained by government. For proof of this, one need look no further back than the global economic turmoil that began with the Asian financial meltdown in the summer of 1997.

In addition to the bookish types, there were plenty of "hairy

apes" on board, and I had to learn to navigate around them. I didn't
have Jack O'Keefe to protect me, so after being knocked about several
times and suffering a broken nose, I learned to watch my step. One
time, I made the mistake of becoming friendly with a young Black
steward, and a hulking Southerner informed me that if I hoped to
reach port, I had better watch my ways. I told the steward, who
understood the situation perfectly well, and we agreed to see less of
each other. Shortly thereafter, the Southerner insulted him in such a
disgusting manner that the steward snapped back with a challenge.
Those assembled in the mess room demanded they decide the issue
on the hatch cover. The Southerner was half again as large as the
steward, so all of us thought that it would be over very quickly. What
neither I nor any of the other Whites who gathered around knew was
that the young Black man was a professional boxer. The fight could
not have turned out any better from my point of view. The steward
very methodically beat the Southerner to a bloody pulp. First, he cut
his face to ribbons, then worked over his body and finally knocked
him down, let him get up, and knocked him down again. When the
Southerner could no longer get up, the fight was over.

Even after that I thought it better not to continue a public friendship with the steward—I knew the Southerner was capable of pushing me overboard if I continued to provoke him. However, when we
made port in Baltimore we went ashore together and directly into a
nearby bar. The bartender informed us that Negroes were not served.
When I protested, he informed me that he didn't serve high-yellows
like me either. I now realized that with a deep tan and my kinky hair,
I was still "Nigger John."

In addition to giving me my love of reading and my political
awakening, life at sea began to repair some of the psychic damage of
childhood and youth. Mainly, the noise died down and life was simpli-
fied to a small set of choices that I could deal with successfully. As I
learned a somewhat skilled trade, my confidence improved and, in
going ashore with my shipmates, mainly to bars designed to draw
seagoing customers, I learned to drink to excess and enjoy the companionship of women; in fact, I become a fairly popular member of the
crew. Not only did the close society of the ship give me a better purchase on life, I also got to see much of the world—Hawaii (not just
Honolulu but the outer islands), Japan, Shanghai, Hong Kong, Singapore, Manila, Panama, and the ports along the East Coast (most partic-

ularly, New York City). With money in my pocket, I was able to buy suits and fancy shirts not only in Hong Kong, but also in New York.

The most exciting city of all was Shanghai. We were there for a week, anchored in the river just off the Bund and with lots of time off. Shanghai was under siege by the Japanese; we could hear the gunfire in the distance, but the danger did not seem to disrupt the life of the city. Its citizens seemed as indifferent to the danger as I was. (It is rather scary to think that had my timing been off by a few months, I could have been interned in a Japanese prison camp.)

Much as one now finds bookstalls along the Seine, the Bund was a book bazaar. Ignoring copyrights must be an ancient Chinese tradition, because in the stalls and set on the paving was every book a young sailor would want to buy at pennies per volume, all with simple paper covers. My more knowledgeable shipmates helped me select books that were then banned in the United States plus authors I had never heard of. I bought a couple of dozen, including books by Henry Miller, Kraft-Ebbing, Nietzsche, and Spengler.

In Singapore, I could also afford to go to the bars in the luxury hotels. The hotels had Sikh doormen who shooed away any "Chinaman" who attempted to enter, but the doors were promptly opened for me. The lobbies and lounges were staffed mostly with beautiful White Russians, and it did my ego no harm thinking about this Missouri country boy spending time with glamorous and mysterious women. Books and bars plus rickshaw rides around the city pretty much encompassed my activities, but together they gave me a delicious sense of being a world traveler.

Other than the chance of being shoved overboard by one of my shipmates, I had only one life-threatening experience, but it created such vivid memories, that I relive the experience every time I have a close call. It was a hurricane off Cape Hatteras, North Carolina, that came on quite suddenly—60 years ago weather forecasting was not sufficiently timely to enable ships to avoid such dangers. Our ship was of WWI vintage and did about 10 knots at full steam. At first, everyone thought it was just another storm, but then it grew progressively worse until we were in seas with 40-foot waves. The ship would plunge into the trough, the screw coming out of the water would race and shake every rivet, then the bow would knife into the wave and a wall of water would course over the ship driving her deep into the water. The ship would stop for a moment and then plunge into the trough again. We were barely making headway, and it was clear to the experienced seamen that, if the ship stalled, that was it.

Our Swedish captain was a skilled seaman who read the danger accurately. He sent down word that he was going to turn the ship and run with the wind. Every hand knew that if he did not time the turn just right, we would lie lengthwise in the trough and the next wall of water would founder us. All hands were to find a secure handhold. The captain timed the turn just right as we headed into a wave. The ship went along the crest of the wave at the top and finished the turn as she ran down the face of this mountain of water. She plunged deep, shuddered, then righted herself. We all waited until she moved forward with the wind, and then some of us cried, some of us prayed, and some of us cheered, and we all thanked whatever gods there be for our survival.

Because I sailed mostly in the tropics and the ships never sailed faster than 12 knots, it was wonderful to lie on the hatch covers at night in a gentle breeze and watch the sky tilt back and forth. It created for me conditions for contemplation that I had never had before and have seldom had since. Lying there night after night gave me a chance to review my life and think about such things as why, now that I thought of myself as intelligent, had I been such a poor student all those years and why, now that I felt myself to be socially ept, I was so inept for so long. I also had to deal with the shame I felt because of my father. I realized that one of the reasons I had so few friends was because that shame meant that I never invited anyone home with me. That sense of shame, and all the quarrelling, made me vow to put as much distance between myself and my family as possible. Mostly, I vowed to myself to be as different as possible from my father. I would work hard, finish whatever I started, be effective, get an education, make something of myself, and be someone that people could admire.

Higher Education, The First Steps

I left seafaring for the final time in August of 1941, and, as luck would have it, Jack O'Keefe had decided to "go on the beach" at the same time. We got an apartment together downtown on Sutter Street. As soon as we were settled, I enrolled at San Francisco City College, and got myself a night job at a Philips filling station a few blocks from our apartment. I decided on a pre-engineering program with only one

English course; the rest of the courses were math, physics, mechanical drawing, and surveying. This time school was wonderful. All the classes were easy for me and I got straight A's. It was like, "Look Ma, no hands." My best class was physics, which was taught by a doctoral student from U.C. Berkeley. I did so well that he tried to recruit me for the physics program at Berkeley and, if the War had not started, I probably would have gone.

That December 7th, all of our lives began to change. Very quickly Jack went back to sea, but I had had enough of that—I wanted to fly. I went back to Portland to enlist in the Navy Air Corps and, once enlisted, waited to be called. Having time on my hands and little money, I got a swing-shift job in the shipyard and enrolled at Reed College. There was some irony in someone with mostly D's and F's, with a few C's at Portland's Washington High being able to enroll in the Northwest's most selective liberal arts college. Had it not been for my one semester of junior college A's plus the fact that Reed desperately wanted males to replace the ones leaving daily, I would not have made it in.

The Navy

Reed during the war years was pretty laid back. It would be quite different when the veterans returned, but then it was a nice easy introduction to higher education. There was a surplus of attractive women and, instead of continuing in math and science, I enrolled in literature and social science courses. I didn't make it through the semester before I was called to enter preflight training at Gonzaga University in Spokane, Washington.

Preflight training was back to math and science, and the Jesuit priests were wonderful instructors. I would later have much to dislike about some Jesuits, but this first experience was all positive. In addition to academics, we also learned to fly light planes and had lots of time to wander around Spokane in our dress uniforms. Looking at myself in the mirror, with my cap at a jaunty tilt, for the first time in my life I felt attractive, not handsome, but attractive; maybe women were not going to be an ongoing problem. Immediately upon completion at Gonzaga, we were transferred to another preflight program, this time at St. Mary's College in Moraga, California, just over the hills to the east of Berkeley.

Gonzaga was like going to college, St. Mary's was being in the

Navy. Our instructors were all naval officers and, compared with the Jesuits, were about on the level of teaching assistants. The curriculum repeated what we had covered at Gonzaga, only on a lower level. In addition to boring academics, we had a grueling physical training program and even more boring lectures on how to be a naval officer. Although I was something of a malcontent, and in regular conflict with my C.O., I was careful not to do anything that would get me washed out, because I really wanted to fly airplanes.

Just before we were finished at St. Mary's, we received notice that the terms of our joining the Naval Aviation Cadet Corps had been changed. When I had signed up, a cadet was allowed to resign from the Navy if he washed out. Now, if you washed out, you were automatically enlisted as a Seaman Second Class. However, if you did not like the terms of enlistment, you could resign. It did not take much imagination for me to figure out which cadet would be one of the first to wash out. Like Eliza and Uncle Tom, I needed another cake of ice to jump to.

As soon as I could get to a phone, I called the Army recruiting office in San Francisco and inquired whether I could transfer from the Navy Cadet Corps to the Army Air Corps Cadet Corps. They said they would find out and to call them back. The next day I called again, and they said I could make the transfer. I resigned from the Navy the same day. As soon as I was discharged, I went to San Francisco and joined the Army Air Corps Cadet Corps expecting to leave for training immediately. Instead, they put me in the queue. I was to go home and wait to be called, so the next day I was on the train to Portland.

Fortunately, I was discharged in August so I enrolled for the fall semester at Reed and returned to the shipyard, where I was now promoted to junior engineer. That semester, I took all arts and social sciences courses, so I had enough time to fall in love and become engaged to a brainy senior who was a great tutor. She was a political science major and, although I liked the subject, I was drawn more to history and economics. Ultimately, I decided on history and declared that as my major.

The Army Air Corps

Fortunately for my education, the next call to arms did not come until after finals, in January 1943. I was sent to basic training and then directly to flight training. From primary training, to basic, to advanced, and then on to training in combat fighters, I was always in Texas. I loved the flying, but all else was pretty dull. This was especially the case after completing operational training, when I sat around three different air bases waiting to be named to a combat unit. Some of my colleagues bemoaned the fact that perhaps the war would end and they would not get into combat. I was not of that persuasion. I was ready to go if called—obviously, I had no other choice—but I was not displeased with the thought that if I was lucky, the war might end before the call came. I was lucky, and it did.

During basic training I married Barbara, my Reed College sweetheart, and the boredom of the Army was compounded by the boredom of being married with nothing more than a small Texas town in which to seek diversion. I became so bored that I learned to sew and I became quite proficient at it. I enjoyed shopping for cloth, then figuring out the pattern, then sewing and fitting. I made my wife two very stylish suits, a coat, and several dresses. She was easily the best-dressed wife on the base. The boredom was just as great for my wife as it was for me and before I finished advanced training she returned home to Tacoma and got a job. When the war ended, with wife in tow, I returned to Reed.

Compared with my two years at sea, the four years of being in and out of the Navy and Army were not a period of great change in the way I viewed myself or the world. True, I had gained a great deal more self-confidence in both my mental and physical abilities and in my sense of self-worth and attractiveness to the opposite sex. I had wooed and won an intelligent and attractive woman. At St. Mary's, I had become a member of the boxing team, fighting as a lightweight and acquitted myself respectably in the ring. I had the highest scores in my unit on the tests to determine suitability for pilot training, and I was a competent pilot. When I mustered out, I was hard as nails and in the best shape I had ever been or would ever be again.

My Serious Academic Education Begins

I mustered out in the fall of 1945 and returned to Reed for the spring semester 1946. I graduated in 1948 and those were two of the hardest years of my young adulthood. I was simply not ready for the level of competition I now faced; although I performed well above average academically, I paid a high price mentally, emotionally, and physically. The Reed College I returned to after the war was vastly different from the one I had enjoyed so much during the war. The returning veterans took over the campus and most of them had actually seen action. They were not newly minted Air Corps pilots; they had mustered out as captains, majors, and even a few colonels. They were not just physically hardened, most of them were also battle hardened, and they were in a hurry to make up for the four years they had lost. Most important for me, they had all come either from elite private schools or very good public high schools, and they were simply far better prepared than I to be juniors or seniors. They were intellectually aggressive, and this was the first time I had been faced with that kind of competition. During the war, classes had been relatively leisurely and fun; now they were intense, competitive, and stressful.

Before the end of the first semester, I began to suffer psychosomatic symptoms that grew progressively worse. Slowly, a variety of symptoms turned into chronic colitis, which first took me to the College infirmary, then to a series of doctors and constant medication; I began to think of myself as someone who would be in ill health for the rest of my life. Intense competition, chronic illness, and an increasingly unsatisfactory marriage finally led me to get serious about why I was having so much trouble. That led to brooding over the fact that, as someone raised poor with a lousy education, I was in an unfair competition with the privileged sons and daughters of the middle class—often the upper-middle class. These students had been acculturated to value education and they looked forward confidently to future careers in academe, government, business, and the professions. By contrast, my culture was that of hardscrabble survival, and I had no sense of where my future might take me. It was my first intimate experience with what I then perceived as class-based entitlement, and my response was class-based resentment. This period of my life might well be entitled, "How I Learned to Hate the Middle Class."

I realized that distancing myself from my family was my first action in carrying out my desire to rise in class and that marrying a middle-class woman had been a deliberate decision to use marriage as a way up. Now the competition with the members of the middle class I had worked so assiduously to join was making me sick and miserable, and finally, I was having to confront the costs of rising above one's station. Class migration upward is a theme of two of my favorite novels, *Tom Jones* and *Great Expectations,* but I was not made of the lighthearted and resilient stuff of Fielding's Tom or the mental toughness of Dickens' Pip. Apparently, I had no capacity to learn anything practical from literature.

The only friends I made among the middle-class students were those on the socialist left, mostly Jews with a smattering of goyim, who were ideologically anti–middle class. Once I had an ideological rationale, I was able to feel justified in my new class consciousness—I now hated the middle class without realizing that my hatred was mostly self-loathing. My rationale was a new ideological identity, that of an intellectual dedicated to ameliorating the condition of the working class. Even though my origins were agrarian, not working class, my two years at sea and my membership in the Marine Firemen, Oilers, and Watertenders Union were, in my mind, a sufficient basis for my new class identity and my political commitment.

There is much irony in my attitudes toward the middle class, because "now I are one," and my own son, plus several other young people for whom I function as a surrogate father, enjoy a host of middle-class entitlements. As an ideologue, I don't think they deserve those perks; as a father, I am pleased that they can enjoy them. In short, I am in a condition of chronic ambivalence.

Miserable as I was, I slogged along. I wrote a senior thesis that was really bad, and looking back, I was so appalled that it made me wonder if the College had any standards. It was, however, an accurate reflection of my totally muddled mind. I was experiencing some sort of intellectual anomie in which ideas flowed through my mind unattached to any reference that could make real-world sense. I simply piled idea on top of idea on top of idea. Had I had any sense of intellectual marketing, I might have invented deconstruction. Muddled though I was, I made enough sense for the College to nominate me as a Rhodes Scholar applicant. Given my utter intellectual and emotional confusion, it was a blessing that I was not chosen. Oxford would simply have been too great a challenge.

By the time I graduated in June 1948, I was a basket case. My wife was from Tacoma and we moved in with her family—bad decision. I turned myself into the Army Hospital at Fort Lewis, a base near Seattle, and they really tried to find out what was causing the colitis that had made me into a functioning invalid. It probably took my shrink a nanosecond to determine that my illness was psychosomatic, and that the only cure was to straighten out my head. He liked me and, having nothing better to do, he was willing to give me counseling. To stay in counseling, I got a job with the Federal Labor Relations Board in Seattle. It didn't take long to figure out that my marriage was a disaster, that I had a very hazy idea of who I was or who I wanted to be, and that I was bitterly unhappy. To this day, I have a very hazy idea of what constitutes happiness, but I have an acute understanding of unhappiness.

By the summer of 1949, I had been through a couple of affairs and had pretty much gotten over my colitis problems. My psychiatrist, who was from Berkeley, suggested that maybe I should try graduate school and, if I was of a mind to do so, he was willing to help me get into the U.C. Berkeley graduate psychology program. At that time, Reed graduates had an almost moral obligation to go on to graduate school or, at the very least, to law school or med school and some 65 percent did so. Deciding to attend graduate school was the easy part; the hard part was deciding whether to take my wife with me. I ultimately decided that it was time for something completely different, but I did not have the guts to tell her that she was not in my plans for the future. As is my wont when dealing with women with whom I am emotionally involved, I cannot look them in the eye and tell them the truth, so I did all of the negotiation for admission into graduate school off-line. When it was time to go, I quietly quit my job, organized my simple affairs and then, one Monday morning, after Barbara was safely off to work, penned a note telling her that I was off to Berkeley to graduate school and that after I had gotten things worked out, I would write to her.

Berkeley

Because life is usually too complicated and there are too many ties to too many people, one seldom has the opportunity to leave all of one's troubles behind, and this is probably the only time it has happened to me. The exhilarating sense of leaving stayed with me as long as the landscape retained the varied greens of the Northwest; it was not until I got to the yellow California hills studded with dark green live oaks that I had the sense of arrival. I remembered how dry and desertlike I considered the Bay Area during my time at St. Mary's, but now it appeared as one of the most beautiful landscapes I had ever seen. The hills were sensual breasts and buttocks that shimmered as the late summer breeze played over them. On my last stop before Berkeley, I had turned off the main highway and found a roadside restaurant with outdoor tables. As I sat there eating and sipping a glass of wine while looking out over the yellow hills, I wallowed in my seeming good fortune. I had simply walked away from my problems and gotten away with it, or so it seemed at the time.

Berkeley in 1949 was not an easy place to find lodgings. I didn't want to share a place with strangers, and the only thing the student housing office had to offer was a tiny room with utility kitchen and bath in a housing project built for shipyard workers. It was in Richmond, about 20 minutes by car from the campus. I didn't realize how limited my social skills were until I had been in this dismal place for a month without making any friends. As my feelings of loneliness increased, my euphoria over leaving Tacoma decreased, then vanished, and I was as miserable as ever.

I had come to Berkeley to seek a degree in psychology, but when I was told that I would have to take a whole series of prerequisites, including statistics, I wilted. Instead of psychology, then, I turned to the history department where I felt safe and where I was welcomed. Once I had registered for classes, I recovered my intellectual self-confidence, but my social self-confidence was at zero. Fortunately, about a month into the semester, I did finally strike up a friendship with Betty Weigel, a history grad student, who lived at Throckmorton Manor, a weird graduate co-op housed in a dilapidated, two-story Victorian not far from campus. Betty invited me to a party at the Manor, and it was all I could ask of an academic party. There were some 50 guests—in addition to the male and female graduate students, often with their undergraduate dates, there was a contingent of faculty members. This mixture, plus copious amounts of alcohol and sufficient marijuana, provided the guests with animated conversations and vociferous arguments on any subject one could desire. And, more important, ample opportunity to begin new relationships and, if one were fortunate, to arrange future liaisons. When, some time later, Betty told me Throckmorton had a vacancy and asked if I would like to be interviewed as a potential member, I jumped at the chance.

In typical Berkeley fashion, the original denizens had chosen the name Throckmorton when they happened on a *San Francisco Chronicle* story of a Lord Throckmorton who had contributed his manor to the British war effort. The reigning Lord of the Manor was Don Kalish, a philosopher of the logical positivist persuasion. Having been evicted from several dwellings because of a penchant for playing Mozart operas at ear-splitting level, he rented Throckmorton to run his own show. Rent on the Manor was $60 per month (rentals were then under wartime rent control), so rent for the 10 residents was $6 per month plus shared utilities. Occasionally, the landlady, a rich eccentric who had been born in the Manor and now lived somewhere in the Berkeley hills, would storm into the Manor, demand that we all leave immediately—"I want you out, out, I say"—as she went from room to room before storming out in the same manner she stormed in. We would not see her again for months.

Moving into Throckmorton was one of those life-defining moments. Instantly, I had a family with an ever-changing cast of characters that ranged from serious to eccentric scholars but all totally dedicated to a life of the mind. So long as we paid our rent and share of the utilities on time and didn't cheat on the amount we drank from the communal bar, we were allowed our individual eccentricities. As might be expected, the nice middle-class neighbors did not appreciate Throckmorton, but their complaints to the police elicited nothing more than requests to turn down the music.

When Kalish, after exhausting his excuses for not completing his dissertation, reluctantly took a position at UCLA, I inherited his office and the responsibility of dealing with the Berkeley police department. Sometime after I assumed office, the neighbors lodged a complaint that Throckmorton was a whorehouse and a dope den. I was not aware of the complaint until I answered the door one day to greet the police lieutenant in charge of the vice squad. He informed me that his officers had investigated the whorehouse and dope-den complaint and that the complaint had not been sustained by the facts. He had told the head complainant, "Lady, the same men that go in, come out; if there are whores in there, they're starving to death." As to the dope and matters in general, his advice was brief and to the point. "Sperling, I don't care who you screw, what you sniff, or what you smoke, just keep it out of sight."

To me, Berkeley was the intellectual capital of the world. All of the grad students were either on the GI Bill or were TAs or both, so almost no one had to work. Our campus-based duties were usually not arduous, so we could spend a good part of every day in the cafes and bookstores that began at Sather Gate and ran down Telegraph Avenue for four blocks. In the cafes, we honed our academic skills by expounding and arguing theory, fact, and fiction—it was a moveable intellectual feast.

Compared with Reed, Berkeley was a cakewalk when it came to classwork. My first-year program was composed of upper-division courses in my major and minor fields plus a large proseminar. In the first semester, I was able to buy FyBate Notes (a professional note-taking service) for all of my upper-division courses. Consequently, I only went to class to turn in my registration card and to take the midterms and finals, and I spent my days in the cafes.

It would be hard to imagine a more ideal society for someone preparing for an academic career. We were part of what we considered to be the greatest university in the world, and now looking back, I think Wordsworth's lines from his *Comments on the Revolution in France* best expresses how I felt: "Bliss it was on that dawn to be alive, but to be young was very heaven."

Not only was I enjoying my intellectual life, Throckmorton also provided a rich social life with all of the sensual pleasures of a bohemian society in which the cliché of wine, women, and song happened to be an accurate description. When we could afford it, we rented a box at the opera, filled a thermos with martinis, and pretended we were rich. The night I heard *Don Giovanni* with Ezio Pinza as the Don, John Brownlee as Leparello, Jan Pierce as Don Ottavio, Bidu Sayao as Zerlina, and Joan Sutherland as Donna Anna, I was hooked on opera forever.

Unfortunately, this graduate student idyll was disrupted by the woman who was to become my second wife. Shortly after our meeting she moved into Throckmorton with me and quickly became the social secretary. Virginia was interestingly beautiful and a talented artist, but partying and making the scene consumed most of her time. Unfortunately, this lifestyle conflicted with my need to prepare for my doctoral written and oral exams and we were soon in conflict.

I certainly was not loving wisely. I wanted to accede to her desires but not deny my own. Being essentially of a weak will, I was not just pulled in conflicting ways, I was torn. Even worse for my fragile ego, shortly after we married she began to seek other males to play with; I was too cowardly to bring her to heel and I lacked the needed sophistication not to care. I was able to tolerate the conflict until I began preparation for my doctoral qualifying exams, at which point I experienced another psychosomatic crisis. This time it was vertigo. The attacks occurred mostly at night when I was lying down, but sometimes they would strike during the day while sitting in class or walking down the street. If I was sitting down, I would have to sit bolt upright or, if on the street, steady myself against a wall or shop window and stare at a fixed point to slow down and stop the spinning. I also developed a compulsion to jump from any height that was higher than the second story of a building. Once more, I was a mess.

As the date for the qualifying exams approached, I fled Throckmorton and moved into a hotel on Telegraph Avenue. To eliminate the temptation to jump out of my third-floor room, I placed all the furniture except the bed in front of the window. From this safe haven, I was able to prepare for my exams and I did quite well. The exam had three parts and, of the 28 candidates, I was 1 of 4 who passed all three. Once the exams were over, I moved back to Throckmorton because it provided the support I needed to prepare for my qualifying orals, which would cover my major field of Modern English History and my philosophy minor of British Empiricism. My orals were at two o'clock on a sunny day in mid-May. Virginia, who had just received a Fulbright scholarship to study in Munich, was feeling quite generous, so she served me lunch in the backyard of Throckmorton. I began lunch with a substantial martini and was feeling pretty good as I walked up Telegraph to the campus. I passed both parts of the oral with distinction and, although I was not to find out until the following fall, my performance on the writtens and the orals was to win me a richly endowed three-year studentship at King's College Cambridge. Unlike the Rhodes Scholar competition, this time I would be ready.

3

The Education
of John Sperling
Part II—1954 to 1960
Voyage to Europe

Over the course of studying British history, I had become an Anglophile and, although I knew it was an intellectually indefensible position, I was emotionally committed to the Whig interpretation of history. For those gentle readers who are unfamiliar with this term, I can define it simply thus—it is history as teleology; the English-speaking nation is on the march, if not to perfection, at least to ever higher levels of excellence culturally, economically, and politically. The sheer grandeur of the history of the English-speaking peoples was both compelling and seductive.

I had decided to write my dissertation on seventeenth- and eighteenth-century financial history, but I most enjoyed the history of the English common law, how wonderfully practical it was in codifying not abstract principles, but rather the experience of the people. If I may be pardoned this long aside, I can report that I am puzzled by the fact that for a long while, I had two incompatible loves—the common law and socialism. Socialism had an emotional appeal to my sense of social justice and equality that was absent from capitalism, but it simply did not occur to me that, unlike the common law, socialism's abstract principles reduce human experience to a limited set of categories, which, had I ever been subjected to them, I would have found intolerable. I suppose I had allowed my negative feelings toward the middle class and its historic commitment to capitalism to muddle my mind.

This digression is my way of reporting that having decided to do my dissertation on English financial history, I would have to do my research in the British Museum and the Public Record Office, both located in London. I accompanied Virginia to Germany, and once she was settled in Munich, planned to go to England to do my research. The Fulbright Scholars received their orientation in Bad Honef, a small city across the Rhine from Bonn. We were only there for a few days when one of the Fulbright scholars came into the dining hall to ask me if I had seen the story in the Manchester *Guardian* announcing that I was the new Ehrman Student at King's College Cambridge. I was at a total loss, but there it was in the *Guardian,* which, incidentally, became my favorite English newspaper.

I had never known such a studentship existed, but in verifying that I had indeed won the award, I discovered that the Ehrman student was chosen once every three years from among all the students at all of the University of California campuses. I was ecstatic, but my wife was less so. She insisted that before I left for Cambridge, I should accompany her to Munich and make certain that she was well settled. Had I done so, I would have missed the beginning of the Michelmas (fall) term, and that I was not about to do. Ambition had given me an unaccustomed courage, so I informed her that I was leaving forthwith for Cambridge. I left her in a pout that was to last for several years.

Once arrived at the Cambridge station, I took a bus down bicycle-filled streets to the market and then by foot to the King's College gate on King's Parade. The Porter checked, found that I was expected, and directed me to my lodgings in the Garden Cottage. The walk from King's Gate, through the College, over the Cam, past the Backs, and on to Garden Cottage so enthralled me that I was now willing to give my Anglophilia full expression.

No one seemed eager for me to begin my academic endeavors, so I had ample time to wander about the town and to spend time in the pubs with the very congenial English students. There were no women in the College, and students were still required to wear an academic gown when in the town, and there were still curfews and proctors to enforce them—I was delighted with the whole scene.

I had picked up a bit of the way things were done from the students, but I did not figure out what I was going to do academically until I met with the head tutor. I had arrived in Cambridge with the intention of doing research and writing my Berkeley dissertation.

However, at this meeting, I was informed that, as a research student, I could write a dissertation and take a Ph.D. from Cambridge. If I were so inclined, I could do a second version and submit it to Berkeley. Snobbery immediately took hold of me and I agreed on the spot—I would not only have a doctorate from Berkeley, I would be Dr. John Sperling, PhD, Cantab.

I only attended three lectures while in Cambridge, which was not unusual. When a lecture was scheduled, the professor often would send a runner down to the Mill Lane auditorium to see if anyone had shown up. If no one had, the don didn't have to leave his rooms.

As at Berkeley, most of what I learned was outside the classrooms and meetings with my dissertation supervisor. My Cambridge education took place in the pubs, the cafes, in the library, in my rooms, and, given the nature of my research, in the British Museum and the Public Record Office. A typical day would begin with breakfast at the Arts with my College chums, most of whom were bright working-class students whose scholarship at King's was as improbable as my own. After breakfast, I worked all day in the University Library or in my rooms with only a break for a pub lunch. All of us worked at hard, intellectual labor all day so we rewarded ourselves with high tea in one of our rooms or, more often, with a trip to a pub (usually the Pickrel) for dinner, followed by beer drinking and darts until bedtime. It was an all-male world.

Once I had agreed on a dissertation topic with my supervisor, my research took me to London several days a week, and that pretty much ended my Cambridge life. I took the morning train, the Fenman, to Liverpool Station, then the Underground to either the Museum or the Public Record Office, then back again on the Fenman that left the station at 4:10 P.M. I had breakfast on the train and read the *Guardian* and the *Times,* plus reviewed my notes; on the trip back, I read the tabloids and reviewed the day's work. Back in Cambridge, I was too late for high tea, but I could usually find my chums at the Pickrel where I would have a late supper, beer, and darts.

London

At the Christmas break, Virginia joined me in London. I rented a pleasant set of rooms in Hampstead and prepared myself for the joys of a London Christmas. Alas, it was not to be. Virginia, who had always preferred homosexuals as friends, had fallen in love with a fellow art student at the Munich Kunst Acadamie. He was five years younger than she and, by her own admission, fickle, bisexual, and not a fit subject for a long-term, serious relationship. In addition, she was not reluctant to inform me that it was these things which made him so much more attractive than I.

This cast me into a slough of despond during which I contemplated suicide, murder, catatonia, and flight, all to no avail. Unfortunately for me, I was still in love with her and didn't have the courage to end it. Furthermore, neither of us had anyplace else to go, so we slogged through the vacation. When Virginia returned to Munich, I stayed on in London.

At this point, I had only been in residence at Cambridge for one term and I needed three terms in residence to take my doctorate. All it took to qualify as a resident, however, was having rooms in Cambridge and taking at least three meals in College during a term. I satisfied these conditions by taking the cheapest room I could find in Cambridge and traveling up to Cambridge three times during each of the next two terms so I could take dinner in my College. I suppose one could have called me an absentee scholar.

Once I had made the proper arrangements at the University, I took a room in the Golders Green section of London and concentrated on my research. It was a cold winter and London in 1954 was still recovering from the War. The only thing warm in the British Museum was the water in the restroom washbasins. I would sit bundled up all day in the Reading Room, and when my hands got so cold I could not untie the red tape with which seventeenth- and eighteenth-century bureaucrats used to tie up bundles of documents (thus, red tape), I would go to the washroom and soak my hands until movement returned. The Public Record Office was somewhat better because there was a coal fire in the room where one could examine the historical documents. If one arrived early enough, it was possible to get a seat within the "warm" area, and one could always warm one's hands at the fire. I really was into my research, but I could not stomach working alone in a half-cold room at night. My nighttime solace was the theater. In San Francisco, I fell in love with opera, in London I fell in love with theater.

After the day's research, I would head for the West End, find a play with a cheap seat and then have a pub dinner before curtain time.

That was only good for weekdays and Saturdays. On Sundays, only theater clubs were open, so I joined all the major ones. In good weeks, I could see a play every night. When there was no play I wanted to see, or could afford to see, I would substitute a movie, a symphony, chamber music, or an opera, which meant that almost every night was filled with some sort of entertainment.

Somewhere about this time, I realized that, from inclination or necessity, I had become a misanthrope. As Sartre commented, "If you feel alone when you are alone, you're in bad company." Fortunately, most of the time that I was alone I felt that I was in pretty good company.

In the spring I went to Munich where I met Virginia's friends. Then, after a brief stay, my wife and I took the train to Italy. By this time, Virginia was slightly over her infatuation with her bisexual art student, so things were pretty good between us. Baedecker in hand, we did an academic grand tour—Florence, Venice, Rome, Naples, Pompei, Paestum, and Amalfi. Even though our dollars were few, the dollar was King, so we lived very well, and by the end of the tour we had pretty much patched up our relationship.

That spring I was joined in London by Alby Mott, a graduate school friend from Berkeley and his Swedish wife, Sev. They had met while Alby had been teaching for the army in Japan and Sev had been an army nurse in Korea. They had saved their money so together we could afford a flat. Luckily, we found a lovely attic place in Southampton Road just across from Bedford Square and only a few blocks from the British Museum, so Alby and I could walk to work. Virginia finished her Fulbright in June and immediately joined us in London, and it was a pretty congenial arrangement. Alby and I worked at research all day, Virginia enrolled in an art school just down the road, and Sev kept house. None of the others had my passion for the theater, so I spent more evenings at home and substituted English novels for the theater. During that period, Virginia and I read most of Dickens, all of Evelyn Waugh, *Tom Jones* twice, Stella Gibbons' *Cold Comfort Farm*, and most of Restoration drama. It was an eclectic foray into literature, but it certainly filled up my evenings.

By the following spring, I had finished my research and, because I write fairly quickly, I was able to complete my dissertation in eight weeks. Six weeks later I sat for and passed my orals. By May, I was a Ph.D. Cantab.

Girsha

In anticipation that I would soon have my degree and a job in the United States, Virginia returned to Berkeley to await my coming. Unfortunately, or perhaps fortunately, there were no jobs immediately available, so I found work teaching in the European program of the University of Maryland. It was a stopgap measure that would last for nearly two years. My first assignments were all in England—Rislip, Mendenhall, and the U.S. Embassy in London were among them. My disappointment at not having a real academic job soon passed as I discovered that my teaching stipend was sufficient to support comfortable rooms, first in Radnor Place, then in Lancaster Square. An added benefit was access to the PX, which allowed me to buy alcohol and cigarettes at prices one-quarter of those on the English market, and which, subsequently, added much to my popularity among my London friends. Soon after Virginia left, I gave a party at the Southhampton flat and met the first great love of my life—Girsha. I learned what little I know about love or women from her, but as was my wont, I was hardly forthcoming. I did not tell her I was married, but wonderful woman that she was, when quite by accident she did find out, she forgave me.

By the time I met Girsha, Alby and Sev were gone, so I gave up the Southhampton Road flat and Girsha and I moved into rooms in Radnor Place, a few turnings west of Paddington Station. Life in London could not have been better. I taught two nights a week and spent most of my days at the London Historical Institute hacking articles out of my dissertation. Girsha had a nine-to-five job in the garment district, which gave us three nights free plus weekends.

Girsha was from a lower-class Irish family that lived in some dismal town east of London. She had quit school when she was 16 and had come to London, where she lived by hard work at less than a living wage and by her wits (meaning that, when necessary, she slept for her supper and whatever else she might earn with her charms—rent, clothes, transportation). She was fiercely independent and took crap from no one.

By the time we met, she was almost self-supporting, so together we had plenty of money to support the lifestyle we enjoyed. And enjoy it we did. When we were not working, we spent every minute together. We devoured London—parks, museums, restaurants, films, and plays, with weekend trips to places like Bath and Brighton and, on holidays, to Paris or drives through the Normandy countryside. One of our greatest pleasures was walking around London. Girsha was a head taller than I, so she would throw her arm over my shoulder and, whenever I got too cheeky, whack me on the head or put me in a neck lock until I agreed to behave. Why, I still ask myself, did I not keep her—divorce Virginia, marry her, and take her to America. The answer, dear reader, is that I was still a snob. I wanted an academic career and I couldn't see an academic community accepting a lower-class, uneducated woman as a proper academic wife. In my defense, I am certain that, had she become one, she would have longed for London and been miserable in a dismal academic town. Had I known then that I didn't want to be an academic husband, perhaps I would have made a different decision. Anyway, I left her and went off to Ohio State to continue my academic "career."

Hello to Columbus

Virginia and I arrived in Columbus in a 1949 Chevy we had driven from Berkeley. We were nearly broke and knew we had to exist for at least a month before the first check arrived from my salary, a princely $4,000 a year. Eking out the first month's expenses was only the first of the petty shifts I stooped to in my life as a junior academic. We spent the first week in a rented room while we searched for an apartment, with, I might add, no help from my department. However, luck smiled upon us and we found a vacant flat above a college bookstore right across the street from the campus.

Fortunately, Virginia was a genius at finding bits and pieces of furniture and furnishings at little cost, so she soon made the place quite livable. Before the first month was out, I had soured on the University, and it rankled me that after three years in Europe and a Cambridge Ph.D., the best I could come by was an instructorship in the history department—compliments of a graduate school friend. In my first quarter, and for all subsequent quarters, I was assigned only survey courses. In fact, in my 20 years of academic life, I never once taught a course in my so-called specialty.

The quality of life in the department was vividly illustrated by an evening reception that the chairman gave for the new faculty. His name was Harold Grimm and grim he was—pale and bloodless—and the reception was of the same quality. We sat about the Grimms' front room making forced conversation with the high point of the evening being coffee and ice cream. I have seldom longed so much for a drink to dull a social pain. Except for a couple of instructors, one maverick full-professor, and a handful of lively graduate students, there were only pompous tenured professors in the department. Their conversation was bounded by disquisitions on their narrow specialty and petty academic politics, especially who had left what job and who was likely to get the appointment.

In addition to the boredom of my job in this boring college town, there was the yawning boredom of my marriage. The most awful moment of the week was Friday afternoon after my last class when I had to look forward to two days at home—at school I only had a desk in the instructor's bullpen so I had to work at home—and the undiluted companionship of my wife. How I longed for Girsha.

Although I avoided most of the department's social life, what few invitations Virginia and I accepted were to dinner at parties at which the hostess almost invariably served either a tuna or macaroni casserole and cheap red wine. It was all very grubby and only then did it begin to dawn on me that academic life, especially for the stay-at-home wives, was a depressing affair. How in hell, I thought, can anyone raise a family on these kinds of salaries? The answer was "not very well." Virginia had gotten a position teaching art at the University's demonstration school, so we were able to live slightly above the subsistence level. Just as boredom had led to my learning to sew in the Army, boredom now led me to learn how to cook so, even though we were poor, we were able to entertain somewhat close to Throckmorton standards; that is, with regard to food and drink.

Needless to say, my attitude toward academic and social life at Ohio State did not bode well for someone supposedly building an academic career. However, there were two bright spots in my two years in Columbus. The first was going to counseling with a psychotherapist on the staff of the hospital at the state prison. I went to see him to deal with a depression compounded by a lousy job, a lousy marriage, and a bleak future. I am not an introspective type, but I dwelt on the same garden-variety complaints that had plagued me for 20 years—an overbearing mother, a wretched father, difficulty in making friends, difficult relations with women, and so forth. After listening to me for a couple of sessions, the therapist told me he thought my problems were more philosophical than psychological and suggested a set of readings from Dostoevsky, Nietzsche, Camus, and Sartre. I had read a good deal of philosophy, ranging from the Greeks to the linguistic philosophers, plus a concentrated study of British empiricism, so it was hard for me to see how this new reading list was going to ameliorate my philosophical confusion. Instead of arguing with me, he simply asked me to trust him and to make a good-faith effort at reading what he had recommended. Our remaining sessions covered the assigned reading, and the concept of life as an existence that only the person living it can imbue with meaning and purpose slowly seeped into the way I perceived the world. The shackles of resentment arising from both real and imagined assaults, abuses, injustices, and malevolently bad luck fell away. I realized that many of my traumas were self-inflicted and that I could continue to make myself a miserable loser or, in the hackneyed language of self-help, "take control of my life."

Having this *existential apperçu* is as close to a religious experience as I have ever had. This awakening ended any further need for psychological counseling, then or since. It ended my periodic psychological crises and turned me into a chronic optimist. I no longer wallowed in problems, especially those with women—I just got on with life. From Virginia onward, women have accused me of refusing to work through "problems," of never looking back while I busily buried the past by piling up new experiences. I can only plead guilty.

The second bright spot of my dismal sojourn in Ohio was getting involved with the Civil Liberties Union. I think it was the wife of a math professor whom I met at one of those dismal faculty parties who recruited me. I was taken with her because of a story she told to illustrate the pomposity of academic life. Her brother taught at Princeton and, when she and her husband went to visit him, they could not find his house. They stopped at a service station in what they were certain was his neighborhood, and when they inquired for her brother by asking for professor X, the service station attendant replied, "Oh, '*Associate*' Professor X. He lives just down the street, third house on the left."

At any rate, she was the president of an almost moribund chapter of the Union, and that first meeting I agreed to attend was an essay in hopelessness. Here they were, a room full of academics, at the dawn of the civil rights movement, with no clue as to what to do. The immediate issue before them was the intolerable condition of prisoners in the State Penitentiary there in Columbus, especially one particular Black prisoner whose cause they had adopted. I agreed to organize some action to address the matter, and I did so by persuading a professor in the Law School to visit the prisoner. The law professor filed a writ of *habeas corpus* and managed to get the man released. Following this triumph, I was asked to recruit some of my fellow professors to the cause. I did so by using the phone to confront the liberals in the English and social science departments with their failure to support that to which they were verbally committed. Phrased more bluntly, I asked them to put their money where their mouth was.

This too was a success, and soon I found myself the president of the Central Ohio Chapter of the Civil Liberties Union. It was my first essay in political/social activism, and I discovered I was as talented in this endeavor as I was untalented in the academic one. Although I found it intolerably sycophantic to curry favor with a senior professor or dean, I had no hesitation in hustling a junior or senior professor to join the ACLU.

As soon as I became involved in social activism, my depression lifted, but I also became even more of a bastard in my marriage. Virginia had attempted to get pregnant for several years. She suffered a miscarriage while we were in Germany, and I had been totally unsympathetic. Now, she was once again pregnant and I was equally unsympathetic. In looking for some redeeming element in my behavior, I can only think that I was still haunted by the fear that any child of mine would have the same deformity suffered by my brother Leon—a short Achilles tendon that caused him to walk on his toes with a cane. Leon's first child, a boy, was normal, but his second, a girl, had the same short tendon and was lame in exactly the same way.

Whatever the source of my emotional confusion, I forced a separation and sent Virginia off to live with her parents in Stillwater, Oklahoma. Six months later, my son Peter was born.

A Sea Change by Land

Once Virginia was gone, a fellow instructor moved into the apartment with me, and I took up with Shirley, the wife of an economics instructor. When my apartment mate took another job, Shirley left her husband and moved in with me. At the end of the academic year, I took her to Berkeley with me. Why Berkeley? Because, I considered Berkeley home, and because Virginia had also returned to Berkeley. I wanted to be near the son that I had feared to father.

At the end of the summer, Shirley and I returned to Ohio State for one more quarter. During that quarter, I negotiated an Assistant Professorship at Northern Illinois University, but before assuming my new position, I received a grant from the Council of Learned Societies to complete a chapter on seventeenth- and eighteenth-century public finance for the New Cambridge Modern History. This required a trip to London, and I again moved in with Girsha. By this time, she was working in television and moving up in the world. It was as if we had never been apart, but we also knew this was the last time we would ever be together. Our lives were very different, and nothing either of us could do could bring them together. Both of our upper lips were stiff when I left London to return to the States.

Columbus had been depressing, but to me DeKalb, Illinois, was the dregs. I took up residence there at the beginning of the spring, taught my classes, wrote a monograph on the South Sea Company for Harvard's Baker Library, and somehow managed to survive. A month before the semester ended, I informed the chairman, who was one of the nicest academics I ever met, that I was quitting. He had seen recruiting me as snaring a budding "academic star," and now, in less than a semester, he was losing me. He offered me a promotion to Associate Professor for which I was most grateful, but I told him, and I meant it, that I was simply not cut out for the academic life, and that I was going back to Berkeley.

While I was in London and DeKalb, Shirley had also gone back to Berkeley. She had been a biochemistry graduate student before her marriage, and now she was reenrolled at U.C. and taking a research exchange at a German university. After a brief stay in Berkeley, I planned to join her in Europe.

Once back in California, though, I began to spend part of every day with my one-year-old son. Peter enriched my life in ways I could hardly fathom, but he also gave me, for the first time, a sense of my own mortality. I realized how little time I had left if I was to achieve anything of significance, and I have wasted little of my time since those first intimations of mortality.

On the day I was to leave to join Shirley in Europe, Virginia and Peter drove me to the Oakland airport. When my plane was ready to board, I picked up my son and I couldn't put him down. I turned to Virginia and said, "I'm staying here." We went back to the car and the next week I moved in with Virginia and Peter.

San Jose State

Having decided to stay in California, my first task was to decide on a new career and then find a job. However, then fate intervened in the form of the only father figure I have ever known.

A former colleague from Ohio State was now an Assistant Professor of English at San Jose State. He and his wife invited Virginia and me to come down from Berkeley for the day because they were giving a garden party for the English department. One of the guests was Clint Williams, Professor of English and Director of the Humanities Honors Program at San Jose. Clint was a charming conversationalist, and I spent most of the afternoon with him. Once the academic pleasantries were past, our conversation turned substantive. I tried to explain why I had decided to leave the academy, and to express my considerable anxiety as I faced a career change with no skills other than what I had picked up in some eight years of higher education, namely, knowing how to read and write reasonably well.

Clint was unconvinced by my rationale for leaving, not academe, but a teaching career. He flattered me by saying that too few interesting minds stayed in the field and that he was prepared to offer me a job on the spot. Had I not been so drawn to him, I would have thanked him and politely declined. Instead, I felt compelled to match his boldness and I accepted on the spot, but with a caveat: I would only stay for 1 year. That 1 year eventually would stretch to 12.

4

San Jose State and the Transmogrification of John Sperling

Reentering Academe

For the first year at San Jose State, 1960, we lived in Berkeley and I commuted to work in my 1949 Ford. Because one had to be assigned a home department and humanities was only a program, Clint had arranged for a dual appointment in humanities and history. Humanities classes were Monday, Wednesday, and Friday, and, fortunately, I was able to arrange my history classes on the same schedule. Unfortunately, this soon led to trouble with the Dean of Social Sciences.

San Jose State had been a normal school when the dean first arrived, and professors were expected to work five days a week. Even though the normal school had been promoted to state college status with the usual Monday-Wednesday-Friday and Tuesday-Thursday schedules, the dean was in a time warp and expected professors to report five days a week. This was something I was not about to do.

Some snitch in the history department soon informed the dean of my insubordination, and I was summoned to his office to explain myself. I was only too happy to oblige. I explained that the history department expected me to publish, and Tuesdays and Thursdays were my research time; furthermore, I was not going to drive 100 miles twice a week to satisfy an outmoded regulation. The dean was not impressed; either I conformed or he would fire me.

When I told Clint, he was angry with me for getting myself cross- 47 wise with the dean, but he was pleased that I had stood my ground with someone he considered to be somewhat less than a cretin. Clint thought that the worst the dean could do was not to renew my contract and, having planned to stay for only a year, I was not terribly concerned. However, by this time, Clint was really pleased with my teaching and was determined to keep me. He did not find the task easy but, wily academic politician that he was, he managed to persuade the Academic Vice President to break the home department rule and allow Clint to hire me full-time in the Humanities Program. Clint thought the sort of research going on at San Jose State was mostly a joke, so I was relieved of that task and, by the end of the year, I had come to so enjoy my teaching that I was content to extend my stay at San Jose State.

I would remain at San Jose State for the next 12 years. Without my being even faintly aware of the process, I learned the lessons and developed many of the characteristics that were to make me a successful entrepreneur. During these 12 years, in addition to what I considered powerful, emotional experiences, there were a number of social and intellectual influences and hard-earned lessons that prepared me for yet harder lessons. The totality of those experiences—intellectual, emotional, and practical—allowed me to articulate and reify the philosophy and organizational principles that undergird the companies I founded: the Institute for Professional Development, the University of Phoenix, the Apollo Group, and since 1998, the Kronos Group, Kronosgroup.com, and Apollolearn.com.

The Humanities Program

Freshman and sophomore humanities was a twenty-four credit hour, two-year honors program that satisfied all general education requirements. Enrollment was restricted to freshmen who had high SATs and high grade point averages, and, despite San Jose's third-tier status, these students were among the best and brightest I had ever had. There were, however, other reasons I found the end of my scholarly career and the beginning of my teaching one so instructive and satisfying.

First, there was Clint. He presided over the program as a benign Buddha—witty, charming, and always ready to discuss one's problems and give counsel, especially on teaching matters. As a manager, he was a superb role model; he was unflappable and never allowed discord among his charges to get to him emotionally. He would listen to all parties, ascertain the facts, and gently but firmly direct the discord into productive channels.

Beyond Clint, there were my fellow humanities instructors. All the courses were taught by a four-member team, and I was never assigned to one that I did not enjoy. My colleagues came from English, Art History, History, Political Science, Economics, Anthropology, Sociology, and Foreign Languages, as well as Speech and Drama. They were intellectually lively, dedicated to teaching, and totally unpretentious. If Clint couldn't deflate pretentious egos, he made sure they did not stay long in the program.

The curriculum was decided by a committee under Clint's watchful eye. Only original works were assigned for student reading; any gloss or commentary came from the twice-weekly lectures or from instructors during the thrice-weekly discussion sections. The program always began with the *Iliad* and the *Odyssey,* progressed through the Greek dramatists, Thucydides, Aristotle, and Plato, with lots of lectures on poetry, drama, philosophy, and art history. Then, the program went to Rome for Virgil and the Roman dramatists and on to pre-Christian Europe, anchored by *Beowulf* and *Sir Gawain and the Green Knight.* Once into Christian Europe, the committee was faced with a literary embarrassment of riches, in which the only anchors were Chaucer, Shakespeare, and Milton. After that it was a free-for-all. In philosophy and science, Hobbes, Locke, Berkeley, Leibnitz, Hume, Kant, and Darwin had a secure place, and then it was another free-for-all.

Teaching humanities provided a yearly reeducation, especially if one taught both the first and second years at the same time. I could not have undertaken the educational reforms embodied in the University of Phoenix without the Humanities Program experience. It taught me the importance of small intimate learning groups, the need to have a challenging curriculum, and the learning power of expecting a first-rate performance.

Berkeley, Peter, and Joan

Meanwhile, back in Berkeley, things, as usual, were not going well at home. Although Peter was a daily joy, I found myself wishing I were somewhere else, but only if I had Peter with me. For most of this year when he was three, he was my Berkeley life. Just as Girsha and I devoured London, Peter and I devoured Berkeley. Either on my shoulder or walking hand in hand, we made the scene on Telegraph Avenue and then on to the campus to the Student Union and the next-door outdoor café. We walked the length of Strawberry Creek and explored every crevice of Live Oak Park where the Creek disappeared underground. Occasionally, we would ride the carousel in Tilden Park or visit the Marina to examine the boats and sit on the deck of one of the restaurants sipping our drinks and enjoying the view of the bridges and the spires of San Francisco. In a setting sun, it was a beautiful and romantic tableau.

I do not remember a moment of boredom. Peter talked nonstop, pausing only for an answer to some important question, such as, "Why do ships float? Why do planes stay in the air? Why is the sky blue? Why is grass green? What's the largest number you can think of?" His questions were not unusual, but their number was endless, because his curiosity was endless. During those walks and talks, I never talked down to him, and by the time he was five, he had a vocabulary my college students would have found quite satisfactory. Not only was Peter a great companion, he inspired me to plunge into early childhood education, and it was this new interest that led me once more to stray from marriage.

When the strains of cohabitation became too great, I rented a room some blocks away from our apartment. Virginia was convinced that it was a trysting place, but it was not, it was sanctuary. Having this additional space did not complicate my life until summer when the dedicated Berkeleyites returned home for their summer vacations from colleges and universities across the country. One of the returnees was Joan, wife of a graduate school friend of yore and mother of a daughter a year older than Peter and a son, a year younger. Her husband taught at Wesleyan and she was nearing insanity from the inanities of university society and her husband's serial infidelities.

Joan and I had been casual friends for nearly 10 years. Her husband and Virginia had been Fulbright Scholars together in Munich, and Joan had worked at Radio Liberation From Bolshevism, a CIA operation, which she referred to as "Radio Hole-In-The-Head." I had seen her briefly when I visited Munich to see Virginia. She also had a dear Berkeley graduate school friend whose husband taught at

Ohio State and I had had several long and interesting conversations with her when she visited Columbus. We had even had a desultory correspondence over the past few years. That summer, we discovered that we had both become fascinated with early childhood education and arranged, children in tow, to spend time in Live Oak Park or Tilden Park watching the children play and discussing our new obsession. Those conversations soon turned personal and inevitably to our dissatisfactions with our marriages. One evening she invited me to dinner at the house she had rented for the summer. After dinner we talked for a long time and just drifted into bed.

Again, I was not an unwilling adulterer, and the affair soon blossomed into my second great love; it has lasted on and off throughout the ensuing 35 years. For the rest of the summer, we met every night and, after the children were asleep, we would slip out to the bar just down the street, drink beer or mineral water, and talk until anxiety about the children's safety ended the conversation. I would arise before dawn and make my way back to my room. During our endless conversations, Joan made a firm resolve to ask for a separation and enter Montessori training. Her return to Middletown began a domestic drama that was to last for years and with a most bizarre resolution, which she has recounted in two recently published books—*Reeling and Writhing* and *Change of Circumstance*.

Once Joan returned to Middletown, Berkeley lost its savor and I decided that, if I were going to stay at San Jose, I might as well move there. Not only would I no longer have a 300-mile-per-week commute, we could afford larger accommodations; Peter could have a room and, with more space, I might find it easier to cohabit with Virginia. Virginia was all for the move because she thought it might help save a deteriorating marriage. While we were in Berkeley, Virginia had taught in the Oakland schools and, because the Santa Clara Valley was undergoing explosive expansion, she was able to obtain a position as an art teacher in a Santa Clara middle school. This living arrangement lasted for two years until I could no longer tolerate cohabitation and moved out permanently.

I was a bad husband but a responsible father, as least as far as money was concerned. San Jose State was an urban college that abutted on downtown San Jose. Because of the huge supply of new houses in the burgeoning suburbs, houses in the inner city were really quite cheap. I was able to buy Virginia and Peter a gracious two-story house about six blocks from campus for $28,000. (Virginia still lives there and she was recently offered $500,000 for the place.) Two years later when my finances were somewhat improved, I was able to buy a house around the corner from Virginia—tricycle distance for Peter.

The only domestic crisis I faced in those years was Peter's dyslexia. He was fine in kindergarten, but as soon as he faced the challenge of learning to read, things deteriorated rapidly. He became hyperactive and his first-grade teacher informed me she had never had a pupil before who could fall off his chair in a hundred different ways; also she thought, that as a professor, I should know that he was mildly retarded and that I should not expect him to do much more than finish high school. Given Peter's vocabulary, I concluded that she was the one who was mildly retarded, but her message got my serious attention. I immediately had a child development psychologist colleague examine him. He determined that he had mirror vision, but that he would slowly develop out of it. The pressing problem was to deal with his hyperactivity without resorting to Ritalin. By the clever use of operant conditioning, the psychologist quickly cured Peter's hyperactivity with a simple program. He hired a graduate student to read to Peter three afternoons a week. The student would sit in a chair with Peter on his lap. He would read as long as Peter sat quietly. As soon as Peter jumped down and ran around the room, the student would sit silently, staring straight ahead. If Peter came back and sat quietly in his lap, he got an M&M. Within a month Peter was an attentive student, and he did very well in second grade. In the third grade, he was transferred to a mentally gifted minors' program. By the time Peter had entered second grade, I had moved out of the house I had purchased for Virginia and Peter and into my own apartment.

The English have a saying that, "It's difficult to distinguish old friends from old enemies," and this fits my relationship with Virginia. Although we had a stormy marriage and were one-time enemies, I think we are now good friends. There is no doubt in my mind that I am a much better ex-husband than I ever was a husband.

In addition to teaching, I was involved in union organizing and in the quest for a large research grant. To pursue these research funds seriously, I had hired a much-needed secretary, who worked out of the office I shared with an English professor.

Between the mortgage payments, the apartment rent, and my secretary's salary, I had, against Mr. Micawber's advice, allowed my outgo to exceed my income. In addition to these expenses, I had monthly service costs on a bank loan for a piece of land on the east side of San Jose that some colleagues and I had purchased with the intention of a quick resale. Unfortunately, the City moved west instead of east and we had either to service the debt or lose the land. It was a struggle, but that loan payment turned out to be a form of forced savings from which I would one day enjoy incredible returns.

I have never been afraid to go the unconventional route to invest in my own meager talents, so rather than give up the house, or the secretary, or the land, I simply dispensed with my apartment. I moved in briefly with a recently divorced colleague who had a place in the Santa Cruz Mountains. After that, I became a gypsy.

I left some of my clothes with Virginia and some with a friend. I showered and shaved, catch as catch can, and I slept in my office. It was not the most comfortable arrangement, and my office mate was appalled; first it was the addition of a secretary, and now I had turned a two-person office into a three-person office and then into my bedroom. To keep the peace, I made certain to have stowed my cot, and to be washed, shaved, and dressed for work before he arrived, so he didn't turn me into the College authorities.

Fortunately, the risk and the discomfort paid off. I began to receive a stipend from my position as a teacher's union official, and the large research grant I'd been after was approved.

I had only been at San Jose State for a short time before my tropism for organizing exerted itself. My options were the Faculty Senate, which demanded years of kowtowing to the Administration for one to have a chance at election; a conventional faculty association; and the almost moribund local of the American Federation of Teachers (AFT). The AFT offered the best opportunities, so I joined.

My introduction to the AFT came at a desultory meeting during which the leadership bemoaned the fact that professors were not organizable and, even if they joined, would not come to meetings. I began to offer suggestions on how to recruit members, and I soon found myself chosen chairman of the organizing committee of one.

My only organizing experience was with the Civil Liberties Union, but I figured that, if I talked to enough professors, I would find out their grievances, articulate a message that expressed those grievances, then deliver it in as many forms as possible. My strategy worked, the local began to grow, and meeting attendance shot up. At the next election of officers, I was overwhelmingly elected to a presidency that no one else wanted. For the next 10 years, I was committed to building and running the union; in the process, I learned most of the skills and developed much of the toughness that are the basis of my later business success.

The San Jose local was a member of a council of locals, the College Council, which was dominated by the largest one at San Francisco State. I began to attend the monthly Council meetings and, because the San Jose local was the only one that was growing, my voice was heard. I quickly became chairman of the Council organizing committee, and this time I had some members who would work if I gave them specific tasks. Soon, I was visiting other locals to assist them in membership growth, and this allowed me to construct an effective systemwide political network.

I figured that the College Council would not grow into a formidable statewide organization unless it had statewide policies and strategies focused on Sacramento. I studied the appropriations process and which committees had jurisdiction over the State College budget. I also kept account of the issues that came before the committees and the persons who gave testimony. More important, I kept account of the members of the Assembly and Senate committees, the location of their districts, and whether we had a Council local in the district and a union member who would maintain a relationship with the legislator's local office. In this way, I was able both to identify issues that would resonate with the faculty and work out policy positions that were persuasive enough to cause the local leadership to lobby their Assembly members and Senators.

When the president of the College Council left office, I was the choice of all of the locals except the one at San Francisco State. Once president, I sacked the incompetent Executive Director (a protégé of the San Francisco local president) and hired an ally from the faculty at San Diego State. The office followed the Executive Director, and having the Council office 600 miles away was not to my liking. Furthermore, my ally proved to be only marginally more competent than his predecessor. As soon as his local support dwindled, I forced him out and moved the Council offices to San Jose, just across the street from the campus.

I hired a labor economist as Executive Director. He brought political sophistication earned from years in state politics and a much-needed knowledge of labor history and labor economics. I raised the dues, which enabled me to hire a secretary, two clerk typists who computerized the membership records (we still used punch cards), and for the first time, allowed the Council to communicate directly with the membership.

These changes drew the attention of the state and national AFT offices, and I soon found myself appointed to state and national committees, finally ending up as chairman of the National AFT Higher Education Committee. Both the state and national organizations responded positively to my requests for organizing subsidies, and these enabled me to buy out my time for one semester while I mounted a statewide organizing drive. Within three years, I had established locals on all but 1 of the 11 State College campuses, and the Council membership approached 4,000. I now traveled regularly to other states to assist in organizing campaigns and, in the process, put together a network of national union contacts.

The Strike

The 1968 professors' strike at San Francisco State and San Jose State took place against a backdrop of assassinations—Bobby Kennedy, Martin Luther King—and violent protests against the war in Vietnam, especially those at the Democratic National Convention in Chicago. At the beginning of the 1968 fall semester, the Black students at San Francisco State began an increasingly militant agitation to force the administration to upgrade Black studies from a program to a department. As the agitation continued, it drew in the Chicanos and the Asians, all demanding departmental status and increased enrollments for their ethnic groups. The more the administration resisted, the higher the demands went, and in October, the Third World Strike began at San Francisco State.

The only group that had currency with the students was the local AFT and slowly, almost inexorably, the AFT was drawn into the conflict. Once the AFT strike at San Francisco State was under way, I saw it as a possible avenue to force the State University Trustees to grant collective bargaining to the faculty, and I was confident the Council would win any vote for bargaining agent. In pursuit of this strategy, I persuaded the leaders and membership of the AFT local at San Jose State University to mount a sympathy strike.

I soon learned that almost no one has sympathy for a sympathy strike, and this proved to be the case with the members of the San Jose local. The week prior to the scheduled walkout, I decided that the response to the strike call was too weak for the strategy to be successful, and I tried to cancel the action. Unfortunately, the local president had by this time wrapped himself in the cloak of leadership and was determined to be a hero. The only way I could have stopped the strike at this point was to oust the president and tear the local apart. Reluctantly, I decided to let the strike go forward, and, instead of tearing the local apart by stopping the strike, I tore it apart by letting the strike occur.

It was not a glorious action; only one-fourth of the membership participated, which left us with 100 professors and a like number of student sympathizers walking around in the January rain for 31 days. We did what we could to disrupt the University's operation, including a sit-in in the president's office. Fortunately, we had enough popular professors on strike to make a mass firing more agonizing than the administration wanted to endure, so we were able to at least bargain our way back to work.

The strike was the beginning of the end of my union career. Not only did I lose much of my credibility as a leader, I became the most disliked, often hated, man on my own campus and on several others as well.

As the saying goes, pain teaches, and the painful experience of the strike and its aftermath taught me the most important of the many lessons I learned from my union experience—one, without which, I could never have been a successful entrepreneur. The lesson was simple: Ignore your detractors and those who say that what you are doing is wrong, against regulations, or illegal.

The strike was one of the most liberating experiences of my life because, after that, I was immune to the disapproval of the University administration, my peers, the higher education establishment, and their allies in state government—primarily, the higher education regulatory agencies. Without that psychological immunity, it would have been impossible to create and protect the Institute for Professional Development (IPD) and the University of Phoenix (UOP) from disapproval, hostility, FBI investigations, legal assaults, and attempts to legislate IPD and UOP out of existence.

Even though the strike failed, I retained my Council presidency but, in penance for the error of my ways, I spent the following year wooing the unaffiliated faculty association into a merger with the AFT. To do this, I needed to broaden the Council's reach, so I turned my organizing talents to the University of California. I gave the tiny AFT locals at the Berkeley and Davis campuses staff organizing subsidies that enabled them to reach respectable size. With membership spread to the University of California, the Council now had sufficient respectability to seduce the leadership of the faculty association, and I organized a convention that would merge the two organizations into the United Professors of California. I expected, as did all of my faithful followers, that I would be elected president of this new organization, but fate smiled upon me, and I was overwhelmingly rejected in favor of a colorless president of a small local. After that humiliation, I was elected chairman of the organizing committee by acclamation.

That night, as I lay in bed, I thought my useful life had come to an end. Ten years of hard work and exercise of talent had come to naught. I thought of Yeat's "Ode To A Friend Whose Work Has Come To Naught," but I was not comforted. How could they have rejected me when every one of them knew that I was the most talented union leader they had ever had and would probably ever have? Crawling out of that abyss was one of the hardest things I have ever done, but this time my love of literature served me well. I thought of Tom Jones the morning he discovered he had spent the night making love to his mother. His first thought was, "I must kill myself." Then, at least in the film version, he reflects on that rather drastic act and concludes, "No, I will not kill myself, I will go to America." Like Tom, I would not let my useful life end. I too would travel to America, to the America of business, an America I had always held in contempt.

ECON-12

I had begun serious prospecting for research money in 1963, and in 1964, Susan Wiggins, an economics professor, and I hit the big time.

We received a $350,000 grant from the U.S. Office of Education to design a 12th-grade economics course. Our first grant was for three years, but we greatly underestimated the difficulties of the task. The first grant was followed by a second, a third, and we finally finished six years later.

What I learned about concepts of learning and instructional design form the infrastructure for the educational programs I developed for the Institute for Professional Development and the University of Phoenix. It has taken another 25 years of building on that infrastructure to produce what I call the University of Phoenix teaching-learning system—a system that is now considered by many to be the nation's most effective system of education for working adults.

Once we got into the project we discovered that, to explain economic theory to high school students, we had to understand what the theorists called the *structure of the discipline*. That took many months of study and conversation with leading economists. We then restated the structure in the form of a conceptual framework the students could use to organize the material we presented. Once we had that fairly well in hand, we then had to study how teenagers learn. That took us into learning theory, developmental psychology, and instructional design. The end product was a teaching-learning system with defined inputs and learning outcomes. In addition to the readings, we had programmers write short text programs that taught the basic theoretical concepts, suggested classroom activities, and developed testing procedures to ensure student achievement of the learning outcomes.

Susan Wiggins, who was a superb economics instructor, did most of the teaching, and although she was able to obtain the designed learning outcomes, this was not true when we field-tested the materials with high school teachers who knew little economics. To carry out the needed teacher training, we applied for and received a grant from the National Science Foundation that allowed us to conduct a series of summer economics education institutes. Once the teachers had absorbed a modicum of economic theory, the results were excellent.

These were the heady days of the Great Society. I remember telling the teachers in one of the institutes that, with Johnson in the White House, there was going to be a renaissance in K–12 education. With support from the U.S. Department of Education and the National Science Foundation, we would be able to train economists to conduct the institutes so teachers all across America would be able to teach real economics in their 12th-grade classes. Secure in this delusion, Susan and I wrote five short textbooks: *Concepts and Institutions, Industrial Organization, The National Economy, Third World Economies,* and *Communist Economies.* By the time the textbooks were published, the Vietnam War had sucked up the money we had hoped would go to K-12 education. There were no more teacher institutes, and feedback from the districts that adopted the texts without proper teacher preparation was largely negative. Sales soon dried up, the publisher dropped the project, and Susan and I went on to other things.

Fortunately for me, I applied what I had learned from Econ-12 to my university teaching (by this time San Jose State College had been promoted to San Jose State University), and to the curriculum I developed for three government-funded projects that followed Econ-12. The first was in environmental education, the second was a program to prepare learning disadvantaged Hispanics for higher education, and the third was a project to design an educational program that would help teachers and policemen cope more effectively with the problem of juvenile delinquency. It was this last project that allowed me to apply almost all of what I had learned about learning over the previous decade. Also, it presented a set of problems that in 1970 was unique to higher education—how to deliver effective higher education to working adults.

In 1970, adults lacked effective access even to ineffective higher education. Supposedly, the mission of my own university was to serve the entire community, but a working adult wanting to pursue a degree was offered courses designed for kids just out of high school, taught by professors who considered it their job to deliver the subject matter in lectures scheduled for two or three nights per week. With great persistence, an adult learner could expect to earn a degree in 6 to 10 years—for some, it took 20.

What was needed was a product that was equivalent in learning outcomes to traditional campus-based education, yet could be delivered at times and places and in a format that adults found desirable. It was the challenge of dealing with these adult education problems that led directly to the founding of the Institute for Professional Development and, consequently, to the founding of the University of Phoenix. I take up this part of my story in the next chapter.

Humanities 160

The junior and senior humanities students were a breed apart; they only enrolled in Humanities 160 (an elective devoted to a contemporary issue) if they wanted not just three credit hours to study a contemporary issue but an experience as well. I set the learning objectives; the students were responsible for determining how they would achieve them. Naturally, this meant that no two Humanities 160 courses would be the same. Each semester, the course allowed me to lead 20 or so talented and imaginative junior and seniors on some of the more memorable trips of my life, as well as theirs. These were trips that allowed me, and them, to conceive and carry out projects that were audacious and, to our detractors, outrageous and unseemly.

The most memorable was the class that began in the fall of 1969, a time marked by student protests, draft card burnings, and agitprop. As this class got under way, environmentalism was making daily headlines. This class decided to celebrate the first Earth Day with something they called Survival Faire.

In a one-semester course, these 20 students organized a series of events that consumed the attention of the entire campus and whose climax made news around the world. At a time when police were being called onto many California campuses to control student activism, it is remarkable that the administration let us get away with it. Perhaps environmentalism was still like Mom and Apple Pie, or maybe it was the weariness that followed the anti-Vietnam protests, but, for whatever reason, the administration let my students literally take control of the campus and hold it for over a month.

The editor of the student newspaper, the *Spartan Daily,* was a member of the class, as well as several members of the Student Council. With direct access to that kind of influence on campus, Survival Faire took occupancy of all three floors of a large Student Union and converted it into a venue for environmental art, film, and seminars. However, this was child's play in contrast to the main act to follow.

What really set the stage for this to become an unforgettable experience for the students, for the University, and for me as a teacher was the students' "big idea." In retrospect, I recognize it as a stroke of PR genius. Here in San Jose, with its decayed inner city and endless land-eating suburbs, they decided to buy a new car and bury it on campus to protest the role of the automobile in polluting the atmosphere and degrading the environment. That decision set off a set of activities that constituted the best learning experience any of them had ever had. They raised the money for the car—they decided on a yellow Ford Maverick—obtained all of the permits and permissions for burying it, arranged for the equipment to dig the grave, and planned the landscaping that would memorialize the grave.

What happened next, no one anticipated. As soon as the Humanities students announced their plans, students from the Black Studies Program expressed outrage that rich White students would buy and bury a new car when poor Black people had no transportation. The Chicano Studies Program immediately organized to oppose the Blacks. They raised high the banner of environmental ethics and reverence for the earth as practiced by their indigenous forebears. The controversy then spilled over into the public press and radio and, in a stroke of good luck, Governor Reagan denounced the whole affair as a stupid idea.

On the day the yellow Maverick was purchased, the students pushed the car from the showroom to the center of campus where they cordoned it off with red velvet ropes provided by a local movie theatre. As the day of the burial drew closer, tensions on campus rose. As the chief instigator, I was warned that if the students didn't back off, I would be assassinated, but I was not about to tell them anything of the sort. On the day of the burial, the Blacks began to walk past the Maverick and whack it with whatever was at hand. With the clock ticking down to the time of interment, scuffles broke out as the Blacks began to attack the Maverick in earnest, first with fists and then with baseball bats, and the Whites and Chicanos acted to protect it.

We had built a platform with a PA system from which we would officiate at the burial. The class representatives and I were on the platform taking turns explaining our position—automobiles were environmental criminals. They devoured scarce resources, polluted the air, and sucked people out of cities into depressing suburbs. Americans had to free themselves from the internal combustion engine and embrace public transportation if cities and the earth were to survive.

Two hours before the burial was scheduled, a crowd of several thousand people had gathered. There was a human being at every point offering a view of the action. They were on the ground, at windows, and on rooftops eagerly awaiting either violence or just the burial of a new car.

While I addressed the assembled throng, the University's Executive Vice President mounted the platform to inform me that there really *was* a plan to assassinate me if I did not step down. There was too much adrenaline flowing in me to care what happened and, in the back of my mind, was the thought that this would be a great time to go.

By this time the Maverick was a sorry sight. The Blacks had broken all the windows and smashed every surface they could attack. Then, as the Maverick sat at the top of the ramp, ready to be pushed into its grave, an Indian Swami and his lady friend broke through the crowd and, clinging to the Maverick, insisted that they should be buried with the car. They were dragged free just as the Maverick was pushed over the edge, sped down the ramp, and hit the wall of its grave with a thump. A waiting bulldozer quickly covered it with the pile of dirt that had formed the ramp.

With that part of the spectacle completed, much of the crowd repaired to the Student Union for a final Survival Faire celebration. That night the Humanities 160 class gathered together in a circle on the floor of the Student Union auditorium, exhausted, happy, and emotionally drained, bonded in a way students and instructor rarely are. In terms of fulfillment as a teacher, it was the high point of my career.

The Humanities 160 students had one more run at saving the environment. In the following year, 1970, Santa Clara County placed a rapid transit initiative, Measure A, on the ballot in the general election. The students created the Atmospheric Liberation Front (ALF) and turned an old city bus into Survival Ark, which traveled to various high schools around the county to pick up interested students. Once the bus was filled, it would go to a neighborhood, park in the middle of the street, a siren would go off, and to the sounds of rock music the students would pile out of the bus, go door-to-door handing out leaflets and buttons. After four minutes, the siren would sound again, the students would pile back onto the bus, and go off to another neighborhood.

They also resurrected the yellow Maverick. They wanted to dig it up, crush it into a two-foot square, and use it as the corner "stone" of the transit building that would be built with funds from Measure A. That took some doing. They had to retrieve the title to the Maverick from the State of California, talk the architect of the transit building into using it as the corner "stone" of the building, a construction company into digging it up, and hauling it to a metal fabricator they persuaded to do the crushing. The campus daily editorialized, "We encourage Dr. Sperling and his class to continue their experiments in relevant education. SJS and the community could only benefit by their ventures."

Several Humanities 160 students were to play significant roles in the companies I was to establish. Two of them went on to obtain their doctorates at the University of Michigan and became my cofounders of the Institute for Professional Development and the University of Phoenix.

Right to Read

One day I received a call from the Academic Vice President inviting me to his office for a chat. When I got there, I found him with one of the senior members of Mexican-American Graduate Studies (MAGS). This gentleman informed me that he was looking for a director for the Right to Read project, and asked me if I would consider taking it on.

Right to Read was a program to remediate 40 young Chicanos and Chicanas and get them ready to enter the University as regular freshmen. My first response was, "Why me?" Certainly, I was a most improbable director of such a program. I did not speak Spanish, I had only a passing knowledge of Chicano culture, and I hardly knew anyone in MAGS, where the Right to Read project was housed. However, as I quickly learned, it was just these disqualifying characteristics they were interested in.

The problem, he explained, was that there were two factions within MAGS, neither of which would accept a director from the other. The program needed an outsider whose reputation would dissuade either faction from screwing with him. These two senior administrators had been discussing possible candidates and eventually hit on me as the perfect outsider. It wasn't that I was well liked. Quite the contrary, it was because I had a reputation for organizational competence, the ability to deal with discord, and indifference to disapproval.

There was only one caveat: I had to accept as my assistant and primary instructor 22-year-old Jorge Klor de Alva, the youngest member of MAGS. He was teaching in the Philosophy Department as well
as in MAGS while taking a law degree at U.C. Berkeley. I opined that
he seemed a bit overcommitted but, if he could do the work, it was
fine by me.

I accepted the offer and the two-year Right to Read program
turned out to be a great success. Jorge not only did the work, he did
it brilliantly. Instead of following the proposal that had obtained the
funding, we used the program as an opportunity to try out my pedagogical theories on what to me was a totally new population of students. I also saw it as a chance for a new approach to helping the less
advantaged. Instead of treating the Right to Read students as remedial basket cases we treated them as I would have treated students
entering the Humanities Program.

We began with 40 students; our first decision was how to avoid
the horrendous dropout rate that plagued similar programs. We
solved that problem by establishing discipline—assignments were to
be completed on time with no excuses accepted, and attendance
required at every class session. If students did not appear, we telephoned them to determine why. If it was car trouble, or they had
overslept, or claimed they were ill, someone went to check on them.
Unless they were seriously indisposed, we brought them to class. It
was not long before the students realized that they had two choices—
conform to the discipline or drop out. Of the 40 students, two years
later we still had 30.

As with the regular Humanities students, they only read original
sources. In the first year, Jorge covered the Pre-Socratics to Hegel, and
in the second, Darwin to Malcolm X. Jorge would set forth the key
issues and arguments in each of the readings, and the students would
then meet alone in small groups to prepare for the next class. In addition to demanding academic assignments, we made the program an
exciting intellectual experience. We were well funded, so we could
afford to take the students, many for the first time, to San Francisco
for museums, symphonies, operas, visits to Chinatown, to the Mission,
and to North Beach for dinners and fun. We treated them as elite students and they performed as elite students. All but a few of the students remained at San Jose State and 20 graduated; of these 20, 9 of

them went on to graduate school at Berkeley, UC Santa Cruz, and Stanford. A larger percentage of these young Chicanos and Chicanas went on to graduate school than did the students who enrolled in the standard Humanities Program.

Right to Read confirmed my belief that no matter how poorly prepared students might be, if conditions for learning are properly designed, innate intelligence will win out and the students will perform at the level expected of them. One of the most important lessons I took from the Right to Read program was the importance of discipline. Today, at all Apollo Group companies, student attendance is mandatory, the expected performance is set at a challenging level, and no excuses are accepted for failure to complete assignments.

My continuing friendship with Jorge has been one of the delights of my life. One might gather some understanding of the depth of our relationship by the fact that, in 1996, Jorge, by now a distinguished scholar, resigned an endowed chair at U.C. Berkeley to become president of the University of Phoenix.

5

The Unintentional Entrepreneur

Summing Up

As a struggle to survive hardship, the first phase of my life provided the raw material from which character is made. The second phase—gaining an education—provided a route out of that hardship, built on the strengths it had given me, at the same time that I struggled to overcome and undo the concomitant psychic damage. The third phase, a consolidation of the two preceding, was a period of learning basic lessons related to my work. At this point, I began to move beyond those lessons imposed by the circumstances of my birth.

I was now entering the fourth phase, which would bring together all that had come before and apply it to something uniquely mine—a distinctive alloy of my origins, education, and experience.

Union organizing had shown me the importance of action and the assignment of focused tasks as powerful motivators for learning. Action and focused tasks give emotional meaning to that learning. The Union also gave me organizational skills that would help build a business. More specifically, it gave me the political skills necessary for battle with the educational establishments.

The Humanities Program had given me three years of experience with small-group instruction. I had learned that students in small groups can be formed into cohesive learning units by the careful nurturing of mutual respect for opinion, social origins, and style. Once cohesive, members of the group are more willing to take intellectual risks.

Econ-12 taught me the importance of structuring learning so that students are introduced to, and acquire, the theoretical concepts needed to organize information on any subject. Just as important, it taught me the technique of setting forth, as precisely as possible, the learning outcomes the students were expected to achieve. It taught me then to measure them, not only to evaluate the students but also to evaluate every element of the teaching-learning process—the curriculum materials, how they are sequenced, the activities designed to make their presentation effective, and the effectiveness of the instructor.

Finally, Humanities 160 had convinced me that in the best of all possible pedagogical worlds, learning is an adventure and should be made as exciting as possible for both instructors and students. Excitement requires a liberated classroom with empowered, assertive students willing to make an emotional commitment to learning. It also requires instructors who will join in the learning process as full participants, not as aloof sources of knowledge or expounders of a discipline. It should be a process of the discovery of new knowledge in which the students, using already-mastered concepts, apply them to new events, facts, data, and so forth, and discover new relationships that, in turn, require new concepts if the relationships are to be understood.

This fourth phase began in 1972 with a federally funded project to lower the juvenile delinquency rate among lower-middle- and working-class youth in the city of Sunnyvale, California, a largely White community just north of San Jose. This project led, through implacable opportunism, to my first entrepreneurial venture.

In addressing the delinquency, I identified three groups of adults who could act on the problem by changing the way they dealt with the delinquents. There were parents, teachers, and the police. I knew that it would be difficult, if not impossible, to change parental behavior, so I concentrated on the teachers and the police.

To drive change without resorting to some tedious behavior modification program, I enrolled 30 teachers and police officers in a Humanities 160 course and set about turning them into change agents. I had never instructed adults before, but I found that all of the techniques I had developed for high school students in Econ-12 and for college students in Humanities worked even better with adults. I broke the class into small groups, each of which was directed to design, conduct, and evaluate a project that addressed the problem of juvenile delinquency. For this task, I tapped into my friends at Stanford, who were willing to do what I asked them. They provided instruction in action research design, statistics, and program evaluation. The students responded eagerly and each group completed a viable project.

Somewhat miraculously, education became for them an appetite that grew by what they fed upon. All but two of these new, adult learners signed up for Humanities 160 the following semester and they brought friends. During the course of the second semester, the students began to lobby me to create degree programs for them—BAs for the police, all of whom had associates degrees, and MAs for the teachers. This seemed like a good idea to me, so I sketched out a possible curriculum, once again formed around a core of theory that could be applied to action research. The students loved it and insisted that it would draw hundreds of working adults into the programs.

Thus emboldened, I took the plan to the Academic Vice President, one of my few friends on campus, as well as someone I could count on to give me good advice. I presented the plan and my estimate of how many students we would attract. He was impressed and sympathetic but utterly discouraging. It would not fly, he said. The people who would have to approve the program didn't like me, and didn't give a damn about having more students, especially adults. Furthermore, new degree programs would have to go through two departmental and two school curriculum committees and then to the Chancellor's office—a process that would take several years. If and when they were approved, they would be unrecognizable. His advice was, "John, go back to teaching and writing, and forget about any new degree programs."

Fortunately, I sought further advice from an academic acquaintance at Stanford, Frank Newman, who was then Vice President for Development.[1] His response went something like this:

> John, you'll never get a public institution to accept a truly innovative program or even an innovative program. The same thing is true of private institutions, especially if they consider themselves to be elite institutions. In fact, no institution that is financially healthy, including all public and most private institutions, will innovate— they don't have to. Educational bureaucracies are dedicated to the

status quo, and the only time they innovate is when they have to. The primary spur to innovation is financial necessity. What you need to do is find a school in financial trouble and convince the people running it that your adult education program will generate a profit beyond the cost of the program.

Acting on that sound advice, together with two of my former Humanities 160 students, Dr. Carole Crawford and Dr. Peter Ellis, we established the Institute for Community Research and Development (ICRD), a private organization dedicated to making higher education available to the working community. We then wrote a proposal setting forth a description of the program that had been rejected by San Jose State. The task remaining was to find an institution, any institution, willing to provide us the opportunity to put our ideas to work.

Some six weeks following my conversation with my friend, the Stanford VP, in what in retrospect appears as a minor miracle, he turned up an institution that had both financial difficulty and a president willing to take risks. It was the University of San Francisco, a Jesuit institution headed by Father William McInnes, to whom we sent a copy of our proposal for an innovative adult education program. In March 1974, Newman arranged an introduction to Fr. McInnes for Peter Ellis and me. Unbeknownst to us, McInnes, who had come to the USF presidency from the presidency of Fairfield University, Fairfield, Connecticut, had already sent a copy of our proposal to the Academy for Educational Development for review and evaluation. The Academy was a respected organization that did contract work for various federal agencies and foreign governments, as well as development consulting for colleges and universities. Our proposal went to Sidney Tickton, a senior vice president, and a man who strongly supported innovation. Tickton gave the proposal a favorable evaluation, and Father McInnes informed us that he had decided to proceed. At that point, I took a year's leave from the University, and because fortune smiled, never returned. At age 53, I began a new career as an entrepreneur.

The University of San Francisco Contract with ICRD

In April 1974, I began a series of visits to USF to discuss implementation of the proposal we had presented to President McInnes. At the end of May, in a meeting with the Vice President for Academic Affairs and the Deans of Education and Continuing, it was decided to proceed with contract negotiations and to prepare to offer two ICRD-designed programs in the fall semester. These included a Bachelor of Arts in Public Service and a Master of Arts in Education. In early August 1974, I submitted a draft contract to USF and began preparation of brochures for the two programs.

Although matters were progressing at the university level, at the school level, which was controlled by the deans, they were not progressing at all. Despite the President's enthusiasm, we could not find a dean willing to adopt the programs. Until that was accomplished, the registrar informed us, no students would be enrolled.

Our financial resources consisted of $26,000, which I had salvaged from the aforementioned soured land investment, and free rent gained by converting my house into an office. As September approached and cash dwindled, we had to move quickly, enroll some students, and get cash flowing into the operation or we would be out of business before we got into business. Fortunately, we had a cadre of true believers among the police officers, public service officers, and teachers with whom we had worked during the previous year. They were eager to enroll in any institution that would offer an ICRD-designed program. If we could simply find an academic home for them, we would be on our way.

The approval process was multifold. Because the program for police officers was undergraduate, it required approval from the undergraduate dean, the dean of one of the schools, and a department chair within the school. The masters program for teachers required approval from the graduate dean, the dean of the School of Education, and a department chair within the school. Each of these officials also had advisory committees that they used to ratify risky decisions or bury proposals they did not like. In this instance, all but the Dean of Education either disliked the programs outright or considered them too risky, so the approval process expanded to include most of the committees.

The Political Process at USF

Our political resources on the USF campus were almost as meager as our cash reserves. As with most busy CEOs, Father McInnes's involvement with the ICRD project pretty much ended with his decision to recommend University approval. Furthermore, we soon found that the blessing of a new president, who was both feared and disliked by many members of the Jesuit community, the Administration, and the Faculty, was of limited usefulness. Our only enthusiastic supporter was an absolute beginner in academic politics. This was Peter Fries, a youthful, recently resigned Franciscan Friar, whom McInnes had appointed to a new position—assistant to the provost for Special Academic Programs.

Peter was a delight to work with—energetic, optimistic, and determined to succeed. However, it was obvious to us that the Jesuit community would not tolerate for long a resigned and recently married Franciscan friar who wore a gold ring in one ear. Fortunately, Peter also recognized that his tenure as assistant for Special Academic Programs would be brief. He knew he would have to work quickly. We all realized that the ICRD programs would be dropped if we did not enroll the students and begin instruction, but how to enroll them? A student had to be enrolled in a school, and there had to be an approved curriculum for a degree to be granted. No school dean was willing to sponsor the program, though, so no curriculum approval was possible. With our noses flat against this brick wall, we decided on action.

Our first move was to inform our cadre of police officers and public service officers from Sunnyvale and San Jose that USF had agreed to sponsor the ICRD program. Given our assurances that we probably would be successful in having the program accepted for a bachelor's degree, 35 of these officers stepped forward, and we collected the first trimester's tuition. We now had over $40,000 in checks made out to USF, but getting them cashed was not nearly so easy as getting them written and signed.

I began instruction in the Bachelor of Arts in Public Service program on September 9, 1974, with only Peter Fries' authority to sustain me. Weeks passed as I wrote curriculum in the morning, did academic politics during the day, and taught at night. I commuted to USF almost every day, and the only way I could keep going was to pull off the freeway going and coming and take half-hour naps. September faded into October with no dean willing to accept the 35 officers as students. Even though we had 35 committed students, skepticism about our ability to deliver a USF-sanctioned degree program grew with each passing week. We responded to the skepticism by offering to give the students back their checks and drop them from the program. None of them took the offer. We all knew that so long as USF kept the checks, there was a chance they would cash them, which would mean acceptance for the 35 officers. So, we waited.

If it had been left up to academic politics, we might be waiting still. However, as institutions living on the margin often do, the University of San Francisco turned up short for a payroll. For over a month, Peter Fries had carried the $40,000 in checks in his briefcase. He and his uncashable checks had become something of a joke among members of the administration, but the joke turned on the jokesters one October day when there was no cash in the University's till. The Vice President for Finance ordered Peter to stand and deliver the checks for immediate deposit. Peter happily complied, and immediately the question changed from "Will some dean accept the program?" to "Which dean will accept the program?"

The deans proved more resistant than any of us expected. Even though the University had cashed the checks, still no dean would accept the students. Eventually, the Academic Vice President solved this problem by resurrecting a failed experimental program, called Inner College, and assigning the bachelor degree programs there. The other half of ICRD was the Master of Arts in Education program, which had a higher profile than the bachelors program because of the extensive approvals required and the large number of deans and committees involved in the decisions. There could have been no better person to handle this complex of problems than Dr. Allen Calvin who, in August, had become Dean of the School of Education.

Dean Allen Calvin: Turning IPD into a Company

To our great good fortune, Allen Calvin had never been in a department of education and was not bound by habit or preconception as to what a dean of education was supposed to do. He had just returned to academe from a decade as president of Behavioral Research Laboratory, an aggressive education publishing firm that had been embroiled in a series of textbook adoption battles in school districts across the country. The most notable of these was the 1969–1970 battle in New York City in Oceanview Brownsville, where a Black local school district was trying to break away from control by the central school administration and make a deal with BRL. In this fight, Calvin was not only in conflict with the central school administration, he was also in conflict with my union, the New York Federation of Teachers. I did not know it at the time, but Calvin's activities in Oceanview Brownsville had caught the attention of the FBI. Later, this was to complicate my dealings with the federal authorities when I was under investigation for violation of the RICO statute arising out of my own battles with the education establishment.

Calvin was brilliant—an academic, a businessman, an entrepreneur, an astute politician—and I could not have found a better teacher. As a psychologist-cum-entrepreneur, he had most recently taken BRL from start-up, to IPO, to paper wealth, to bust. Having experienced the excitement of business, he was not about to retire into an academic deanship. More than any of us, Calvin saw the business possibilities in ICRD and it was immediately apparent that he also saw ICRD as an instrument he could use to further his own interests. In fact, he would use ICRD to build his political support, and I had to balance his demands with my need for political support. Ours was a test of wills that usually ended in a standoff. The fact that I constantly had to fight being dominated by him in no way diminished his importance to our success.

Not only did Calvin help me develop and carry out our political strategy, he taught me the rudiments of business—how to structure a company, price our products, negotiate a contract, change potential enemies into allies by making them stakeholders in the enterprise, and how to use a legal offensive when reason fails. Losing control of the United Professors of California, after I had built it with my own two hands, made me quite wary of creating another nonprofit organization that some board could yank away from me. Calvin confirmed my decision to make the Institute a for-profit corporation—one of the best decisions I have ever made. Once this was determined, Calvin led me to the legal and accounting talent that made the Institute not only a reality, but was critical in helping make it a successful company.

Under Calvin's tutelage, my learning curve became almost vertical. He literally transformed me into an entrepreneur.

Within a few weeks of meeting Calvin, he directed me to accomplish the following:

- Change the name of the Institute from the Institute for Community Research and Development to the Institute for Professional Development (IPD).
- Give Father Martin, the graduate dean, the task as well as the credit for establishing the Master's in Education as a legitimate program.
- Begin the development of an external Bachelor of Science in Business Administration program reporting directly to the dean of the School of Business.
- Create IPD as a for-profit corporation.
- Set aside the vague contract under which we had been operating, and draft and sign a new contract between USF and IPD that set forth the financial and administrative relationships between USF and IPD.

Calvin was insistent that IPD could never succeed unless the people upon whom the IPD programs depended became stakeholders, with Calvin being the chief stakeholder and beneficiary. IPD had to offer these stakeholders the opportunity for professional advancement and for doing new and exciting things. It also had to produce an extra income for those being asked to participate. To this end, he arranged for a portion of the income from the IPD programs to flow directly to the schools and departments. He also made certain that senior professors had the first choice of teaching assignments and consultancies for developing curriculum. Although Calvin had not been assigned responsibility for the Institute's campus operations, the President and the Academic Vice President regularly deferred to him. Without their unflagging support, however, we never could have established our position within the USF community.[2]

Calvin also set us to work creating the organizational structure of the business. He arranged for John Kelly, a senior partner at Morrison and Foerster, one of San Francisco's largest law firms, to handle IPD's incorporation and to draft the USF-IPD contract. Kelly had been corporate counsel for the Behavioral Research Laboratory and was the first of many of Calvin's BRL associates who played major roles in IPD. Once I met Kelly, there was no doubt that we were in business. Because we had a new and desirable educational product, we were an immediate financial success. In the first full year of operation, which began September 1, 1974, the company had revenues of $210,297; in the second year, revenues were $2,838,134. As enrollments and revenues grew, our first business problem was controlling growth. We had to learn very quickly how to collect all the tuition due, control expenditures, and keep the quality of services at the desired level.

During the fall of 1974 and the spring of 1975, several key people from BRL joined IPD and played major roles in helping to make our new venture into a viable company. Nick Cochran and Rodger Ricard were the two most important. Cochran, who ultimately became IPD's CFO and Vice President for Finance, not only established an orderly accounting system, he retained Price-Waterhouse as our auditors. It was the P-W signature on our financials that thwarted many of our academic enemies who hoped for an IPD defector to bring tales of financial malfeasance. It was also the P-W signature that would protect us from the FBI agents who, inspired by these same academic critics, would later investigate us for bribing academics and public officials. Ricard, the other critical BRL recruit, was a spectacularly good salesman and a first-rate builder and leader of sales teams. Under his direction, the sales and marketing function drove IPD to success. Ricard also brought a vital cultural change to the Company, instilling in us the critical importance of marketing and sales. "If you can't sell it, you can't afford to make it," was his mantra. From that time forward, the student recruiters were the highest-paid people in the Company, and it was over a decade before my compensation equaled that of the highest-performing recruiters.

Building the Company

During the 1974–1975 academic year, IPD principals worked 80-hour weeks building the company in San Jose and positioning the company in the USF community. In San Jose, they recruited a curriculum development team from the Stanford School of Education that was willing to work within the theoretical structure I had laid out. For students who had just completed or were completing their doctorates, this was a wonderful opportunity to write a curriculum, field-test it, revise it, and test it again until they got it right. The principals built an administrative structure, recruited and trained faculty in the proper use of the curriculum, and monitored their performance. Although the business changed daily, we still managed to provide an acceptable level of service to the increasing number of students that Ricard and his staff were recruiting.

My job was now mainly political. In San Francisco, I spent endless hours in meetings with administrators, faculty, and faculty committees as I explained the IPD philosophy, its theories of teaching and learning, and why changing American demographics required changing higher education. With Calvin's help, I identified the USF stakeholders—senior professors and deans—assessed their needs, and created the mechanisms whereby tuition monies could be directed to satisfy those needs. The stakeholders viewed IPD as a candy store, which meant that each assessment required a negotiation. Still, on the whole, there was general satisfaction with the arrangements I worked out.

By the end of the 1974–1975 academic year, it was evident that IPD was a success. Its products had strong appeal for the educational market, it was operating at a profit, and it had gained a solid, if grudging, acceptance in the USF community. This success brought inquiries from institutions that were eager for innovation and whose officers recognized the demographic changes that were making adult programs not only desirable but imperative.

IPD under Attack

With success, however, came increasing concern from competing institutions, from the California State Department of Education, and from the Western Association of Schools and Colleges (WASC), the accrediting association which had jurisdiction over California. Although the IPD principals had spent almost their entire lives as students or instructors in public educational institutions, we were only dimly aware of the governmental organizations that controlled higher education, and totally unaware of the private ones, such as WASC. WASC was run by Dr. Kay J. Anderson, an educational reactionary who had established a reign of terror among the small colleges and universities in California. Any of these institutions that did not heed his word were quickly disciplined by the threat of loss of accreditation—a fatal penalty.

As sheltered academics, we also were unaware of the sharp competition for students among colleges and universities, both in the public and private educational markets. We had no idea the extent to which education is a highly politicized and regulated activity, nor the extent to which innovators were to be searched out and destroyed as quickly as possible by the academics who controlled the institutions and by their allies in the regulatory agencies.

Our awakening to the realities of the education industry was rude and not long in coming. The first indication of trouble came when the administrators of competing institutions began to denounce the quality of the IPD programs and to claim that IPD was turning the University of San Francisco into a diploma mill. Thus emboldened, the USF internal critics resurfaced with a vengeance. They denounced the scandal of IPD peddling 400 years of Jesuit tradition to non-Catholics and various others of the great unwashed.

Competing institutions turned to the educational regulators for help, and that help was immediately forthcoming. The California Department of Education, together with its various commissions, began a campaign of negative comment and regulatory harassment. Local governments and school districts, which had initially supported the program, withdrew support, and some of their officials denounced the programs to the press.[3] IPD was now getting more publicity than it wanted, but the worst was yet to come. At this point, the struggle for educational innovation moved out of the realm of theory and philosophy into the realm of politics at its dirtiest.

Fortunately, my Union training had prepared me for the battle, and Dr. Peter Ellis brought his own organizing skills to the enterprise. He had almost a decade of experience in community organizing, was active in local politics, and had done a superb job as director of the juvenile delinquency project. Without our combined skills, we could never have protected IPD from its enemies at USF, at WASC, in the competing colleges, in the State Department of Education, and in several of the city governments and school districts that employed students enrolled in the IPD programs.

Our organizing skills also had worked their way into the curriculum. It was action oriented. Learning was designed to be of use to the students in their work life, and we expected students to have a positive impact on the organizations that employed them. Not only did this characteristic of the curriculum lead to action by the students, it also produced a group of students passionately committed to the program. Being professional adults, many of them held influential positions in their organizations, and they were valuable allies in working to protect IPD from its growing number of enemies. Many of the faculty became equally committed, and they also were invaluable in helping us within the University and in the business firms and public agencies where they worked.

By the end of the first year of operating the USF program, it was apparent that there was an untapped market in providing higher education for working adults. More important, it became obvious that an institution could make money at it—at least, they could make money if IPD ran the program. In early 1975, two institutions beat a path to our door seeking a contractual relationship. The first was St. Mary's College, a Christian Brothers college located in Moraga, California, a small town east of Berkeley; the second was the University of Redlands, located in Redlands, California, another small town some 50 miles east of Los Angeles. Using the USF contract as a model, negotiating a contract was relatively easy; all we had to change were the names and the percentage split between the college and IPD. Needless to say, these two contracts, concluded in 1975, were much more profitable than the one with USF. There was, however, one great weakness in all three—their term. They were annual contracts that had to be renewed each year. It placed IPD in a very precarious position, but we were not yet strong enough to negotiate a more favorable arrangement.

Fortunately, the St. Mary's and Redlands programs grew almost as rapidly as the one at USF, and by the end of 1975, IPD was profitable and rapidly growing. Unfortunately, our success spawned both envy and hatred.

The battles fought by IPD and UOP against the educational establishment were, in a formal sense, regulatory battles, but they were largely proxies for cultural battles between defenders of 800 years of educational (largely religious) tradition, and an innovation that was based on the values of the marketplace—transparency, efficiency, productivity, and accountability. To me, the defenders of academic traditions were protecting undeserved middle-class entitlements and, although I was part of the academy, I was not of it, had few emotional attachments to it, and was indifferent to its disapproval. These attitudes, shaped by what is now called a disadvantaged childhood and

years of union organizing and politics, made it possible for me to
undertake battles against very long odds and persist in those battles for
two decades.

Now, some 20 years later, UOP is widely regarded as the very
model of a twenty-first-century university, but it still needs to fight
regulatory battles even if they are no longer passionate. Today, they are
wars of attrition in which both sides know that UOP eventually will
prevail against the rearguard action of educational bureaucrats
doggedly protecting the market share of their local institutions. However, in the mid-1970s, our ability to prevail was hardly a foregone
conclusion.

USF's War with WASC

In a memorandum to the University's priority committee at the
beginning of the 1974 academic year, Vice President Luckmann had
pointed out that the 19-campus California State University (CSU)
system had established 17 external degree programs.

> Clearly, the Chancellor's Office [CSU] accepts the External Degree
> Program as the instrument which will do the most to help preserve
> the integrity and strength of the campuses which are now faced
> with declining enrollments. The system has seized the opportunity
> to serve a new population . . . It is clear that the University of San
> Francisco must prepare to enter this field immediately.

IPD was to become USF's competitive weapon.

It did not take long for CSU to react to the competition, first
from USF, and then from the IPD programs at St. Mary's and Redlands. The CSU administration appealed to WASC for help and, as
the state's largest institution, WASC was quick to respond.

The three California institutions with which IPD had contracts—the University of San Francisco, St. Mary's, and Redlands—
were under-endowed, lightly funded private institutions lacking the
resources of the State of California to fund the development of their
external degree programs. It was my $26,000 and expertise that had
enabled USF to launch its adult education programs, and now IPD's
program at USF provided the financial resources and expertise for St.

Mary's and Redlands. WASC seized on IPD's role as a plausible reason to undertake a program of harassment.

At this point, WASC's Executive Director, Kay Anderson, emerged as our major enemy and he would remain so for the next 10 years. One of the arguments Anderson used as a reason for the attack upon USF and the IPD contract was that it had not received careful academic scrutiny. This charge was well off the mark. McInnes performed due academic diligence before entering into the IPD relationship. His decision came only after the IPD proposal and programs had been evaluated and recommended by the staff of the Academy for Educational Development, an academic project management organization. In addition to the Academy evaluation, the USF administration had been careful to abide by WASC regulations regarding contracts with nonaccredited entities.

Anderson's attack was fairly easy to mount, because USF was due for a five-year accreditation visit in December 1975, a little over a year from the beginning of the IPD contract. The IPD program had occasioned enough hostility among the USF faculty and administration to provide Anderson with a wealth of complaints, both about IPD and about the USF administrators who worked with us. Anderson had begun the softening-up process by conducting several preaccreditation visits during the fall of 1975, which gave him an opportunity to express his growing concerns. By some strange coincidence, the turmoil on campus was played to the accompaniment of the previously mentioned "public outcry" from the officials from competing institutions and officials from school districts, and from city, county, and state agencies whose employees were enrolling in ever larger numbers in the USF-IPD programs.

Father McInnes's academic sin was not failure to exercise due diligence. His sin was his failure to pay deference to Kay Anderson. After this one false step, there was a steady deterioration in the WASC-USF relationship.

As Kay Anderson acted to force USF to bend to his will, the USF administration fought back. This only resulted in harder blows from Anderson in the form of more campus turmoil as IPD now emerged as a threat to USF's accreditation. There is no doubt that neither Fr. McInnes nor his chief administrators could match Anderson in political skill or toughness. As an outsider from New England, McInnes was in a weak political position and soon became unacceptable to many members of both the Jesuit community and the lay faculty. Anderson knew that USF was a factionalized campus with serious financial difficulties and he exploited every division. It was the financial crisis that had brought McInnes to USF and, with every school and department fighting for its share of a shrinking budgetary pie, it was not difficult for Anderson to exploit the turmoil.

As enrollments dropped in programs offered by competing institutions, they turned to WASC to help them deal with this "unfair competition." Now that these IPD programs made educational access possible to working civil servants, public agencies throughout the Bay Area suddenly found themselves spending far more money to support their tuition assistance programs than they had ever dreamed possible. Their response was not, "How wonderful that our loyal civil servants now have education available." Instead, it was, "My God, the University of San Francisco has become a diploma mill that is draining our educational assistance fund, and thank God WASC is willing to shut these programs down."

WASC Visits USF, December 1975

The team that Anderson appointed for the five-year accreditation visit was composed of WASC heavies. Two members, including the Chair, were members of the WASC Senior Commission, and four of the remaining five were from the State University system, the institution that had first complained to WASC about unfair competition from the IPD programs. As part of the three-day visit, IPD received a half-day visit by the two team members from the WASC Senior Commission. They visited the IPD offices in San Jose, and they were not friendly. The Chair, a University of Washington Dean, dominated the proceedings and directed most of his questions to me. Both his demeanor and his questions were hostile, contemptuous, and contentious, and I replied in a vigorous and not overly respectful manner. He declared that IPD was selling USF's 400 years of Jesuit tradition and stated that, even though USF faced bankruptcy, there was no justification for seeking additional revenue from IPD programs. I pointed out that his employment at a publicly supported university gave him the luxury of such a high-minded position and that USF had every right to fight for survival in a marketplace increasingly dominated by tax-supported institutions. When the two sides departed, there were only the barest shreds of civility left.

The team produced a 23-page report that was negative, carping, and filled with errors. It began by stating that "the present financial situation of the university is so grave as to jeopardize its existence as a high-quality, private, and independent institution." Then, alluding to the new external degree programs, the report continued, "Unfortunately, the fiscal crisis of the university has appeared simultaneously with a compelling need to clarify the rationale for the new educational missions being adopted by the university . . ." The report dealt with IPD by characterizing the USF-IPD arrangement as "controversial" and pointed out that the program was established without adequate consultation with the faculty; the quality controls in faculty selection and curriculum content were rudimentary; and the program's administrative and academic relationships were unclear to faculty, students, and the surrounding community.

Father McInnes had done due diligence on the issues of quality, but he had not consulted the faculty, because he knew they never would have approved the program. That's the reason the program's administrative and academic relationships were unclear to the faculty—the program had been forced on them before they had a chance to evaluate it. Had Fr. McInnes acted in any other way, USF never would have developed an outreach program for working adults. Of course, Anderson was aware of this, but his concern was neither academic quality nor service to the working adult students. His concern was to stop any change he had not first approved. Wrapping himself in the banner of faculty prerogatives, as he well knew, was a sure way to stop any innovation.

The WASC report also pointed out that the program was unexpectedly successful and was a "lucrative source of new income" for the university. The report concluded its comments on IPD by recommending that "all aspects of this off-campus program be placed under careful university controls" and that "no future programs of this sort should be established without review and approval in accordance with regular institutional procedures." USF, with IPD's assistance, prepared a comprehensive response to the WASC report and pointed out all the errors of fact and interpretation. The response was ignored, and the final report was issued with all of the errors intact.

The Senior Commission Meeting, February 1976

In February 1976, the WASC Senior Commission considered the report of the December visit. President McInnes, Academic Vice President Donald MacIntyre, Dean Calvin, and I were there to defend USF and IPD. McInnes was no summer soldier; he was committed to educational reform and so were MacIntyre and Calvin. All of us presented a vigorous defense to a hostile and contemptuous Senior Commission, and the Commission's response was vintage Anderson—it voted to defer the reaffirmation of the University's accreditation until the next meeting, scheduled for the following June. Any doubt as to the basis of the Commission's action was dispelled when Mrs. Frances Heller, a public member of the Commission, bluntly informed Fr. McInnes, "Father, the issue is not the University of San Francisco, the issue is John Sperling."

During the period from February to June there was a steadily rising concern about the University's accreditation status among all groups on the campus. Following the WASC December visit, complaints about the USF-IPD programs came from academics from competing institutions, school superintendents, and local government officials. Golden Gate University's long-established program in public administration, for example, was suffering from the competition presented by the USF undergraduate and graduate programs in public service. Not only did Golden Gate's president complain to WASC, but he, his deans, and his faculty solicited complaints to WASC from public officials throughout the San Francisco Bay Area. The Bay Area cities of Concord, Fremont, Menlo Park, Oakland, Richmond, San Leandro, Santa Rosa, and Sunnyvale, all of which had administrators who were adjunct professors at Golden Gate University, withdrew tuition support from the USF-IPD programs.

One of the more vocal complainants was Mr. Theron Nelson, director of Administrative Services in the East Bay city of Concord, as well as a Golden Gate adjunct faculty member. Writing to Anderson, Mr. Nelson declared, "I consider the contract education programs offered by USF/IPD to be an outrageous situation. Is it not the responsibility of the Western Association of Schools and Colleges to take remedial action by removing its accreditation from such programs?" Soon articles appeared in local newspapers with headlines such as "BA Degree Given in 9 Months," "Quickie Degrees—A

Taxpayer Rip-Off?" and "Row Over USF Degrees." To this litany were added complaints from school superintendents and, of course, from the officials of other competing institutions. One letter to WASC from Andrew Pringle, Jr., a City bureaucrat from Martinez, California, was typical of the vitriol and error that characterized the complaints:

> The University of San Francisco is engaged in a degree awarding program that I consider appalling. This institution has begun to award baccalaureate degrees to students who possess less than minimal qualifications.
>
> I feel that California has one of the finest college and university systems in the nation, both in the public and private higher education sectors. This reputation should not be tarnished by literally allowing students to buy college and university diplomas.
>
> This disgraceful practice should be halted immediately and its instigators disciplined. In my opinion, this practice boarders on the rim of consumer fraud. A thorough investigation should be conducted into this matter.

It was evident that Anderson was building a dossier on USF that would go to the WASC Senior Commission and any WASC team that visited USF.[4]

As a result of the WASC December visit, the USF-IPD contract was available to WASC, and it seemed no coincidence to USF and IPD principals that copies of the contract reached the hands of our critics. A negative analysis of the contract by an anonymous author, plus an anonymous paper modeled on the *Protocols of Zion,* were soon in circulation and provided our critics with ample ammunition for continuing slander. One report stated that "there is a lawsuit pending against the IPD programs from the Attorney General's Office," the insinuation being that the lawsuit was over "shady dealings" between USF and IPD due to USF's "financial problems."[5] It was now widely claimed that IPD controlled Fr. McInnes and was using its financial power to corrupt University officials.

IPD's threat of legal action finally ended Golden Gate's campaign of slander, but that led to even more effective action on Golden Gate's part. It refused to accept credits from the USF-IPD programs or to recognize those degrees. The tactic was soon adopted by other institutions and used repeatedly against IPD, and later UOP. As long as IPD had a contract with an institution, the credits and degrees in the IPD-designed programs would not be accepted. Even after IPD had departed an institution, the credits of an IPD-designed program were not transferable unless the institution first made its peace with WASC. As an example of the persistence of academic feuds, now, 25 years later as I write this chapter, the President of the University of New Mexico, who was previously at Arizona State University, has just announced that University of Phoenix credits and degrees will no longer be accepted at the University of New Mexico. Old cultures die hard.

The Second WASC Visit, December 1976

Anderson continued the softening-up process and, in June, the Commission again voted to defer action on USF's accreditation. On June 18, Anderson wrote to McInnes to inform him that, not only was a decision on USF's accreditation again deferred, but USF was also to have another accreditation visit in the fall of 1976 "under the direction of the Commission's newly appointed Committee on Contract Education."[6] The reason for the deferral and the second visit was explained this way. "Although the university has been partially responsive to the team's general recommendations, the Commission continues to be seriously concerned about the structure, quality, and control of programs offered through the Institute for Professional Development."[7] Anderson finally got McInnes's scalp; the president was fired in September.

The WASC team arrived the morning of December 14 and spent the first day of their three days on-site at IPD. Chairman Lewis Mayhew, a bombastic educational reactionary from Stanford, immediately took charge and promptly turned the visit into a farce. My memo to file for that date provides an *aide memoir* as to the events.

Morning—Committee arrived between 9:30–11:00 A.M., Chairman arrived last.

Mayhew dominated the questioning.

- What does IPD do that the University couldn't do better for itself?

- What does IPD do?
- How does IPD do what it does?
- How can IPD provide the services it does and not lose money? State University budgets would be astronomical if they tried to compete with a similar delivery system.

No organization to questions, no one was in charge of the meeting, and team members were only able to ask questions when Mayhew stopped talking.

Afternoon—2:30–4:30 P.M.

Oral report:

- Good program for which the University (not IPD) should be commended.
- Faculty is not given enough freedom.
- Curriculum is sterile.
- Too much credit for life experience (14.7 credits, mean).
- Only individual projects should be permitted.
- Financial relations negative for USF, positive for IPD.
- IPD making excess profits—when offered the opportunity to receive a full financial report from Nick Cochran [IPD Financial Vice President], Mayhew refused.

Characterization of visit:

Confused, unorganized, seemingly more concerned with confirming preconceptions than in doing serious evaluation and were frustrated by not finding much wrong with the program.

Most of the time, Mayhew answered his own questions. This was particularly the case on matters of finance. Mayhew came with an analysis showing that IPD took 54 percent of tuition revenue for its administrative overhead. The fact that IPD's audit, conducted by Price-Waterhouse, showed the correct figure to be 29 percent was of no interest to Mayhew; he rejected CFO Nick Cochran's offer to walk him through the analysis. The 54 percent appeared in the draft report that USF corrected in its response, and it was still there along with Mayhew's original analysis when the final report was issued. The handling of financial matters was characteristic of the way the visit and the report of the visit dealt with administration, curriculum, and instruction. Privately, team members informed Academic Vice President Donald MacIntyre that the program was all right and that IPD was the problem.

The 30-page first draft team report criticized the programs from a traditional viewpoint and recommended changes that would force them back into a traditional mode, for example:

1. Give the faculty more freedom to determine course outcomes.
2. Give the faculty greater academic control.
3. Make what they considerd a "sterile" curriculum less structured.
4. Prohibit group projects and allow only individual student projects.
5. Require more contact hours.

There were errors of fact and interpretation throughout the report, but the errors in the section on finances and administration provide the best illustration of the WASC methodology of program evaluation. That is, the Red Queen method: "First the verdict, then the evidence."

USF's Response to the Team Report

USF prepared a 58-page response to the team report. The response to the team's financial calculations well characterizes the whole report.[8] Some of the relevant sections are:

Financial and Administrative Arrangements

The University was shocked by and dismayed at the conclusions and inferences contained in this section. We are particularly disturbed at the process, or lack thereof, used by the Visiting Committee in dealing with these important matters. Our post-visit review has revealed that members of the Visiting Committee refused to meet with the chief financial officer of IPD and spent a few minutes with the University's chief financial officer. At no time did any member of the Committee seek additional data or clarification of the matters reported in this section from either the President, the Vice President for Academic Affairs of the University, or the President of IPD. We are, therefore, at a loss to determine the source of much of the "factual" data contained in this section. Members of the Visiting Committee were given the audit statements for the Institute but at no time did they ask assistance in interpreting those statements. Had they taken the opportunity to do so, they would not have so grossly misinterpreted the data and made the numerous accusatory inferences found throughout this section. The University, therefore, respectfully requests that the conclusions set forth in this section as well as the "evidence" cited to support those conclusions not be used as the basis of any judgement by the Commission regarding the Financial and Administrative Arrangements between the University and the Institute for Professional Development . . .

It was evident that the team was directed to charge that IPD was siphoning off monies from the program for other uses. Because there was no evidence to show this, the report used obfuscation instead. Professor Mayhew wrote, "It is entirely plausible that substantial tuition funds paid by students in USF-IPD programs could be used to support programs offered by IPD and other institutions." To this groundless allegation, USF replied as follows:

A brief examination of the enclosed instructional billings, which are prepared on a program-to-date basis, indicate that it would be extremely difficult for IPD to have diverted funds earmarked for instructional and program development purposes inasmuch as all programs are currently in an overspent condition.

The whole response vigorously defended the IPD programs while judiciously agreeing to make changes that did not strike at the philosophy of the programs or the pedagogical theories upon which they were based. The effort expended in preparing a thoughtful and detailed response was wasted energy. The final report followed the draft verbatim.

The Senior Commission Meeting, February 1977

The team report of the December 1976 visit, together with the University's response, was considered at the February 1977 meeting of the WASC Senior Commission. Fr. John Lo Schiavo, McInnes's

replacement as president, along with Academic Vice President Mac-
Intyre appeared for the University. Lo Schiavo was bluntly told that if
the University were to receive reaffirmation of its accreditation, it
would have to terminate the IPD contract by June 30, 1977. Lo Schiavo had no choice but to comply. He promised to terminate the IPD
contract and WASC reaffirmed the University's standing.

In June, Donald MacIntyre wrote informing me that the contract
with IPD was to be cancelled. The most gracious Dear John letter I
have ever received opened as follows:

> Dear John:
>
> Since March, 1975, the University of San Francisco and the Insti-
> tute for Professional Development have been involved in an educa-
> tional venture aimed at bringing education to heretofore
> underserved, if not excluded, segments of the population. Boldly, if
> not apprehensively, we set out together on uncharted seas. As could
> be expected, reception to our new programs was both overwhelm-
> ingly positive and disconcertingly negative. In spite of the many
> challenges to the integrity of our relationship, we persisted; because
> of our persistence countless individuals have realized their dream of
> completing their college education. No one and no thing can take
> from us—or from those students—the satisfaction of knowing that
> justice, albeit protracted, can be served.[9]

In accordance with Lo Schiavo's agreement with Anderson,[10]
IPD ceased recruiting students on December 31, 1977, and the USF-
IPD contract was terminated on September 30, 1978, almost five
years from the date IPD began operations at USF. It was a cordial
parting, and, considering the stress which the war with WASC placed
on both IPD and USF, the relationship was amazingly free of conflict
or hard feelings. Perhaps the cordiality was an aspect of the symbiosis
that had come to characterize the relationship. At the end of the five
years, USF had developed a capability in adult education that it probably would not have had without IPD, and IPD had become a viable
company.

6

Exodus from California and Flight to the Valley of the Sun

Seeking a Strategy for Survival

The two years from January 1976 to December 1978 were brutal. The Company was under siege from competing institutions, their allies in the accrediting association, and the state higher education agencies. In a uniformly hostile press, the Company was regularly referred to as a "diploma mill." It is not an exaggeration to describe that period as a struggle between the totality of the higher education establishment and an idea. The idea was of a different educational vision embodied in a small, insignificant company dedicated to providing a college education to working adult students who, at the time, were denied effective access.

In 1976, the only access available to working adults was to enroll in night classes, one class at a time; and maybe, after several years and stopping work to get certain required courses that only met during the day, they could earn a degree. Today, practically every institution of higher education trumpets its welcome to working adult students, but in 1976, the IPD system was considered a debasement of education. We violated much that was sacred in the groves of academe: an untenured faculty composed of working professionals who taught at night what they worked at during the day; programs developed in 91

cooperation with employers; curricula developed by expert consultants, editors, and instructional designers; standardized courses with
specific learning objectives taught the same way each time the course
was offered; classes held at times and places convenient to the students;
and assertive students who did not consider the instructor as the fount
of knowledge, but who took the responsibility for their education seriously and expected their instructor to respond to their needs.

With so many institutions and individuals intent on destroying
the Company, its survival was problematic. There were literally dozens
of times when its continued existence was decided by chance or by
the unexpected support of persons over whom it exercised neither
control nor influence. The skill, energy, and will of the principals was
the foundation of success, but I will never discount how important a
generous share of good luck was in our survival.

Although it was clear that WASC would drive IPD out of its
three California contracts, I was not going to leave the state without
a fight, and the only two strategies available to me were political and
legal. Legal action would get WASC's attention, but there were three
problems that made it unwise: cost, time, and lack of a credible cause
of action. After careful review by the constitutional law experts at
Morrison & Foerster, I had to conclude that IPD was in no position
to spend hundreds of thousands of dollars and several years in a legal
assault on WASC. Even if we got to trial, the outcome would be in
doubt until a final decision—barring the unlikely possibility of in-
junctive relief, it would probably take years, and years I did not have.
Politics seemed my best bet.

During my time as a union leader, I had collected a few political
chits by organizing contributions, endorsements, and supplying campaign workers to state assembly and senate candidates, so I set about
constructing a new political operation. Lacking access to the campaign
funds and membership base that were available to me as a labor leader,
I had to use ideas as my method of organizing support. I first had to
convince my former colleagues in the teachers' union movement that
WASC was a malign influence on education. Because I believed so
passionately that this was the case, I was able to succeed with most of
them. This backing gave me access to the two politicians who had
been involved in legislation concerning WASC: Lieutenant Governor
Mervyn Dymally, a former teacher and teachers' union activist, and
Assemblyman John Vasconcellos, an educational reformer who headed

the Committee on Postsecondary Education. It did not take me long to discover that USF and IPD were not the only victims of WASC's heavy-handed tactics. There were several anti-WASC bills either currently being considered or lying inactive, so I had a place to start.

Lieutenant Governor Dymally had once attempted to start a university in the Los Angeles area that would serve the Black community, but WASC refused to grant accreditation. Dymally had already sketched out the concept of a bill to substitute state accreditation for WASC accreditation, and he was delighted that I was willing to rewrite the bill and then to work it. He was also able to get the authors in both the Assembly and Senate to schedule hearings. My other contact, Vasconcellos, had long been concerned with the unjust proceedings of the WASC Senior Commission and had introduced WASC sunshine bills in two previous sessions of the legislature. He was also pleased that I was willing to work his current sunshine bill.

My efforts on behalf of the legislation got enough attention to cause WASC to organize a legislative alert within the higher education community and to seek help from the U.S. Office of Education and the Council on Postsecondary Accreditation. By June 1976, it was apparent that WASC was too well organized for any of the bills to go anywhere, but still they were valuable as a diversionary tactic. Although we got the bills put over to interim study, time had run out on political action. With our legislative initiative blocked and having no ground upon which to mount a legal battle, the only recourse remaining was to seek contracts with colleges and universities outside of California.

Seeking Greener Pastures

Escaping WASC would not be easy with Kay Anderson broadcasting to the national academic community that IPD was turning respectable colleges into diploma mills. The effort also would involve us with different academic cultures, state regulatory bodies, and accrediting associations.

In 1976, Peter Ellis and I journeyed back and forth across the country visiting some 20 colleges and universities; in 15 of these we were able to make a sales presentation, and out of these we managed to sign contracts with 4 of them. Among the 20 we visited were: Grambling University, Grambling, Louisiana; Rochester Institute of

Technology, Rochester, New York; Alfred University, Alfred, New York; Lesley College, Cambridge, Massachusetts; Stetson University, DeLand, Florida; Drake University, Des Moines, Iowa; Kalamazoo College, Kalamazoo, Michigan; University of Tulsa, Tulsa, Oklahoma; Philips College, Bartlesville, Oklahoma; Bradley University, Peoria, Illinois; National College of Education, Evanston, Illinois; Elmhurst College, Elmhurst, Illinois; and Regis College, Denver, Colorado.

As an indication of how desperate we were to establish other sources of revenue, I targeted Grambling University, with only the most questionable of contacts to gain me an audience. A Phoenix School District official I knew had taken a position at Grambling, and he assured me that the Louisiana school was ripe for an IPD contract. On my first visit, in November 1976, I stayed in a local hotel while my contact presumably carried on negotiations with University officials. He reported back to me that if I could demonstrate there was a market, the contract was a sure thing. He further explained that one sure market Grambling could own was the Black community in Chicago, his hometown.

My Grambling associate put me in touch with a man named Dan Androzzo who was part of something called the Woodlawn Association on the South Side of Chicago. Actually, it was a front for the Blackstone Rangers, the gang that controlled the Woodlawn housing projects. Innocent as I was, I thought it was just a neighborhood association.

In early January 1977, I went to Chicago and met with Androzzo at his fortresslike apartment in one of the Woodlawn blocks of prisonlike apartment buildings. He assured me that if I could deliver Grambling classes to Chicago, the Woodlawn Association would deliver the students. I told him Grambling would need to be licensed in Illinois. He told me that that would be no problem.

With these commitments in hand, I returned two weeks later to Grambling, to the same hotel to await further word from my contact, which never came. Some months later, I learned that my contact had been arrested, tried, and convicted for embezzling university funds.

At two of the institutions that would have been real coups, we came close to closing, but academic culture intervened to stop them. At Rochester Institute of Technology, the Dean of Continuing Education and the School of Engineering, and most important, the President, were eager to establish extension centers nationwide that would deliver four engineering programs: civil, industrial, mechanical, and chemical. After our initial visit, we met with an RIT task force in Tucson and, together, we determined that it was a feasible plan. We then formed a joint task force, headquartered in San Jose, charged with developing the curriculum and operational plan for a pilot program in the San Francisco Bay area. The task force solved the laboratory problem by arranging with Bay Area community colleges to use their laboratory facilities on weekends; the faculty would be drawn from RIT and from Bay Area colleges and universities.

When the final plan was in place, we presented it to the RIT administration. Unfortunately, the president who had approved the program had just resigned because of poor health. His replacement was the Institute's provost, a young man on the make, who was facing a visit from the regional accrediting association. Although not as arbitrary as WASC, the Middle States Accrediting Association was not known for its support of new ideas, and the new President wanted a smooth accreditation visit with no hit of innovation. He killed the program.

At Stetson University, the President was faced with the same problem—falling enrollments—that plagued most nonelite private institutions in the mid-1970s. He saw an IPD contract in much the same way as had Father McInnes at the University of San Francisco; it would bring a much-needed increase in enrollments and revenue. The President was able to convince all of his Deans that an IPD contract would be a good thing, and to get their full buy-in, we arranged for them to visit the University of Redlands. We put the delegation up at the Newporter Inn where a group of University of Redlands officials extolled the advantages of their IPD contract.

With the management of the Stetson University convinced, the sole hurdle remaining was the faculty. Because of my "impeccable" academic credentials, I was chosen to present the program at a full faculty meeting. After the President gave me a handsome introduction, I set out to present the IPD contract in the most nonthreatening way possible. Unfortunately, some members of the faculty had contacts with Bay Area institutions and it was not long before they were declaring to the assembly that a contract with IPD was a sure way to tarnish the University's reputation and turn Stetson into a diploma mill. When I looked to the President to say something in defense of the IPD program, he was ashen and silent. As one after another faculty member rose to denounce IPD, the faculty meeting spun out of control. After what seemed like an eternity, the President rose to adjourn the meeting and, with profuse apologies, saw me to my rental car and off to the airport.

The four institutions with which we negotiated contracts all proved to be stopgap measures. At Lesley College, we had only a marketing consulting contract that provided very little positive cash flow. The Elmhurst College contract was given only lukewarm support by the College administration, was marginally profitable, and lasted only three years. The National College of Education was enthusiastically supported by the administration, but the problem there was collecting IPD's share of the revenue. The college collected the tuition money, but because of their chronic cash flow problems, they consistently withheld IPD's share and fought us over every dollar. IPD was facing cash flow problems of its own, and it still rankles when I think of the times we had to cajole, beg, and or threaten the National controller to get our money. Perhaps the best result of that contract was the wording of all future contracts. All of them call for IPD to collect the tuition monies, which are then paid into a joint-signature bank account. Neither side gets its money until each party signs. It also brought home to us that, when it comes to money, very few colleges are paragons of ethical behavior.

The last of the four contracts was negotiated in the spring of 1979 with Regis College, a Jesuit institution in Denver, Colorado. Of the four contracts, this was the only one that was substantially profitable and therein lay a great danger. It did not take Father Clark, Regis's president, long before he viewed IPD's profits as a needless loss of income. Just at the beginning of Christmas vacation in 1981, in the spirit of the season, he declared IPD in breach of contract, and ordered us to turn over all the program records and exit our offices on the Regis campus. This act led to a long and contentious legal battle that was not concluded until the fall of 1984 with a $2-million award to IPD.

Flight to the Valley of the Sun

Early success often contains the seeds of early destruction, and this was the reality I faced in 1976. I was the president of a growing company whose adult outreach programs enrolled over 3,000 students, yet I knew the company was going to die unless I could reestablish it somewhere beyond WASC's reach. Doing this would face me with a whole new set of regulatory hurdles. Since the emergence of capitalism and the struggle to create free markets in guild-dominated cities, to the mercantilism of the nation state, and on to the regulatory structures of the modern state, every new industry has emerged only if the original companies were successful in their battles against regulatory barriers and control-minded bureaucrats. Had IPD and UOP not won the battles recounted here, there would be no Apollo Group, and the for-profit education industry would probably have emerged much later and in a different form.

By 1976, I had not only grown weary of academic politics and the countless committee meetings that IPD contracts required, I had also come to realize that it would never be possible to fully develop my concepts of education within the structure of an existing institution. If my concepts were to survive and prosper, we would have to have a university of our own. At this point, I had no more than the intention to try; how I would accomplish the feat would only emerge from the struggle.

Our only foothold outside of California was in Phoenix, Arizona, where we were operating a St. Mary's College program. Vitally important, Arizona was in the region of another accrediting agency— the North Central Association, making Phoenix an even more attractive site for our new university.

I can pinpoint the exact time I made the decision to create the University of Phoenix. In October 1975, we had moved the company to a 12,000-square-foot executive facility in north San Jose that had been vacated by a downsizing company, and we thought it very appropriate that a growing company take it over. Little did we realize that six months later thoughts of unimpeded growth would be replaced by worries over survival. Our new offices had a large carpeted office for the CEO with attached bathroom, shower, pantry, and boardroom; I can remember sitting at my fancy rosewood desk one March afternoon carrying on the business of the company and suddenly realizing that if I continued to run the company from that office, there would soon be no company to run.

At that point, I turned the IPD operations over to my two cofounders, Peter Ellis and Carole Crawford, and went out to accomplish what my fellow IPD'ers said was quixotic and doomed to failure—the creation our own university.

The St. Mary's–IPD Consortium

I did not study the problem very long before I realized that it would be almost impossible to achieve our goal directly. I had to get the process of university creation started in a way that did not set off academic alarms. My two assets were IPD and St. Mary's. IPD had the system of education and St. Mary's had the accreditation. My solution was to establish a consortium between IPD and St. Mary's, get the consortium accredited, and then spin off IPD as an independent accredited university. It was a godsend for me that Brother Dominic Ruegg, the Academic Vice President at St. Mary's College, believed in the IPD innovations as much as I did. He heartily endorsed the idea of creating a St. Mary's–IPD consortium, and he was able to convince Brother Mel Andersen, the St. Mary's president, that it was a worthy endeavor.

In addition to the serendipity of North Central jurisdiction, Arizona had no law governing private higher education. All that was required to establish a degree-granting institution of higher education was to create a corporation for that purpose. If the University of Phoenix constitutes a valuable educational innovation, then it can be argued that there are some important advantages to leaving private higher education unregulated by state agencies.

Brother Dominic and I decided on a plan whereby we would restructure the Arizona programs so the students would be enrolled both in St. Mary's and in IPD and would receive degrees from both institutions. We researched the history of consortia and found that there were several of them with a similar structure, the only difference being that both members of these consortia were accredited institutions. We intended to finesse that problem by chartering IPD as an institution of higher education in Arizona and making immediate application for accreditation with the North Central Association.

The Valley of the Sun

Apollo is the god of the sun and the Apollo logo is a mandala representing the sun. Little did I realize when I stepped off a plane at Sky Harbor on a scorching June day in 1976 that I would come to love this sere country. Even less did I imagine that it was here that we would build a NASDAQ One Hundred company that would literally create the for-profit higher education industry. Riding the greatest bull market in history it has, at this writing, given investors at its 1994 IPO nearly a thirtyfold return and, in five short years, reached a market cap of $3.0 billion.

When I arrived at the IPD-St. Mary's offices that June day, I found a secretary and a program coordinator in two small rooms in a high-rise. Classes were held in hotel rooms or in space donated by supportive companies or school districts. The coordinator was Sandi Sunde, wife of a St. Mary's graduate then a student at Thunderbird. Sandi was a short-termer but she was clever and, having worked previously on the St. Mary's campus, she brought valuable knowledge of the College departments with which the consortium would have to do business.

Creating the consortium, at a minimum, would require a physical presence and a legal existence. I found minimally acceptable space for offices and classrooms in the Boilermakers' Union Hall, for me an ideologically comfortable choice. Next I had to establish IPD as a degree-granting institution of higher education, and for this, I would need legal assistance.

Fortunately, a San Jose State colleague, Tony Carillo, had been a member of the Arizona House of Representatives; he provided me with some of his political contacts. The most important of them was Dino DeConcini, a member of the most powerful Democratic family in Arizona and a person who would play a vital role in our success. At the time, Dino was Chief of Staff for Governor Raoul Castro. I visited him at the capital, and, having already checked me out, he was most cordial. He recommended two firms, one Democratic and one Republican. After interviewing his contacts at each firm, I chose Snell & Wilmer, the Republican firm. It was a lucky choice. Shortly after making that choice, *The Arizona Republic,* the press power in Phoenix, ran some negative coverage on the Democratic firm.

At Snell & Wilmer, Richard Mallery handled our legal work, but, more important, he helped me recruit two absolutely vital members for the IPD Board of Directors: Ray Shaffer, retired president of the Greyhound Corp., and Dr. John Prince, Chancellor Emeritus of the Maricopa County Community College District. Shaffer was a giant both in size and in influence in the business community; Prince, as the founding chancellor of the Maricopa District, was much honored in the education community.

To have a consulting firm and an institution of higher education with the same name (a strategic decision based on keeping the lowest possible profile), I had Mallery create a new corporation—IPD, Inc. IPD, Inc. was also a for-profit corporation, even though Mallery had questioned the wisdom of creating what turned out to be the nation's first for-profit accredited institution of higher education. Being for-profit removed the siren song of soft money, it forced upon us the discipline of the market, and it left us no alternative but to produce a service for which customers were willing to pay a price high enough to sustain a going concern. Now that IPD was an institution of higher education, the only way to keep the innovation alive was somehow to get IPD accredited.

The North Central Connection

Other than WASC, I had had no previous experience with accrediting associations, but acting on the assumption that all of them couldn't be as predatory and unethical as WASC, I wrote to Dr. Thurston Manning, the North Central Executive Director, to inquire whether his organization would entertain an application for membership from our proposed consortium. My letter went out in early July 1976; Manning replied immediately that such a consortium appeared to be a legitimate educational enterprise, and that North Central would accept an application. He enclosed copies of the North Central rules and regulations and agreed to an August meeting in Denver, where he would be attending a conference of officials of the regional accrediting associations.

The meeting was held at a Denver airport hotel. I met with Manning, along with Bob Terrell, Director of Experimental Programs, representing St. Mary's, in one of the conference rooms during a break in the proceedings. The one ominous note in an otherwise cordial meeting came when I glanced up to see the figure of Kay Anderson standing in the half-open door with a look on his face that was both quizzical and angry. Manning encouraged us to pursue the consortium, and to prepare a self-study as the first step in the accreditation process. With that encouragement, Brother Dominic, Dr. Nancy

Dyar (who had replaced Terrell), and I set to work.[1] I drew up a consortium agreement and together we planned the Arizona joint operation.

Manning was one of the serendipities without which there would be no UOP and no Apollo. He was a Yale-educated physicist who had been Provost at Oberlin College; Professor of Physics and Astrophysics, Vice President for Academic Affairs, and Vice President for Research and Planning at the University of Colorado in Boulder; and thence to the presidency of the University of Bridgeport. In addition to his other virtues, Manning has a wonderfully wry sense of humor and looked upon all the *sturm und drang* attendant on our reeling and writhing within the coils of regional accreditation as simply part of the human comedy.

Only an Executive Director who was academically and professionally secure could have approved the idea of an IPD-St. Mary's consortium. It took great confidence to ignore Kay Anderson's charges that the North Central was whelping diploma mills, and to appoint academically secure visiting team members who would make disinterested judgments when examining IPD/UOP. It also took courage during battles yet to come to persuade the members of the various North Central bodies, those who would decide the fate of IPD/UOP, to focus on the integrity of their regulations and processes and ignore the opprobrium of the other five regional accrediting associations.

In November, Brother Dominic and I visited with Dr. Manning in the North Central offices in Boulder, Colorado, to seek further direction. We presented a progress report, obtained his advice on a timetable for submitting the consortium self-study, and scheduled a visit by a North Central accreditation team for sometime in the spring of 1977. When we left Boulder, we were in a state of euphoria.

Kay Anderson Kills the Consortium

Fortunately for us, Kay Anderson was busy with USF and did not turn his attention to St. Mary's until after the February 1977 meeting of the WASC Senior Commission, when the USF accreditation was again deferred. However, when he did, he immediately drove a spike through the heart of the consortium.

Shortly after the February commission meeting, Anderson sent Leo Cain, a Cal State professor, to St. Mary's on a reconnoitering visit; on March 24th, Anderson and Cain then paid St. Mary's a second visit. On March 29th, Anderson wrote to Brother Mel Anderson to inform him that "Discussion during the meeting reveals some rather serious problems with your off-campus programs as they relate to Commission policy." This was followed by a list of seven items needing correction, five of which applied directly to IPD.[2]

All of the charges were designed to force St. Mary's to break its contract with IPD and place control of the off-campus programs in the hands of the faculty. Most of the data cited as documentation of the problems was inaccurate. Kay Anderson's bill of particulars was simply preface to his conclusion: "Now that the Institute for Professional Development is incorporated in Arizona and has applied for recognition to the North Central accrediting association, the programs offered in that state can no longer be considered part of St. Mary's accreditation." By removing St. Mary's accreditation in Arizona, Anderson killed the consortium.

There was no precedent for such a decision. There was nothing in academic tradition or WASC regulations to bar an institution from entering into a consortium with another institution. Brother Mel responded by return mail demanding to know "under what guidelines or regulations do you determine that accreditation of Saint Mary's College does not cover the programs which we sponsor in conjunction with IPD in Arizona? It seems to me that many questions must be answered before a determination can be made as to what Saint Mary's may accredit and what we may not."

Not only did Kay Anderson write to inform Brother Mel that the Arizona programs were null and void; on the same day he had replied to a solicited letter of inquiry from the Mesa, Arizona School District, that St. Mary's Arizona programs were no longer accredited.[3] Brother Mel responded to this act of arrogance with a letter to Anderson reviewing the history of the St. Mary's-IPD contract and its conformity with California and Arizona law and WASC regulations. He closed by requesting that a telegram be sent to the Mesa school authorities "indicating that new information regarding IPD and Saint Mary's College has come to light" and to inform the people in Arizona that the programs were being operated in conformity with the applicable WASC guidelines.[4] I also sent a letter over the signature of Richard Mallery, IPD's corporate counsel. It reviewed the legal status of the St. Mary's-IPD programs and the current WASC regulations and pointed out that there were two IPDs—the original IPD, which was incorporated in California, and the new IPD, Inc., which was incorporated in Arizona as an institution of higher education. The letter closed with a request for an explanation as to why Anderson had taken the position that WASC accreditation did not extend to the Arizona programs. "I am also interested in knowing whether this position is a formal position adopted by WASC or its Board of Directors and how that position can be reconciled with the fact that WASC currently permits many educational institutions . . . to offer programs outside of California."[5]

The letters were a means for the consortium to stall for time until the North Central Association sent a visiting team to Arizona. Neither I nor any of the St. Mary's officers had any illusions concerning Anderson's power and how he used it. St. Mary's had no grounds for appeal. However, neither Brother Dominic nor I had any intention of abandoning the consortium. We knew that Brother Mel did not dare sign the letter of agreement for the consortium, but that did not prevent us from operating as the consortium in Arizona. We simply changed the terminology and billed the consortium as the "St. Mary's-IPD Cooperative Program."

IPD, Inc., Receives Candidacy for Accreditation

Based on our conversations with Manning, we anticipated a North Central visit in April. In late April, Manning scheduled a visit for mid-May and then postponed it. At this point, I was certain that Anderson had been successful in either dissuading Manning from scheduling a visit or at least postponing it until WASC could drive St. Mary's out of Arizona. I was convinced that all was lost, and then a miracle happened: Manning scheduled a visit for June 13 and 14, and my spirits soared.

However, when I received the names of the North Central team, my spirits immediately collapsed. Everyone was a traditional academic and they were not lightweights: the Chairman was Dr. Donald Roush, Academic Vice President of New Mexico State University;

the two other members were Dr. Wade Ellis, Professor of Mathematics and Associate Dean of the Graduate School at the University of Michigan, Ann Arbor; and Dr. Roy Troutt, President of the University for Sciences and the Arts of Oklahoma. My apprehensions about our chances with such a team were not ill placed. Years later, Dr. Ellis told me that it was his intention to do what he could to stamp out this new for-profit diploma mill that had opened for business in Phoenix. It was only after being shocked to find that we were not only serious about education but also knew more about the teaching-learning process in adult education than he did that he reversed field and, together with Roush and Troutt, voted to recommend that IPD, Inc. be granted status as a candidate for accreditation.

The North Central team's recommendation was affirmed by the Review Committee and the Commission on Institutions of Higher Education. Once IPD, Inc. held candidate status, it could emerge as an independent institution. One of the recommendations of the Review Committee was to clarify the relationship between IPD (the consulting firm) and IPD, Inc. (the institution of higher education) by changing the name of one of them. We chose to change the name of IPD, Inc. and, after long discussions and with much trepidation, the Board of Directors decided on University of Phoenix. It was an ambitious choice and in the long run, it has served the University well, but in the short run, it added to our list of enemies. Usurping the city's name appeared as an act of arrogance to the two entities that controlled civic life—the Phoenix Forty, a group of self-elected civic leaders, and *The Arizona Republic,* owner of both morning and evening papers and the major TV station. As with one voice, they all expressed shock that this upstart institution would even dare call itself a university and then have the audacity to appropriate the name of their fair city.

The battle for the consortium and for North Central candidacy for accreditation had involved neither any Arizona academics nor their supporters in the North Central Association, in any of the government agencies, nor in the Arizona legislature. It was simply the calm before the storm. As soon as word leaked out that UOP had been granted candidacy, the WAR IN ARIZONA began.

7

The War in Arizona

Setting the Scene

In achieving candidacy for accreditation, the University of Phoenix had managed to clamber over one huge barrier, but a more formidable one loomed ahead. The whole regulatory structure of higher education is designed to favor nonprofit and public colleges and universities, which it does by placing added regulatory burdens on those institutions organized for-profit. This difference in treatment represents a cultural prejudice that arose from centuries of practice. Beginning with the University of Bologna, founded in the twelfth century, down to Harvard College and its American offspring, ranging from large state universities to community colleges, to small church-related colleges, education for profit simply doesn't seem right; it violates the established order of things.

The instant disability facing UOP in 1976 was a U.S. Department of Education statute-based regulation. That regulation grants Title IV eligibility to nonprofit and public institutions that have achieved candidate-for-accreditation status, but only grants Title IV eligibility to for-profit institutions *after* they have achieved full accreditation. Title IV eligibility was crucial to UOP because it would give its students access to federal grants and guaranteed loans. In addition, the standard practice among U.S. corporations is to limit employee tuition assistance grants to students enrolled in accredited institutions, not institutions that are merely candidates. In 1976, the only way for a student to attend UOP was to pay the tuition by cash, check, or a credit card.

In the first year, only eight students were willing to pay cash to enroll in a nonaccredited university that the dominant press regularly described as a "diploma mill." Money from the California contracts would last, at most, for two more years. With that span of time, UOP had to achieve accreditation.

Kay Anderson was also aware that UOP could not survive long without accreditation, and UOP's receipt of candidacy gave him the issue he needed to rally the academic conservatives and destroy this hated Son of IPD. It was apparent to us that only Anderson could have orchestrated the denunciation of UOP by Arizona's educational leaders. The same criticisms IPD had faced in California were now used against UOP in Arizona. The University's for-profit structure and its refusal to abide by the canons of academic orthodoxy were again seized upon as violations of everything academically acceptable and accreditable.

The Regents' Grasp for Control of Private Higher Education

Once UOP was granted candidacy, the academic conservatives tried, but found they had little ability, to force a recession of the grant. It was evident that pressure on the North Central would not be effective until UOP applied for accreditation, so the conservatives turned to the state legislature for relief. This took the form of a bill that had been introduced some years before but had languished in committee and was now being reintroduced in the 1977 session. The bill would give the Arizona Regents of the three state universities—University of Arizona, Arizona State, and Northern Arizona—control over both public and private higher education. If the bill were to pass, UOP would very quickly be regulated out of existence.

The person coordinating the legislative effort was Larry Woodall, the Regents' Executive Coordinator. Woodall knew little about education and spoke only in garbled sentences. Yet, no matter how off the mark his utterances, the Regents and the officers of the state universities formed a faithful amen chorus. Woodall was a perfect cat's paw for Anderson.

I had informed Woodall of IPD, Inc.'s intention to apply for candidacy with the North Central Association, and he had assured me that any institution that could achieve accreditation by the North Central was welcome in Arizona. When the 1977 legislative session opened, he chose to forget that conversation and, instead, organized opposition to UOP in the universities and in the Legislature. After working the Regent's bill for several years, Woodall thought that he was close to success.

Until this point, I had done all the political work. Fortunately, I was then joined by John Murphy, a student activist from San Jose State days, who came equipped with lobbying experience gained in California. He was to stay with me until 1996. Together we lobbied against and testified against the bill in the House Education Committee and were effective enough to slow its progress.

Woodall needed something to dramatize the need for his bill, so he seized upon North Central's award of candidacy to UOP as evidence that the educational "flood gates" had been breached, and Arizona now would be inundated with diploma mills. With Woodall in full cry, the Arizona Board of Regents took up the cause of defending traditional education from the scourge of the nontraditional. At the November 1977 meeting of the Regents, Woodall offered the following gem:

> It would appear that the North Central Association has lowered their accreditation requirements to the extent of actually recommending accreditation for people who have no campus, who have no classrooms, who have no libraries, who use evaluation of life services, meaning that in flying or practical nursing or any of that sort, that it be evaluated and cranked into your BA and, in some cases, you can bypass your BA altogether and go straight to a masters or a doctoral program . . .[1]

The Regents and the presidents and vice presidents of the three state universities all agreed with Woodall and entered into the record their opinion that UOP represented a clear and present danger to higher education in Arizona and that the North Central Association had abandoned its standards.

The portion of the Regents' meeting devoted to diploma mills and UOP was widely reported in the press and about the only solace we had was the fact that they spelled my name right. Having no access to the media, I initiated a correspondence with Woodall, and in a letter to him of December 1st, I reviewed our adversarial encounters before the House Education Committee. I listed the press distortions attributed to him, the corrections as I saw them, and requested an opportunity to attend the next meeting of the Regents "for the purpose of accurately describing the structure, operations, and goals of the University of Phoenix. . . ." Regarding his attack on UOP as a tactic to further his legislative agenda, I wrote:

> I hereby demand either an assurance that you did not make the following statements reported in the newspapers, or a public retraction of them: "The University of Phoenix offers quick degrees." "If you're real skillful in what you say about yourself, you may get a master's without having completed second grade." (In reference to UOP's position among the imaginary hordes of diploma mills) "There are many of them that are just as bad and some a lot worse.[2]

I closed with a request to attend the next meeting of the Board of Regents and to be given the opportunity to describe the "structure, operations, and goals of the University of Phoenix. . . ." I then sent copies to the following persons:

- Members of the Arizona Board of Regents
- The Governor
- The Superintendent of Public Instruction
- Members of the Arizona Commission for Postsecondary Education
- Presidents of the three state universities
- Speaker of the Arizona House of Representatives
- President of the Arizona Senate
- Majority and Minority Leaders in both houses
- Chairs of the Education and Appropriations Committees in both houses

Woodall replied in his letter of December 8th. It began:

> Your letter of December 1, 1977 has been received. I too am dismayed at the controversy which has arisen over this matter . . . Due

to the wide distribution which you gave to the letter addressed to me, I feel it is incumbent to put this matter of the University of Phoenix and its proposed accreditation in focus as soon as possible . . . In fact, one reading the newspaper account would be inclined to think that I had centered my remarks on accreditation around the University of Phoenix. Such was not the case. In fact, I neither mentioned the University of Phoenix nor diploma mills during my initial address to the Board.[3]

Woodall was being less than candid. He might have omitted reference to UOP and diploma mills from his initial address but, as the transcript of the meeting showed, he was not misquoted by the press. Woodall now had little choice but to extend an invitation for me to attend the next Regents' meeting and to make a presentation.

I made the presentation to a stony-faced group of Regents and to their academic minions, and I was not apologetic:

To me, the most disturbing aspect of the present situation is that the persons who provided the Regents with information concerning the University of Phoenix violated every tenet of scholarship which is the foundation of any university. Their allegations were not based on research, showed no respect for fact or sound argument, and were uttered with no concern for the harm which they surely knew these allegations would cause.

I then reviewed the diploma mill fright and its lack of substance, concluding:

It seems an inescapable conclusion to me that the purpose of such misrepresentations and alteration of facts had as its objective, one, to intimidate the Legislature into passing an ill-considered "degree mill" bill, and two, to irreparably damage the University of Phoenix and thus to force it to cease operation.

I followed with a description of UOP and at the close of my remarks, I offered to respond to any questions. None were asked.[4]

The Regents' alarm over "the invasion of the diploma mills" and their problems with UOP were reported in the press, and on radio and

TV and the connection between the two issues was lost on no one. Woodall saw diploma mill operators under every bed. At one point, he claimed that there were 300 diploma mills operating in Arizona and, when asked to show proof of the assertion, he lamely replied that if something wasn't done, there might be 300.

To refute his assertion that the diploma mills were flooding into Arizona from Texas, we telephoned the Texas higher education authority and found that there had been no new legislation, and that Texas did not have a diploma mill problem. As to the problem in Arizona, we visited the Arizona Attorney General's office and found that, relying on the commercial fraud statutes, it had eliminated the one or two diploma mills that tried to operate in Arizona. Woodall, the Regents, and the academic high command of the three state universities were undeterred by facts in their resolve to eliminate UOP. These high-volume efforts eventually caught the ear of the Christian conservative legislators who feared possible extension of state control to religious K–12 schools, and they became our quiet defenders.

Woodall's patent distortions, our fact-finding efforts, my correspondence with the legislative leaders, and testimony before the House Education Committee, along with John Murphy's work in the corridors, drew enough support away from Senate Bill 1340 to cause its narrow defeat on the House floor the final night of the session.

For us, the 1977 legislative session was the arena for the battle between the spirit of education past and present versus the spirit of education future. Even though we had stopped S.B. 1340, we finally realized that, to the academic traditionalists, IPD and UOP were the embodiment of heresy and we were locked in a jihad with an army of true believers.

The Battle for Accreditation

The battle for accreditation was a battle for survival. The minimum time that could elapse between the grant of candidate status and the application for accreditation was two years. Only one or perhaps two newly created institutions of higher education had ever achieved accreditation in that short time, but UOP had no choice but to make the attempt. As far as UOP was concerned, the pending loss of IPD's three California contracts proved to be a blessing rather than a tragedy.

Once a contract was cancelled, most of the expense of administering the contract ceased, but the revenue from the contract continued to flow into IPD and on to UOP for the next 18 months. Because of this enhanced cash flow, which began with the phase-out of the USF contract, UOP did not lack for financial resources in its hour of peril. Although we had only eight students enrolled, UOP was able to retain the most competent academic consultants available: Doctors Donald Roush and Wade Ellis.

Roush and Ellis were chosen on the recommendation of Dr. Thurston Manning, Director of the North Central Commission of Institutions of Higher Education. Both had been members of the first North Central team to visit the University, so they were familiar with its operation. Both men had extensive experience in evaluating institutions for accreditation, and both had served as members of the North Central Commission on Institutions of Higher Education. Dr. Roush had chaired the Commission and had then gone on to serve as the President of the North Central Association. I decided to act upon their advice, whatever it cost. If Roush and Ellis recommended a change in the University's structure, personnel, or capital equipment, we made the change. During the two years they acted as our consultants on accreditation, we wrote two draft self-studies and Roush and Ellis conducted two mock accreditation visits. At the end of the two-year period, they believed we were ready for accreditation, and we fully intended to fight for it.

Unfortunately for me, 1978 began with a routine physical that revealed a prostate tumor. This was followed shortly by an operation, called a transurethral resection (TUR), at Stanford University Hospital. In addition to its primary purpose of removing an obstruction from my urethra, the TUR provided tissues for a biopsy that would determine whether the tumor was malignant. Besides leaving me physically exhausted, the operation induced a depressing sense of foreboding as to my future.

Depression not withstanding, I had only a few days for recovery before I had to drag myself aboard a plane for Phoenix to meet with officials of the Arizona Regents and their minions from the three state universities. It took all of my energy to get through the meeting. Dr. Roush, our North Central consultant, had invited them to visit UOP in hopes that better information of what we were about might

dispel some of their misconceptions and, perhaps, soften their opposition. It was a vain endeavor. When the ambassadors arrived, we prof-
fered coffee and soft drinks, which were declined. Dr. Roush and I
then made a presentation and asked if there were any questions. There
were none. Our guests left without shaking hands or saying good-bye.
Two days later I had to appear before a legislative committee hearing
to rebut the testimony of these same ambassadors. Fortunately, returning to combat allowed me quickly to throw off both weariness and
depression.

About a month after my surgery, I received the results of the
biopsy. The surgeon, Professor Tom Stamey, phoned to inform me
that the tumor was malignant. When I visited him to discuss the matter, he laid out my options: do nothing, a radical prostatectomy, or
radiation. My being 57 would have given the cancer a long time to
grow, thus he thought doing nothing would be most unwise. The
nerve-saving prostatectomy had yet to be invented, so a radical prostatectomy would leave me incontinent and impotent. There were two
options for radiation: the linear accelerator or radioactive Iodine-125
implants, and both were experimental. I decided that before making a
decision, I should practice due diligence review. Because I was working 70- to 80-hour weeks, the process took several months. In the
meantime, the battle went on.

The First Accreditation Visit

We spent the better part of the spring of 1978 preparing for the
accreditation visit. By this time, we had moved to a two-story court-
yard office, somewhat upscale from the Boilermakers' Union hall.
Most of the University functions—receptionist, registrar, curriculum
developers—were housed in a large open space on the second floor.
This is where John Murphy and I fought the crucial battles of accreditation with our minds and pens. An institution prepares for an
accreditation visit by writing a self-study that, for us, was a carefully
reasoned argument as to why UOP should be granted accreditation.
We wrote two mock self-studies and countless drafts of the self-study
itself. We sat at a long table with yellow pads scribbling away with
pencils and editing with scissors and paste sticks. When we had a
"final" yellow-paper draft, we had it typed. Then, this being the good

old days before word processing, we further edited by literally cutting and pasting. Working in this fashion, we had constant contact with all of the staff and with faculty and students who dropped in. It is not an exaggeration to say that every member of the University was involved in the process and all had immediate input. They all understood that the future of the University depended on the quality and persuasiveness of what we were writing.

Again, Manning had chosen three distinguished academics for the crucial visit that occurred in June 1978. The team was chaired by Francis Heller, the Roy Roberts Professor of Law and Political Science at the University of Kansas; the other members were Alfred Sussman, Dean of the Graduate School at the University of Michigan, and Ray Heffner, Professor of English and former Academic Vice President at the University of Iowa. The team conducted a thorough examination of the University and made a legitimate, if conservative, recommendation. The recommendation was not to grant accreditation but to continue candidacy—a decision that was almost, but not quite, fatal. The basis for this determination was not that the University was unqualified for accreditation, but rather that the University had been in existence such a short time that the team could not be certain that the University would continue to operate as it was then operating. In short, they said we needed more time to acquire a track record.[5]

Not only would continuation of candidacy leave our students without eligibility for financial aid, the constant attacks by the officials of the three state universities created a certainty in the minds of both current and potential students that UOP was slowly slipping into oblivion. Accreditation was the only thing that would reverse the fatal slide.

We appealed the decision to continue candidacy to the North Central Review Panel that would make the final recommendation to the Commission on Institutions of Higher Education. At the hearing before the Review Panel, Professor Heller, who had chaired the visiting team, explained the basis of the team's recommendation and, surprise of surprises, informed the Panel that he had voted to grant accreditation. Based upon Heller's testimony, the Panel recommended that UOP be granted accreditation.

Alas, it was not to be. Facing increasing pressure from the three state universities in Arizona, the Executive Board of the Commission on Institutions of Higher Education ruled that UOP would remain in Candidacy status, but it would permit UOP to reapply for accreditation in one year rather than the regular two years. Although the Executive Board probably considered that the best they could do given the political pressure from the Arizona universities, it was of no value to UOP, because UOP would no longer be in existence in another year. We knew that the members of the Commission had been heavily lobbied, and we were informed that the reversal came only after threats of secession from the North Central Association by Arizona's three state universities. The Arizona Regents, in what was certainly an unprecedented action by a governing board of a state university system, had joined with the Arizona academics in the attempt to force the Commission to rule against the University of Phoenix and deny accreditation.

The Battle for the Soul of the North Central Association

The continuation of candidacy was still the kiss of death. Having no other alternative, we appealed the decision and petitioned for a hearing before the Committee on Reconsideration. Murphy and I flew to Las Cruces, New Mexico, to meet with Don Roush in his offices at New Mexico State. With his help, we were able to craft what Roush considered a compelling petition. The petition asked that UOP be granted accreditation based on the accreditation team report and the report and recommendation of the Review Panel. Our petition was only partly compelling. In response to the appeal, the Executive Board ordered fact finding and scheduled another visit to UOP that August, with the charge to the team to make a determination of whether UOP was a stable institution that was likely to continue to operate in an accreditable manner.

By the summer of 1978, I had read numerous scientific papers about my medical condition and had spoken by phone to any of the authors of those articles who would take my calls. At the conclusion of this due diligence, I decided on the I-125 implants. I had the surgery on the first of August—two weeks after the meeting of the North Central Review Committee that recommended UOP accreditation, and three weeks before a North Central fact-finding team would pay UOP a visit. This was rougher surgery than the TUR and left me quite exhausted. A few days later, I began to feel the effects of the radiation. It was not acute pain, yet it did not come and go. It was just a steady, unvarying burning sensation that I could lessen, but not mask, with drugs. When I was awake, even when heavily drugged— Percodan seemed to work the best—I had to move constantly to distract myself, and I could only sleep by consuming handfuls of sleeping pills. It was not too many days until I could not stand my brain being drugged by the Percodan, so I tried smoking marijuana. This allowed me to reduce the Percodan to a nondrugged level.

I managed to continue working through the North Central fact-finding visit and again we were blessed by competent and unprejudiced visitors. Manning had chosen G. Philip Johnson, Dean of Graduate Study at Oakland University, Rochester, Michigan, and Donald Robinson, Dean of the College of Education at Oklahoma State. Their report was substantially favorable and found "the institution better able to abide by Association standards than did our colleagues on the [accreditation] team."[6]

Once the visit was over and the pressure was off, it was impossible for me to be effective, so my son Peter decided that a trip to Hawaii might help take my mind off the pain. He chose Maui, where he believed he could keep me constantly occupied. He arranged helicopter trips up the Wimea Canyon and along the Nepali Coast and Jeep trips anywhere on the island a Jeep could go. In the evening, I would add alcohol to the Percodan and marijuana, which would allow me to fall asleep without sleeping pills. One day, Peter had the helicopter drop us off on a secluded beach where I was able to lie in the shade, listen to the surf, and smoke enough marijuana to mask the burning completely. It was a day to remember. At the end of this vacation I returned to work.

When I returned to work, I had to take several Percodans each day, but I was still able, with John Murphy's help, to draft a petition seeking reconsideration of the North Central's decision to postpone accreditation. The petition, together with the one negative and two positive accreditation recommendations, then went to the Committee on Reconsideration, which heard the matter in the following October. Acting on Manning's advice, the Commission chose five more

distinguished academics from traditional institutions to hear the
appeal: Sr. Ida Gannon, Mundeline College, Chicago, chairperson;
President Tilghman Aley, Casper College; Professor Joseph Cosand,
University of Michigan, Ann Arbor; Professor Robert Keller, Univer-
sity of Minnesota, Minneapolis; and Vice President William Neptune,
Oklahoma Baptist University. Among the Committee's findings were:

> The procedures of the Commission in this case did not provide for
> adequate presentation to the Executive Board of the reasons for the
> recommendations of the Review Committee . . . [T]he Commit-
> tee on reconsideration finds that the action of the Commission
> respecting the University of Phoenix did contain factual error of
> sufficient magnitude to warrant reconsideration, in that significant
> information was not available to the Executive Board at the time of
> the decision. The Committee finds further that knowledge of that
> information, provided to it by the report of the fact-finding com-
> mittee, supports the recommendation of the July, 1978 review com-
> mittee. The Committee unanimously recommends: The University
> of Phoenix be granted accreditation as a master's degree–granting
> institution.[7]

At last, we had reached the finals, but the three Arizona public universities remained astride the path to victory.

We knew that the Arizona academics and their Regental supporters were applying the same pressure to the NCA Board of Directors that they had applied to the Commission. In his letter informing
me of the favorable action of the Committee on Reconsideration,
Manning also informed me that the North Central Board of Directors, ". . . concluded that it would be desirable if each member had an
opportunity to consider the full written record available to the Committee on Reconsideration." Accordingly, action on the Committee's
recommendations was deferred to a special meeting of the Board
scheduled for December 9, 1978. Manning also requested that copies
of our self-study be sent to the members of the NCA Board of Directors and that he would provide copies of the reports of the team visits and the Review Panel.

We knew that the Regents and academics were applying a full-
court press when we were informed that the special meeting sched-

uled for December 9th was to be held in Tucson. The same pressure tactics which the anti-IPD forces had used so effectively in California now appeared in Arizona. Not only were the members of the North Central Board bombarded with stories of UOP's scandalous academic practices, I was accused of purchasing the support of Dr. John Prince, a member of the UOP Board of Directors who had just retired as Chancellor of the Maricopa County Community College System, and Doctors Ellis and Roush, our two North Central consultants.

Manning's letter had signaled the opening of the battle for the soul of the North Central Association. I had immediately responded to express my "shock and concern" over the deferral and made the following points:

Except for its public members, all of the members of the North Central Board of Directors represented tax-supported institutions and are perhaps unaware that UOP is totally dependent on tuition revenues and accreditation is a necessity if UOP students are to have access to federally insured student loans. Not only has the University of Phoenix been subjected "to malicious, unsubstantiated and unprovoked attacks upon its integrity" by officials of Arizona's public universities, but these officials have mounted a sustained attack upon the University of Phoenix within the North Central Association itself.

In the previous April, when these officials were given an audience before the North Central Commission of Institutions of Higher Education, they: 1. maligned the integrity of the North Central consultants assigned to the University of Phoenix and have accused the University of Phoenix of purchasing the favorable opinions of these North Central consultants. 2. these officials have threatened to take their institutions out of the North Central Association," and on September 9th the Arizona Regents passed a resolution containing that threat.

I then closed:

Clearly, the opposition of the Arizona public universities to the accreditation of the University of Phoenix has been heard and been carefully considered at many levels within the North Central Association. The opposition of the Arizona public universities represents a danger to the existence of the University of Phoenix but it also represents a danger to the North Central Association. These well-publicized and heavy-handed activities of the officials of these Arizona public universities threaten the political contamination of the accreditation process as it relates to the University of Phoenix. Unless this contamination is avoided it will destroy the integrity of the accreditation process itself.[8]

When Manning did not reply, I took silence for assent.

Our political advisors believed that the only way we had to counter the pressure and the slander was to appeal to the Governor of Arizona, who was an ex officio member of the Regents. Fortunately, our corporate counsel was a close friend and advisor of the Governor's, and he arranged for a confidential luncheon meeting for Governor Babbitt, myself, and a member of the UOP Board of Directors. The degree of confidentiality was evidenced by the fact that the luncheon was served in a private hotel suite, and the Governor entered the building through the service entrance and used the service elevator.

Governor Babbitt was both understanding and gracious. In his opinion, the University of Phoenix was providing a useful service to the community and the attempt of the state universities to destroy it was territorialism at its most unattractive. The Governor assured me that he was not, and could not be an advocate of UOP, but he was and could be an advocate of fairness and due process. He said that he would urge the members of the Board of Regents to cease their lobbying efforts and to "allow the process to work."

The special meeting the North Central Board of Directors called to make the final decision on UOP's accreditation was held in Tucson on December 9th, as scheduled. The Board members arrived at the hotel the evening before the meeting. This gave us the opportunity to lobby those members who were determined to see that the North Central's processes were not tampered with, as they had been at the meetings of the Commission on Institutions of Higher Education and Board of Directors. To make the University's presence as painfully evident as possible, Don Roush, Wade Ellis, and I registered at the hotel and spent the evening lobbying for the soul of the North Central Association and the survival of the University of Phoenix. At a final session with some of the Board members in the coffee shop the next morning, we were assured that the "matter of the accreditation of the University of Phoenix," would be decided in our favor by 9:00 A.M. That prediction proved to be wide off the mark.

I had rented a suite where Roush, Ellis, and I could wait for the decision, and I had ordered a bottle of Mumm's Cordon Rouge that was iced and waiting for the celebratory moment. The morning passed, lunch was eaten in silence, and optimism turned to apprehension. After lunch, I ventured into the hallway outside the room where the Directors were meeting, and the loud and angry voices from within served only to increase our apprehensions. Eventually, Roush and Ellis, who had scheduled afternoon flights home to appointments they could not cancel, departed, leaving me alone with the champagne. Then, at 5:00 P.M., Manning came in, greeting me as the president of the North Central's newest member institution. I skipped the champagne and settled for two double vodkas.

The "Diploma Mill" Bill

After the defeat of their bill in 1977, the Regents again sought legislative relief. In 1978, they sponsored a "new and improved" anti–diploma mill bill that would give them even more control over both public and private higher education in Arizona. They were prepared to and did give it a maximum effort. Fortunately, we were better prepared for legislative battle than we had been in 1977, and we now had the same level of legislative access as did our opponents.

John Murphy carried the main burden of the lobbying effort, assisted by me and by a most knowledgeable and astute individual who had come to us on the understanding that ours would be a confidential relationship. The University of Phoenix had so many enemies throughout the state and in the legislature that even our lobbyist could not support us publicly. He did not even give us any sign of recognition in public beyond a discrete glance or nod. If he were able to arrange a meeting with a legislator, we would receive a phone call telling us that a senator or representative would see us, but, in the meeting itself, we never mentioned the lobbyist who had arranged it.

The universities had, over the years, practiced sufficient greed and arrogance to gain some powerful legislative enemies who assumed that UOP couldn't be all bad if the state universities were trying to destroy it. In fact, they decided that because the state universities considered UOP to be an abomination, it had to be saved. Working from this base, we and our lobbyists were able to defeat the legislation. It again passed the House and Senate Education committees but lost by a few votes on the floor of the House.

Although the Regents had failed twice to get their bills though the legislature and they had failed in their lobbying efforts with the North Central Association, they did not cease their efforts to destroy us.

The Secession Threat

Blocked at the legislature and the North Central Association, the Regents now tried to rid themselves of both UOP and the North Central Association by seceding from North Central and joining WASC. Had they succeeded, WASC would have had jurisdiction in Arizona, and UOP would have had to seek WASC accreditation. As we and the Regents knew, WASC would quickly have administered the *misericordia* to UOP, and our attempt to create a new model for adult education would have ended in defeat. At the Regents' meeting following our successful grant of accreditation, they voted to secede from North Central and pursue another affiliation.

The Regents and the officials of the three state universities put pressure on the other Arizona institutions of higher education to support the move. All the private institutions agreed to go along, but the community colleges fought to maintain their affiliations with the North Central.

Secession required at least the informal approval of the legislature and the "diploma mill bill" battle had raised enough flags so the transfer of Arizona to WASC jurisdiction was given careful scrutiny. Consequently, it occasioned an investigation by the staff of the Majority Leader of the Arizona House of Representatives, Burton Barr. Barr's staff prepared a report that found that the University of Phoenix was neither a diploma mill nor more dangerous than one. On the contrary, it was found to be a legitimate and very useful institution of higher education that served a student population that was ignored by Arizona's other institutions.[9] The Majority Leader also ordered an investigation of and report on the issues involved in the transfer of Arizona from North Central to WASC jurisdiction.

The investigation determined that, except for their belief that the North Central Association had abandoned standards and that WASC hadn't, the reasons cited by the Regents for requesting the move to WASC were unconvincing. These included the following: that the North Central region spanned three time zones and Arizona and California only two; that the North Central accredits 1,000 institutions and WASC only 250, which would give the Arizona universities more voice than they had in the North Central delegate assembly (in this case they forgot to mention that WASC had no delegate assembly); and that their peer institutions were the other PAC-10 universities. The Majority Leader's staff concluded that the operative reason for the Regent's action was nothing more than hostility toward UOP. Based on these findings, legislative leaders quickly put a stop to the secession effort.[10]

Safe at Last

The only tactic left to the Arizona universities, other than slander, was to refuse to accept UOP credits or degrees. In the western states, the senior land grant university sets the credit transfer policy for all of the institutions in the state. In this instance, the University of Arizona listed UOP in the standard credit transfer guide (AACRO) as an institution whose credits were not acceptable. After a long and acrimonious conflict with the University of Arizona and the association that published the credit transfer guide, we convinced both institutions that we would sue them for restraint of trade if the listing were not changed.

With that credible threat, the University of Arizona did not change its position but finessed the issue by removing the credit transfer status of all Arizona institutions, thereby making Arizona the only state whose institutions of higher education have no credit transfer status. We responded to this ploy by having a bill introduced in the legislature mandating the acceptance of UOP credits. When the Regents, to their horror, found that we had a sufficient number of committed votes in both the House and Senate to pass the bill over their opposition, they called for negotiations. In a meeting moderated by House Majority Leader Burton Barr, I met with the Chair of the Board, Esther Capin, and two other Board members. After two hours of acrimonious argument, and only after Mr. Barr assured them that we had the votes, did they capitulate and agree to adopt the language of the bill as Regental policy.

There are still occasional conflicts with a few departments in the state universities, but, after two decades, both sides have settled into an armed stalemate with regular skirmishes but no pitched battles. It is our hope that Dr. Jorge Klor de Alva, who left an endowed chair at U.C. Berkeley to assume the UOP presidency, will help to set at ease academic critics both in Arizona and at large.

Certainly, this academic range war in Arizona drove home one message: No innovation will survive unless its protagonists are willing to respond to the inevitable attacks by the academic traditionalists with a passion of equal intensity. Furthermore, successful defense of an innovation requires will, political skill, and financial resources. Fortunately for IPD and UOP, they had all three. Plus, they had principals who were happy warriors and who thrilled to the battle.

8

Meanwhile, Back at the Ranch

Part I—1979 to 1981
The FBI Arrives—RICO

We did not have long to enjoy the euphoria of being an accredited institution of higher education. In May 1979, a new danger appeared. FBI Agent Mike Maloney and his silent sidekick descended on the IPD office in San Jose to examine an anonymous allegation that I was guilty of a criminal conspiracy. Their charges were no more specific than that I had somehow bribed officials at the University of San Francisco to gain their support for the IPD contract. They also claimed that I had bribed the Lieutenant Governor of California to induce him to support legislation that would strip WASC of its authority to accredit California colleges and universities. To substantiate the allegations, they sought evidence that I had siphoned money from IPD and had made cash payments to the Lieutenant Governor and a variety of John Does.

Fully expecting to obtain evidence of my malfeasance from disaffected staff members, they systematically interrogated every employee who handled money, from tuition collection to the payment of vendors and staff salaries. When this produced no incriminating evidence, they brought in clerks to examine every check IPD had ever written. Again, there was no evidence.

Having come up empty-handed in San Jose, the two FBI agents came to Phoenix, where they visited each member of the UOP Board of Directors, asking them how they could associate themselves with a company whose president was such a disreputable figure; surely they were aware that I had corrupted both University of San Francisco officials and public officials in California and probably public officials in Arizona. None of the Board members had anything to report, and they properly asked the agents if they were to assume my guilt before I was tried and convicted.

Although the FBI had drawn blanks in both San Jose and Phoenix, the agents made a negative report to a San Francisco Grand Jury that had been empanelled to investigate political corruption. The Grand Jury, whose targets included Lieutenant Governor Dymally and Dean Alan Calvin, recommended that I be called for interrogation by the U.S. Attorney in San Francisco. As an African American, Lieutenant Governor Dymally was a target almost by definition; Calvin was of interest because of a presumed bribe of a school District Superintendent back in New York City. If the U.S. Attorneys could show that I had bribed either one of them, it would not only snare me but would help snare Dymally and Calvin.

In late August, I was in the Federal Building in San Francisco under interrogation by two young and very aggressive U.S. Attorneys backed up by Agent Maloney and his sidekick. The four of them made it clear to me that the government was not even mildly interested in the facts or the truth as I saw them; they were interested in getting an indictment any way they could. The UOP Board had voted to pay for my defense, so the UOP corporate counsel had provided me with a young attorney who, unfortunately, had only a passing acquaintance with criminal law. He accompanied me to San Francisco but played only a minor role. The interrogation went on for hours with the two U.S. Attorneys never giving me any information about the allegations—who made them, what were the specifics, when were they made, when were the dates upon which I had tendered the bribes. When I refused to answer general questions and demanded times, places, and amounts, they changed their tune and said they realized I was the victim and had only responded to solicitations for bribes. For all their sudden sympathy for my presumed plight, the admission they were trying to coax and cajole would still destroy not only me but the Company as well.

They could present no evidence that I had bribed the Lieutenant Governor, and eventually they accepted the fact that Dymally had as much reason to hate WASC as I did. He had helped to sponsor Windsor University, a west Los Angeles institution targeted to serve the Black community but killed by WASC, so he was more than eager to assist me in promoting anti-WASC legislation. As far as I could determine, the attack on Dymally was blatantly racist. He was never charged, but the Grand Jury investigation badly damaged him in California state politics. Fortunately, the story had a happy ending; Dymally was elected to Congress and served until he retired.

When the Dymally line of questioning led nowhere, the Attorneys turned to the University of San Francisco and presented me with a list of payments IPD had made to various members of the University administration and faculty. If I hadn't bribed them, then surely I had been solicited by each of the recipients to pay them a bribe. Clearly, I had had no option but to pay the amounts demanded to continue to do business with the University. If I were the victim, then why wouldn't I cooperate with the government to bring these people to justice?

They then invented the "threshold question," which they asked at least a hundred times. "When did you realize that these were illegal solicitations and why didn't you go to the authorities to report them?" No matter how they asked the question, my reply was invariably the same, "These were payments for legitimate services rendered to IPD. IPD was hated by the higher education establishment and Calvin was working like hell to keep them at bay." And thus it went hour after hour. Finally, when they could get no admission of guilt from me, and no accusations against University of San Francisco administrators or faculty, they discharged me with assurances that they would see me again—perhaps, again and again.

The case was transferred to Los Angeles, and in December I was summoned there to appear before two other U.S. Attorneys and the same two FBI agents. By this time, I had come to terms with the frightening possibility that the U.S. Justice Department might very well manufacture a criminal conspiracy charge under the Racketeer Influenced and Corrupt Organizations (RICO) statute and get it before a jury. It was not a pleasant thought that I might be convicted and be forced to spend several years in prison.

By this time, I had retained Tom Karas, reputedly the best criminal defense attorney in Phoenix. Karas had been a U.S. Attorney and knew the game very well. He accompanied me to the meeting in Los Angeles, and this time the encounter was civilized and noncontentious. After an hour or so of respectful questioning, I was ushered out with no threats of having to return.

The final act came when a substantial number of the IPD staff were summoned to appear before a Grand Jury in Los Angeles. When they arrived, they were forced to sit in a waiting room for several hours, in hopes one of them would come forward with incriminating evidence. When no one volunteered, they were dismissed. That was the last we heard from the Feds. This ended what I perceived as a despicable conspiracy between members of the California higher education establishment and the U.S. Department of "Justice."

The following year, under the Freedom of Information Act, I requested the documents alleging my RICO conspiracy. I received some 50 pages with every name and date blacked out.

Moving the Company

From 1973 to 1979, IPD lead a rather nomadic existence. Our first headquarters was in my two-story house close to the San Jose State campus. When IPD moved in, it took over all of the ground floor and the garage, which we used for curriculum development and printing. This left me a bedroom and my personal office on the second floor. This arrangement lasted until the space occupied by my household furniture was needed for desks and office machinery; at that point, I moved out to an apartment. Even with every inch devoted to the business, my house was still relatively small, and we outgrew it within about six months. IPD's next stop was the recently vacated sorority house I had used as headquarters during the time I was the Union president. This house, together with additional space in nearby office buildings, lasted for another six months.

At this point, we were a growing company filled with optimism, so our next move was into a large executive office complex recently vacated by a printing company that was in the process of contraction. Luckily, our lease was only for three years, because the attacks by WASC would change us from a growing company to a shrinking one, and force us to shift our center of gravity to Arizona.

When I left San Jose for Phoenix in 1976, I divided operations between my two cofounders. I made Peter Ellis President of IPD and Carole Crawford became Chief Operating Officer of the University of Phoenix. By the end of 1978, it was clear that Ellis wasn't up to the job, so I placed an Executive Vice President under him, the Director of the University of Redland's operation, Harry O'Donnel. That steadied things down a bit, but only for a moment.

Our lease on the space in the executive office complex terminated in November 1979, and we planned to relocate to a much smaller open space. Such a move being primarily a matter of organization, I placed Peter Ellis in charge. He still held the title of Executive Vice President, and I had hoped that having a discrete task such as this would allow him to exercise more self-discipline and improve his management skills.

Unfortunately, the move that occurred over the Christmas vacation in 1979 was an unmitigated disaster, and one that almost destroyed the company.

Our new offices were still under construction when we signed the lease. We had never made a critical corporate move before, and foolishly, I accepted Peter's assurances that the space would be ready when we needed it.

Our old space had been leased to a new tenant, effective on the date of our termination, and we had agreed to vacate promptly to accommodate them. When the day arrived for them to move in and us to move out, our new space was not ready. It would not be ready for another month, and Ellis had no contingency plan.

All of our furniture and records, with the exception of the accounting and enrollment ledgers, had been placed in the moving vans. We distributed these critical accounting ledgers to the homes of the employees who had previously had the attendant responsibilities. The only centralized part of the company was a person to answer the telephone and direct the calls to the homes where the ledgers resided. The result was barely organized chaos. Enrollment records were soon out of date, collection of tuition from new students was catch-as-catch-can, both receivables and payables bloomed. On December 20th, while the records were still in the moving vans, CFO Nick Cochran resigned from what he considered a sinking ship, and I had no alternative but to assume the position myself.

Becoming the CFO

Once in the new offices, I tried as best I could to get my arms around the accounting function, but my first priority was dealing with angry vendors, especially the textbook publishers, who daily threatened to force us into bankruptcy. When they pressured me too hard, I simply told them that if they drove us out of business, they would, one, have to absorb a bad debt, and two, see one of their large accounts disappear forever. It was a sufficiently convincing argument to keep them at bay for the six months it took us to become current.

Although Cochran had done a lot of things right—he retained Price-Waterhouse as auditors, established better controls, and produced monthly and quarterly financials in a timely manner—what he did wrong was fail to develop an internal computerized accounting system. All the accounts, including the general ledger, were farmed out to a variety of service bureaus, so his departure left us with a hodgepodge of systems that barely enabled us to keep control of the Company. However, with the help of a barely qualified controller and some clerks, I managed to hold the accounting function together.

Our most critical weakness was our accounts receivable system; it consisted of a clerk, an out-of-date ledger, and a telephone. Our salvation came in the form of a woman I hired to handle the accounts receivable. I can't remember her name but she was a godsend. She was in her early forties with silvered-white hair and a most proper mien, but she was also a lethal collector who brought order to the process, and each month she managed to collect enough of the $1.2 million in old receivables to keep us afloat until we could bring tuition collection current.

Every day while I functioned as CFO, I cursed Nick Cochran for leaving us with a Rube Goldberg set of service bureau–based accounting functions and cursed myself for ignoring the accounting department until it almost collapsed around me. It soon became clear that if I was to watch the accounting department, it would have to be moved to Phoenix and that was not going to be easy. All of the service bureaus were local so moving required that we reduce all the ledgers to paper.

None of the accounting staff intended to move to Phoenix, and they were less than thrilled to cooperate in exporting their jobs. The task was far beyond my competence, so I retained the Price-Waterhouse management advisory service from the Phoenix office to help. They hired a Phoenix-based accounting staff to carry out the actual transfer and found me a Phoenix-based CFO. The lessons from that experience burned into my brain, and from that day forward we have had anywhere from a competent to a superb accounting department.

Once I decided to move accounting, it was a simple step to move the headquarters of the Company to Phoenix. By this time, I had decided that the long-term future of the Company lay with the University of Phoenix. With that in mind, I made IPD a subsidiary of UOP and, by the end of 1979, both companies were marginally profitable and the future looked fairly rosy.

Strategies for a Viable Company

In the five years from 1973 to November 1978, the Company was never more than a heartbeat away from death by regulation. During these regulatory battles, I never had the opportunity to look more than a few months ahead; only after accreditation could I turn the greater part of my attention to running what had finally become a viable company. I knew that many regulatory struggles lay ahead, but they would no longer be life-or-death affairs. Now I needed to communicate a vision beyond survival that could capture the imagination of the troops and gain their commitment.

Visions have to be operationalized and this required that I lay out strategies for internal development and external growth. Most important, I had to develop and communicate a philosophy of management. It took me over a year to gather my thoughts on the future of this now viable company, and in June 1980, I shared them with my managers. Although the following excerpts may seem long, they do much to explain the nature of my leadership and give some insight into why the Company has been successful.

Memorandum dated June 17, 1980 to Division Managers

I have given considerable thought to the process of strategic planning. I have read numerous articles on the subject—about half praise the process, and the other half damn it. The two most common opinions, and to my mind most commonsensical, were the following:

- Strategic planning is a process and the greatest benefit to be derived from the process is the impact which planning has on the people who do the planning. The plan itself is of secondary importance.

- Strategic plans are direction signs, not road maps. Both internal and external environments can change rapidly and dramatically, and these changes often require major changes in a company's strategic plan. There are several articles which provide examples of companies that came to grief because of adherence to a plan which changing circumstances had made obsolete.

In my first consciously drafted strategy statement, I quoted Robertson, an English historian, who had made a long study of historical movements and the men and women who made them. One of the generalizations which he drew from that study, was, "He goes farthest who knows not whence he goes." There is obviously much truth in this since it is clear that the person who is part of a movement with a direction will almost always go farther than one who has a set destination. In my opinion, we should undertake our planning always with the thought that what we do and build today will surely provide us with new vistas and opportunities tomorrow. We must have a coherent philosophy, a clear direction, and the strategies and tactics to make our journey successful, but never let us delude ourselves into thinking that we know exactly where we are going or that our planning is so successful that it eliminates the possibility of surprise and new discovery. If that were to happen, we would have failed.

Strategic Statement

Strategic planning is usually conceived of as an exercise in five-year forecasting in which an organization tries to predict what exogenous changes it will face during the next five years and how best it can respond to them. Planning poses basic questions—What are we? What do we wish to become? Where are we? Where do we wish to go? How do we get there?

One way to approach a five year plan is to begin by looking back at some of the major foreseen and unforeseen exogenous changes which have impacted our company over the last five years and then to pose answers to the above questions.

Five years ago, we were solely an educational contracting firm in a national industry with about fifty other firms, twenty or so of which were in California. The future for educational contracting looked bright; we quickly became the largest and most successful firm in the industry and the possibilities for future growth seemed almost unlimited. Those were really exciting days when we believed that we had discovered an ideal mechanism to be a major force for change in higher education.

We soon discovered that success was not an unmixed blessing since with success came increasing opposition from the educational establishment. That opposition soon thinned the ranks of our contractor competitors and today, there are only two or three marginally successful educational contractors still in business. Through our foresight, we had discovered an industry with the life span of the Mayfly. We also discovered that the establishment was powerful and conservative and had no intention of changing without a bloody war. At this point, we hunkered down for the war and learned to survive, and occasionally prosper, in an extremely hostile environment.

The most difficult part of this situation was the fact that we had no control over our own destiny. We had always to act in the name of another. We knew what actions needed to be taken if we were to meet the assaults launched against us, but we were bound by the restrictions of our contractor status. Sometimes I felt we were like Laocoön and his sons, unable to struggle free from the serpents which establishment had sent to destroy us.

Five years ago, we did not foresee the limits of contracting nor that the solution to the problem lay in the creation of our own university. Fortunately, we had a direction rather than a destination. We were determined to be a major force for change in higher education, and we were prepared to take whatever path that aim required. Five years ago, we had to battle daily for the legitimacy of extended adult education. We did not foresee that five years hence many other colleges would be hawking their wares in the marketplace hoping to attract enough adults to replace its lost youth. Five years ago, there was a huge population of adults who had never had access to higher education; today there are few adults who do not have access to several higher education options. Five years ago, our struggle was for the survival of a new conception of adult education; today our struggle is against the competition of institutions that have adopted the concepts we pioneered.

The rapid changes in our environment have required us to change constantly in order for the company to survive, and there is no indication that the next five will have fewer changes. A strategic plan written five years ago would be ancient history now, and the same will probably be true of our present plan five years hence. Even though we know that there will be unforeseeable changes in our environment, and that these might be the most important changes we will face, we must still plan in order to be able to deal successfully with predictable change and to be in the strongest possible posture when the unexpected occurs. One thing the past five years have taught us is that our future lies with the University of Phoenix; it must always be the focus of our planning. A major dimension of every decision on whether to undertake new activities, or to continue an on-going activity, should be whether or not it is in the best interest of our University.

I would now like to sketch our brief answers to the above questions—answers I hope will open, rather than close, our discussion on what the answers should finally be.

- What are we? We are an educational institution that is a leader in the field of adult education and experiential education. In order to maintain this position of leadership, we must set high standards for ourselves and strive constantly to meet those standards.
- What do we wish to become? Because our primary focus is on the University of Phoenix, our mission is to provide an educational experience that will lead to positive changes in the lives of our students, our faculty, and our staff. Functioning as an exemplary institution of higher education is the only sure path to success.
- Where are we? As usual, we are at the crossroads—is there anywhere else for this company? The particular crossroad we now face is the one which has been occasioned by our parting company with two contracts which have, during fiscal year 1979, produced annual revenues of $3.8 million. There is no immediate prospect of replacing this revenue and, clearly, we must now become smaller before we can again become larger.
- Where do we wish to go? We wish to grow again, to have the divisions grow larger, to expand our non-degree programs so that

they become a significant revenue producer, and to expand geo-graphically. We also wish to increase our influence in the higher education industry by building our reputation for quality educa-tion and sound management.

■ How do we get there? First, we must work to insure quality and efficiency in everything we do—curriculum development, mar-keting, recruiting, academic services and student services. Only through the constant concern for quality by every person in the company can we hope to achieve this. Maintaining quality is a matter of both form and substance. Managers must set an exam-ple for others to measure themselves against. We teach what we are and thus, if we wish to teach well, we must be in form what we are in substance. Unless the students know and appreciate the quality of the services we render, they will never say to others, "That is a quality program, course, institution, etc." If the stu-dents do not say it, we will never become the quality institution that can insure our future.

■ Second, we must become and remain significantly profitable. Quality is expensive, not only in maintaining current operations, but equally important in providing for our future. Only by con-tinuing to invest a substantial portion of our income in research and development can we stay at the state of the art in both cur-riculum content and the system of delivery. We have had spec-tacularly profitable months and even quarters, but profitable times were always followed by equally spectacular losses by months, quarters, and alas, once by a whole year. We have never been able to maintain for any significant period an acceptable level of profitability. We have always focused more on the growth of revenue and on meeting planned revenue than we have on meeting planned margin. In order for this strategy to be consis-tently successful, we would have to be able to predict revenue; and the fact is, we have never been able to do this.

We have focused on growth as a way out of difficulties. It is always more exciting to open a new market, get a new contract, or develop a new program which will increase the revenue line than it is to cut expenses when the revenue line falls below plan. Invest now, collect later is the theory. It is a good theory, but we have seen that it has its limits and that to be useful, it must be coupled with the equally valid theory that a company can maintain its profitability if it can cut expenses by as much as revenue falls below plan.

Consistent profitability comes only with consistent manage-ment, and consistent management is based on effective accountabil-ity. In an effort to create a structure for effective accountability, we have transferred as many powers and responsibilities to managers as we deem possible. In addition we have adopted an incentive system which we hope will stimulate an entrepreneurial spirit. Essentially, we all know that effective accountability is self-imposed; and thus, we must work toward a system that created a desire on the part of every employee to adopt accountability as the most preferred way of performing his/her function.

I'm sure the reader will recognize much of the above as conven-tional wisdom but, insofar as I practiced conventional management, these are the precepts I applied. However, it was the skills, knowledge, and attitudes I acquired prior to being a manager—organizing, polit-ical action, implacable opportunism, doggedness, and indifference to the advice of experts—that made my application of conventional pre-cepts successful.

My notes for January 10, 1981, show that, in addition to execut-ing the strategic plan as previously set forth, I laid out my agenda for the coming year. It was very aggressive:

- Prepare for the annual audit (our fiscal year ended March 31).
- Write self-study for North Central visit.
- Negotiate new line of credit.
- Recruit new Board members.
- Recruit new Advisory Committee members.
- Plan accreditation visit.
- Overhaul accounting department.
- Conduct management review with P-W.
- Refresh all legislative bases.
- Develop a new management information system.
    - Student tracking
    - Accounting and finance
    - Modeling and forecasting

- Electronic mail
- Teleconferencing

Both the strategic plan and much of my agenda were soon over-whelmed by an internal struggle that took up much of 1981. In this instance, it was the expulsion of one of my cofounders, Peter Ellis.

Ellis Challenges My Leadership

Peter was one of the most talented organizers I have ever known. As a former student of mine at San Jose State, he played a role in Survival Faire and other Humanities 160 ventures, but, as I came to know him better, I found that he lacked the consistency of purpose and stability of personality to build and lead an organization. During the time Ellis was involved in the Humanities 160 activities, he was also working with the Community Schools program in the Department of Education. Community Schools had a close relationship with the Department of Education at the University of Michigan, and Ellis went on to Ann Arbor where he earned his Ph.D. in education.

When he returned to San Jose State, Peter assumed a position in the School of Education's Community School Project, where he was the driving force in obtaining the grant from the Law Enforcement Administration for the program with the Sunnyvale teachers and public safety officers. When I attempted to gain University approval to grant degrees for the programs I had developed for the teachers and public safety officers, it was Ellis who urged me to seek another venue. Once I found that venue at the University of San Francisco, Ellis became one of the cofounders of the Institute for Professional Development.

Ellis was dedicated, innovative, and a hard worker who made major contributions to the early success of the Company. Unfortunately for our relationship, when I changed IPD from an informal association between Ellis, Crawford, and myself, in which each of us had one-third ownership, into a corporation, I changed the owner-ship shares to 60 percent for myself and 20 percent each for Ellis and Crawford. I did this at the insistence of Dean Allen Calvin, who rep-resented the University of San Francisco in negotiating the relation-ship between the University and IPD. Calvin demanded that IPD be represented by one person with full authority. Calvin did not think Ellis, with his new Ph.D. in Education, would carry any authority with either the Jesuit community or the faculty. Calvin was right in that I ended up doing 100 percent of the political work of getting IPD positioned within both the academic and the Jesuit communities, while Ellis concentrated on operations. In addition to campus politics, I had to deal with the press and do all of the lobbying in Sacramento.

Even though I later discovered that Ellis harbored a deep resentment over my changing the ownership percentages, I did not detect this at the time, and I designated him as second in command and successor. It was not until he exhibited indifference to my efforts to create the University of Phoenix that I began to entertain doubts as to his loyalty. In fact, a person's willingness to support UOP and to move to Phoenix proved to be the defining decision that would determine who would stay with the Company and who would move on.

Once I had committed myself to creating the University and had made the move, I quickly drew apart from Ellis. However, he was still in charge of IPD, and UOP had a desperate need for the income from the IPD contracts. After my departure for Phoenix, Ellis, in addition to his formal position, quickly established his political control of the California operation, which meant that UOP's finances were hostage to his goodwill.

Although Ellis was a great organizer and salesman, he could not concentrate on the responsibilities of management. Ellis was a seeker. Prior to my meeting him, he was a member of an activist Christian group on the San Jose State campus; he then became a freethinker and, from 1976 to his departure from the Company in 1981, went through EST training, Life Spring (EST-lite), Rolfing, and an Open Marriage which, as might be expected, ended in divorce.

Ellis was also an early advocate of computer-mediated learning and was the driving force behind the Company's first efforts in that area. In 1978, he negotiated a contract with the Source, a precursor of America Online, and established Interactive Educational Systems as the vehicle that would repurpose the IPD curriculum for delivery from the Source via modem to a student's Apple computer. Given the state of hardware and software technology, the effort was doomed to fail. The contractor Ellis hired to write the authoring software for translating the IPD courses worked on the project for two years but was never able to deliver a useable product. When Ellis left in 1981, I killed the project.

Recognizing Ellis' political position in the Company, especially his hold on the all-important California revenue, in 1978 at his insistence, I agreed to rewrite the shareholder's buy-sell agreement and to give Peter the right to buy sufficient shares to take majority control if I sold any of my shares. At the time, I had no intention of selling my shares, but just in case something went wrong, I asked the corporate counsel to include a statement that would give me an "out." Counsel inserted a phrase in the agreement that said the Corporation had to agree to any transfer of shares between shareholders. Because I controlled the Corporation, I assumed that any sale would require my agreement. Unfortunately, I accepted counsel's assurance that I had the "out," and I did not pay due attention to the clause giving Ellis the right to buy a majority of shares:

> *Notwithstanding anything to the contrary in this Agreement,* in the event that any of the Stock of John Sperling becomes subject to the provisions of Sections 2 or 4 on account of a voluntary or involuntary transfer, then as of the date upon which such sections become applicable, Peter T. Ellis shall have the right and option to purchase from the Corporation, at the price and terms set forth in Sections 6 and 8, a number of share of such Stock that, when added to the number of shares of voting Stock owned by Peter T. Ellis, shall be sufficient to give voting control of the Corporation to Peter T. Ellis.

The phrase, "Notwithstanding anything to the contrary in this Agreement," constituted a *virus* that was not activated until the spring of 1981. When I decided to create a holding company that would own UOP in perpetuity, keeping the University free of regulatory difficulties in the event the Company changed ownership or engaged in a noneducational activity, I would have to sell my stock to that holding company. Inadvertently, this would trigger the virus.

I had observed Ellis long enough to become convinced that the welfare of the Company rested primarily with me. I was the only one who had the skills needed to protect it politically and it was clear that, except for the dissidents of the Ellis persuasion, the rest of the Company had accepted my leadership as a given. After the bloody battles of the previous five years, I was not about to turn the Company over to someone whose management abilities I considered inadequate.

By early 1981, it was evident that Ellis was going to be a problem. He and Nick Cochran, the CFO who had resigned during the move fiasco and was still a member of the Board of Directors, formed an alliance with one of the other directors to challenge my leadership. In February, Cochran circulated a report to the Board decrying the move of the accounting department to Phoenix and trashing the work of the new CFO. I responded with an analysis that contrasted the accounting department operations under Cochran with those obtaining under the new CFO. My analysis trashed Cochran in return and shortly thereafter led to his resignation from the Board.

Not only did Ellis attack me at the Board meetings, unbeknownst to me he was busily building what he thought would be the basis for a new company focused on computer-mediated distance learning. He appropriated the programming we had paid the consulting firm to produce, and incorporated a new company, "Adventures In Learning," which, to give the devil his due, was a very imaginative concept. In the prospectus, Ellis set forth his intention to create a national network of education centers that would reach into communities through each community's public, school, and corporate libraries. Through this network, learners would have access to educational programs that had been produced by IPD and would then be rewritten using the authoring language developed by Adventures in Learning. Unfortunately for Ellis, the hardware and software to run such a system would not be available for 10 years. Quite apart from its feasibility, Adventures in Learning was using UOP's corporate assets and would be in direct competition with IPD and UOP. It was in this poisonous atmosphere that I presented my plan for reorganizing the Company.

Creating the Apollo Group

It was not until after the University was accredited by the North Central Association that I became aware of the "change of ownership or change of control" issue. In such an event, an institution's accreditation automatically terminated and had to be reinstated. Additionally, most state licensing agencies had the same stipulation and, more important, so did the U.S. Department of Education. In the latter instance, an institution's eligibility for federally insured student loans terminated and it could take from six months to a year to get it reinstated. My solution to this was to create Apollo Group, a holding company that would own 100 percent of the University of Phoenix in perpetuity and thus protect it from regulatory harm. Prior to this, I had made IPD a subsidiary of the University, so I also proposed to transfer ownership of IPD to Apollo. Apollo would then be the parent company of both existing companies and of any future acquisitions. My plan seemed a corporate necessity to me, but it required that I transfer all of my University of Phoenix shares to Apollo and this, to repeat, would activate the virus.

As soon as I presented the plan, Ellis opposed it as unnecessary and said that if I attempted it, he would trigger the virus and purchase the shares needed to give him control of the Company. However, in return for a six-year, no-cut contract, the right to buy back shares he had had to sell to settle his divorce, an antidilution clause, and the right to enough proxy votes to ensure that he and his supporters would have the same percentage representation on the new Board that they had on the present board, he would support the reorganization.

The thought of having Ellis tied about my neck for the next six years was nightmarish. Not only would I have to pay him far more than he was worth, he and the other dissident directors would control over a third of the seats on the Board. I declined his offer with thanks, whereupon he countered with an offer to sell his 13 percent share in the Company for $1,000,000, which would have meant a valuation of $7.7 million for the whole Company. Given the state of the Company's finances it was a ludicrous offer.

In the period between the University's accreditation in 1978 and 1981, I had been able to attract several substantial members to the Board of Directors, and they were supportive of most of my initiatives, including the creation of a holding company. They agreed with me that Ellis' demands had to be rejected, so I asked corporate counsel to affirm my power, acting in the name of the Corporation, to nullify Ellis' right to purchase majority control of the Company.

At that point, counsel informed me that my supposed power would quickly be set aside by any court asked to rule on the matter. "But, you told me that . . ." only elicited, "Sorry, you must have misunderstood." I was not only furious, I felt trapped. When I went to the senior partner who had drafted the "out," he claimed that it was not his wording, rather it was the wording of the associate to whom he had given the task of drafting the Agreement. When I asked, "Who in hell can get me out of this?" I was directed to Jon Cohen, who became my white knight and who, I concluded, possessed at least half the brains of the entire firm. After the associate and I explained the problem, Cohen dismissed the associate and proceeded to grill me. How did I get into the situation? What was I willing to do to get out of it? What did I want the end result to be?

Once Cohen had grasped the facts, he quickly outlined a plan of attack. To create a holding company without a sale of my stock, the shareholders of the current UOP—"UOP.1"—would vote to sell its assets to an entity to be called "UOP.2." The disappearance of the UOP.1 would terminate the buy-sell agreement and Ellis would simply own the same percentage of UOP.2 that he had owned of UOP.1. As controlling shareholder of UOP.2, I could then vote to sell UOP.2 to the holding company without triggering the virus. At that point, Ellis could remain a minority shareholder of the holding company, or simply sell out. Such a transaction would clearly constitute a change of ownership and would require reaccreditation and relicensing. The transaction could only be carried out if I could obtain prior approval from the North Central Association and from the licensing agencies in three jurisdictions—Arizona, California, and Puerto Rico.

When I had first conceived the idea of a holding company, I had consulted with Dr. Manning at the North Central Association on the regulatory issues. Because the reorganization might be construed as a change of ownership, it was critical that it be preapproved by the North Central Association. Fortunately, Dr. Manning, the Executive Director, ruled that it did not constitute a change of control or a change of ownership because the same people who owned the University of Phoenix would own Apollo and, therefore, would not trigger any of the regulatory issues. However, selling the assets of UOP.1 to UOP.2 would clearly be a change of ownership and would trigger all of the regulatory issues. I visited Manning to present this new and more complex scheme. Again, Manning came to my rescue. He agreed to a pro forma examination of UOP.2 after the sale had occurred and, if the examination confirmed that the same management and Board of Directors were in control of UOP.2, then accreditation would be continued. Then, in turn, I visited the licensing agencies in Arizona, California, and Puerto Rico. Each of them agreed to reinstate their license if North Central reaffirmed the accreditation. I figured I would finesse the U.S. Department of Education eligibility because there would be no hiatus in the University's accreditation.

Shortly after Ellis incorporated Adventures In Learning, members of the San Jose staff, who were no longer enamored of his charisma, informed me of his extracorporate entrepreneurial activities. I had them gather the inculpating information, which I took to corporate counsel, who used the information to draft a complaint charging Ellis with various breaches of his fiduciary responsibilities to UOP. With the complaint as a lever to use on Ellis, and with my regulatory ducks in order, I presented the plan to dissolve UOP.1 and create UOP.2 to the Board for approval. The whole thing seemed rather bizarre to the Board, but they approved the plan. The final item I needed before my showdown with Ellis was a valuation of the Company; P-W had this ready two days after the Board approved my plan. The P-W valuation of the Company came in at a little over $1 million with a share price of $9.20. Ellis owned 13,500 shares, so I was prepared to offer him $125,000.

With these things in hand, I was now ready to deal with Ellis. I presented him an offer of $125,000 together with the substance of the complaint, the Board's action, and the P-W valuation. He asked for time to consult his counsel, and apparently his counsel counseled his acceptance. His resignation letter ended as follows:

> I would like to end this letter with a bit of unsolicited advice in the form of a quote from the famous Chinese philosopher Lao Tzu. I hope you will incorporate some of the spirit of this quote in your personal life and in the life of the university.
>
> > Alive, a man is supple, soft;
> > In death, unbending, rigorous.
> >
> > All creature, grass and trees, alive
> > Are plastic but are pliant too,
> > And dead, are friable and dry,
> > Unbending rigor is the mate of death,
> > And yielding softness, company of life:

> Unbending soldiers get no victories;
> The stiffest tree is readiest for the axe.
> The strong and mighty topple from their place,
> The soft and yielding rise above them all.

Yours in Community,
Peter T. Ellis

On August 25th, the Board approved the offer and revoked the liquidation of UOP.1. After eight months of internecine struggle, I was finally able to create the Apollo Group.

9

Meanwhile, Back at the Ranch

Part II—1981 to 1986

These five years saw inconsistent but positive development. It opened with a legal battle, followed by several political ones that occasioned two potentially disastrous initiatives. It also occasioned some painful personnel changes that formed the basis for future success. The intensity of the previous nine years had left me somewhat weary, and I lost my single-minded focus on reforming higher education. That weariness coupled with my low boredom threshold and tropism toward action lead me into two initiatives that were almost doomed to fail. In the process, I learned a few more basic business skills and by 1986, I was much less prone to risky action than at any time since starting the Company.

A chronological accounting of the events of this decade would sorely test a reader's tolerance for detail. Consequently, I will restrict this account to the events and personalities that had a major impact on the Company and on me personally.

The Regis College Case

The victory over Ellis was concluded on September 25, 1981, and it proved to be a much more costly settlement than the $125,000 we paid him. Six weeks later, on November 6th, Regis College, an IPD   143 contract institution, declared IPD in breach of contract. Ellis had negotiated the Regis contract and would be one of their star witnesses in defending against an IPD suit for breach of contract. The relationship between Ellis and Regis was immediately evident from the fact that the letter claiming that IPD had breached its contract was mailed to Ellis even though Regis knew that he had left IPD.

I heard the news while traveling in California and I remember the day quite well. That evening while driving from San Jose to Santa Cruz, my thoughts totally consumed with the news, I went well over the speed limit and got a speeding ticket. When I explained to the officer the reason for my preoccupation and asked that he cut me some slack, his response was to write the ticket and advise me not to take my work home with me.

The news from Regis was a shock for several reasons—our cash flow was still precarious, the Phoenix newspapers were certain to seize on the news and give it maximum publicity, and, if Regis was successful, the other IPD contract institutions would very likely follow suit with bankruptcy almost certain. This was major trouble.

I left for Denver immediately to calm the staff and assess the situation on the ground. I told the staff there must be some miscommunication with Regis and that I would soon set things aright. However, when I tried to meet with the Regis officials who were in charge of the IPD program, I was informed that no meeting was needed. I then realized that I needed a lawyer and fast.

Corporate counsel Snell & Wilmer recommended the obvious referral, Holland and Hart, Colorado's largest firm. I confirmed this recommendation with our San Francisco firm, Thelen, Marin, Johnson and Bridges, who referred me to the head of litigation at Holland and Hart. The head of litigation assigned a Jack Smith to the case and assured me that he was a top-flight litigator.

Alas, when I met Smith he appeared to me as a clean-cut all American boy who would be far too nice to deal with the Jesuits at Regis College. He was trim, youthful, and soft-spoken, and our conversation did nothing to assure me that he would be the junkyard dog I thought we needed. I immediately expressed my reservations to my San Francisco contact who stood by his recommendation, so I reluctantly agreed to retain Smith.

As soon as Smith contacted Regis, the College agreed to a meeting. On December 9th, Smith and I met with John Brennan, the person charged with overseeing the IPD contract, and Regis corporate counsel, A. Thomas Elliot, bodybuilder and former Mr. America. Elliot was arrogant and dismissive, so it was not a pleasant meeting. When I told Brennan that IPD was eager to cure any breach, "Just tell us what to do and we'll do it," Brennan refused to do so unless I admitted to the breach, a thing I was not about to do. Smith reacted hardly at all to their incivility and I followed suit. We thanked them for their time and departed.

I did not find the behavior of the Regis representatives too surprising because I perceived that they were simply mirroring the attitudes of the Regis president, Father David Clark. I had only met him on two occasions and both meetings were unpleasant. He was secretive, pompous, and arrogant all at once. This attempt to steal a successful program that IPD has spent hundreds of thousands to create allowed me to add greed to his other unpleasant character traits.

After the meeting, Smith gave me one of the toughest assignments I have ever received. I was to make certain that IPD continued to perform all its contractual obligations, including continuing to place ads for the program at IPD's expense, and to enroll students, even though IPD would soon be ousted from the Regis campus. I could hardly believe what he was asking but he said that, to have a chance in court, IPD must enter with "clean hands." If the orders were hard for me, they were trebly hard for the IPD staff, but they followed orders loyally.

The staff dutifully went about their tasks amid the surliness and taunting behavior of the Regis staff, but I was able to keep up their morale by assuring them that we would have our day in court and, better still, if we were expelled from Regis, we would open a UOP campus in Denver. By December 31, 1981, the day of our departure from Regis, we had already obtained a license to operate and rented space. We opened the Denver campus on January 2, 1982.

While the staff worked with almost maniacal energy to create a viable UOP campus, John Murphy and I devoted ourselves to the suit versus Regis. Working with Smith and his assistant, Tim Rostello, Murphy and I did the necessary factual research while Smith and Rostello did the law. Smith filed IPD's claim in federal court and, with Regis's agreement, asked for a bench trial. Why Regis would give up the hometown advantage it would have in a jury trial, we could not fathom, but our pleasure was short lived.

IPD's request for a temporary restraining order and preliminary injunction were heard on December 29th before Judge Kane. Kane refused the temporary restraining order and preliminary injunction but ruled that we had justiciable issues with an adequate remedy at law. Ominously, Kane added an obiter dictum, "I read the contract—and this is certainly no judgment, but as I read the contract, the parties agreed to vest Regis with sole discretion, and the plaintiff would have to show bad faith for its determination." Regis took this as confirmation of its right to act as it wished and immediately sent IPD notice of termination.

I was really depressed by Kane's ruling, but Smith assured me that the phrase "this is certainly no ruling" conveyed no rights to Regis. However, the ruling meant that IPD had to decide on whether it should expend at least $100,000 of its thin resources on what would surely be a lengthy process that might or might not end in a trial. After a long discussion with Smith, who assured me that case law was on our side, I agreed to go forward. Not only was the process costly, it was lengthy and we did not get to trial for 42 months.

Discovery and depositions stretched over 1982 and 1983 and my responsibilities were pretty much restricted to responding to requests for documents, preparing the IPD employees for their deposition, and attending depositions, including my own. It was not until preparation for trial, scheduled for August 1984, that I focused on the Regis case. In late May 1984, John Murphy and I moved to Denver and for three months devoted all of our time to the trial. We were assigned an office at Holland and Hart and we met daily with Smith and Rostello. In addition to conducting all of the nonlegal research, John and I pretty much determined our strategy, which was to assert that the contract was a living document and could only be reasonably interpreted within the context of experience. How was each section of the contract implemented and how did the various Regis employees sanction that implementation, and what were the terms of the contract as amended by experience?

Murphy took all of the IPD employees who would be called to testify through their depositions and conducted mock cross-examinations until we were satisfied that they had their facts straight and could interpret their actions within the context of our theory of the contract as a living document. We also queried the staff on how best to deal with each of the hostile witnesses.

On August 5th, we began an eight-day trial before Judge John P. Moore in the federal district court in Denver. We knew we were ready; our only concern was Smith. How good would he be in court?

By the end of the first day, our worries on that score were laid to rest. Smith was meticulous and lethal. He had the relevant cases at hand, had accepted our theory of the living document, and had absorbed all of our research. Opposing counsel Elliot had seemingly done little preparation and seemed to have relied almost totally on Judge Kane's obiter dictum that Regis had sole discretion. Our witnesses were prepared and Regis' were not.

Although the trial was long because of the factual complexity, we became more optimistic with each passing day. Smith was succinct, gracious, and sensitive to the judge's rulings; Elliot was verbose, obtuse, and insensitive; he would stand at the lectern for minutes at a time, looking deep in thought, and then utter a platitude. When this happened, Murphy and I would murmur, "He's simulating thought again." When Judge Moore could take no more of Elliot, he would swing around in his chair and sit with his back to the court until Elliot had finished. About the 10th time Elliot asserted the "sole discretion" argument, Judge Moore, as I recall, said, "Mr. Elliot, Regis has no sole discretion. That is an argument with no foundation. Please, do not use it again." At that point, I figured that we had won.

Jack Smith was not so sanguine. He suggested that we propose a settlement conference at the end of the first week. I was somewhat hesitant because I thought we were ahead and that it should be Regis asking for a settlement conference. I let him set up the conference and he and Rostello suggested that we offer to settle for $1 million. I agreed and they made the offer, but fortune smiled upon us and Regis rejected it.

The trial ended on August 12th, and I was pretty optimistic as we waited for Judge Moore's decision. The decision could hardly have been better for IPD. Judge Moore dismissed the "sole discretion" argument by saying that it was unfortunate that "Regis apparently took great solace in a gratuitous comment by Judge Kane . . . unfortunately, it is my opinion Regis misperceived the basis for Judge Kane's ruling, for 'sole discretion' plays no dispositive part in this case." Judge Moore then continued:

"In my judgment, there are two matters which are fundamental here. First, the contract contained very specific conditions regarding the right of termination, not the least of which was a provision giving the alleged breaching party the right to cure the breach within 30 days of the breach notice. Second, it is uncontroverted in my eyes that by its conduct Regis effectively deprived IPD of its contractual right to cure the alleged breaches. Indeed, both the breach allegations and the conduct of certain Regis personnel display a pettiness which I find shocking in an institution with the reputation of Regis College."

The ruling then rejected each of the alleged breaches and granted IPD $1,950,000 in damages and attorneys fees. That settlement was soon to save us from bankruptcy.

The Centrality of Political Action

No matter how excellent the education produced by the Apollo companies, or how effective this education is in meeting important social and economic needs, none of the Apollo companies would exist without the ability to protect them from regulatory and political attack. From the Company's inception in 1973 down to the present, the political and lobbying tasks have been the responsibility of three persons—myself, John Murphy, and Charles Seigel.

From 1973 to 1976, I was solely responsible for fighting all of the regulatory and political battles. In 1976, I was joined by John Murphy who slowly assumed the major part of these responsibilities. When Murphy, as will be recounted below, was unable to move from a regional to a national conception of the regulatory/political context in which Apollo operated, I hired Charles Seigel, a Congressional staffer and wily in the ways of Washington. Because of their critical importance to the success of Apollo, I think it is only fair to describe their contributions.

John Murphy

John Murphy came to the Company in a very circuitous way. He was a student activist at San Jose State when we first began our association. As a student activist, he was drawn to the activities of the Humanities 160 classes—Survival Faire, Right to Read, and the Sunnyvale project, but never directly participated in these activities.

His passion was to help the mentally handicapped and their parents who had either to care for them or to arrange their care. John's role in the Company is illustrative of the similarities among the group that began the Company and accounted for its survival and early success. We were all social activists whether we came from union or community organizing, advocacy of the unfortunate, or antiwar agitation. We were all interested in the power of education to effect social change.

In the early 1970s, Governor Ronald Reagan had pushed a bill through the California legislature that closed state mental hospitals, discharging their patients into halfway houses, on the theory that with less medication and greater responsibility for themselves, many of them could be mainstreamed into the larger society. The result of the legislation was to dump these people into any neighborhood that would tolerate halfway houses, and one of these neighborhoods was adjacent to the San Jose State campus.

The 1960s had seen the demise of most of the Greek system and the rooming house culture. Students now lived on campus in newly constructed dorms or in nearby apartments. These largely vacant properties were sold to landlords who turned many of them into halfway houses. What had once been a student neighborhood quickly became a ghetto of the mentally handicapped, and it was evident to any disinterested observer that few of them were ever going to be mainstreamed.

The residents in and around the halfway houses were not about to welcome these new denizens, so the former patients were isolated and had no one to care for or about them. This situation aroused John's sense of justice and his compassion for underdogs, and he set to work to ameliorate the conditions under which they now had to live. John recruited students to work with the halfway house residents to bring them out of their isolation and to provide some of the social skills they lacked. The result was an organization which he named "Community of Communities."

John's organizing instincts soon led him beyond the San Jose State halfway houses project. He organized the parents of the mentally handicapped; created, wrote, and distributed a newsletter for the mentally handicapped and their parents; and lobbied in Sacramento for legislation that would repair the damage done by closing the state mental hospitals. A product of this work were skills that were to prove vital to the survival of the Company.

It was in Arizona that John found his metier. He was magnificent in a fight and I could never have succeeded in those battles without him. Whether we were writing endless self-studies and position papers explaining and justifying our system of education, making presentations before editorial boards and community organizations, or lobbying at the legislature, he was both effective and indefatigable. For months—in retrospect, it seems years—we would work 10-, 12-, 14-hour days, go to a bar for enough liquor to unwind, have something to eat, fall into bed, and get up early the next day to repeat the process.

I suppose the source of much of our energy was the sheer joy of the fight. No one else had the energy to keep up with us, so we pretty much dominated the whole organization; we certainly determined its strategy, tactics, and philosophy. It was in those months that I recognized how important our intellectual labors were to our survival. The position papers for the legislators were critical in bringing them to understand why UOP was a legitimate institution and the self-studies and responses to the often negative reports issued by the North Central visiting teams were equally critical in persuading the various North Central committees to grant and continue our accreditation.

After the battles to gain accreditation and to fight off the fell embrace of the Arizona Board of Regents, John returned to California. In addition to his passion for organizing was his dream of being a writer. He had worked long enough to save up sufficient money to support himself while he wrote a novel and a couple of screenplays. Unfortunately, as is the case with almost all writers, he was unable to publish his novel or sell his screenplays.

At that juncture, I welcomed him back to his first assignment, which was to help me deal with my Peter Ellis problem. No sooner was that accomplished than I was able to provide him with a new challenge he was eminently qualified to meet. To rescind WASC-inspired legislation that would have, once again, driven us from California. It turned out to be a four-year battle ending in legislation that turned back the WASC threat. The importance of that victory can be measured by the substantial presence the University has today in California—with 25,000 students, it now ranks as the second largest private university in the state.

California: Regulation as a Mechanism to Expel Competitors

Almost as soon as UOP gained North Central accreditation, we began planning our return to California and our next inevitable battle with Kay Anderson. Fortunately, in California, a regionally accredited institution had simply to apply to gain a license to operate. With that soon in hand, we marched back into California.

We sited our first campus in San Jose, our original home, followed shortly thereafter with another in Orange County. These were obvious choices because we could operate out of old IPD offices and knew the markets. In San Jose, we began with a business and management course in the spring of 1980 and in Orange County in the following fall. We knew that the first question a prospective student or the employer would ask is, "What is the University of Phoenix doing in California?" That was not too difficult to answer because there were some 20 out-of-state schools operating in California.

The really difficult problem would be dealing with the slander that WASC and competing institutions were certain to broadcast as far and as often as they could. Those first months were hard-rock mining. Students had to be convinced that UOP was not a diploma mill, that it had not been run out of California, and that it was going to be around for a long time. It was very difficult to find and retain managers and recruiters who were tough enough to work for a pariah institution, but the ones who could stand the opprobrium generally stayed around for a long time. As we trudged up an endless hill thinking that things couldn't be much harder, they suddenly got a lot harder.

The Expulsion Notice Arrives

In October of 1981, just 18 months after receiving licensure, the University received a California Department of Education advisory informing it, that one of the provisions of Senate Bill 272, which became law in June 1981, would dramatically change its status. According to S.B. 272, by June 30, 1983, our North Central accreditation would no longer be recognized, only WASC accreditation would be accepted in California for the purpose of licensure.

There was no chance that WASC would accredit UOP's California programs, and UOP had no intention of exiting the California market without a fight. Once again, our main antagonist was Kay Anderson, and this time he had allies in both the executive and legislative branches of California government. This was to be a long, mean, and bitter, but intriguing, regulatory struggle, the brunt of which was carried by John Murphy, by now UOP's Vice President for Public Affairs.

When notice of our change of accreditation status arrived, it immediately placed our substantial capital investment at risk; even more troubling were the exiting costs of buying out long-term leases and terminating or moving employees. UOP really had no choice but to protect its position and we knew that it would require a major legislative effort. Murphy's first task was to find out how the legislation mandating the change of status could move through the legislature without our knowing about it.

Every official, whether public or private, disclaimed any prior knowledge of or responsibility for the change. Murphy finally determined that the change—which constituted nothing more than the deletion from Section 94310 of the California Education Code of the three words—"or applicable regional"—occurred when a bill, S.B. 272 authored by Senator Joseph Montoya, was heard in the Assembly Subcommittee on Postsecondary Education.

When Montoya asked the staff of the Assembly Subcommittee on Postsecondary Education why the three words were deleted, they told him it was a "technical clean-up." Consequently, no analysis of the change appeared in the Assembly legislative record, no discussion of the change took place in any Assembly committee, and obviously, no accredited out-of-state institution was informed that the change was even being considered. There is no doubt that all parties to this secret cabal knew that the change was designed to allow WASC to drive UOP out of California.

Knowing that it was the victim of a conspiracy of the powerful, UOP embarked on what, again, seemed a hopeless battle—pushing a bill through two committees and both legislative chambers that would rescind the fatal clause of S.B. 272. Murphy immediately began an intense lobbying effort as he sought to win the hearts and minds of the members of the Assembly and Senate Education Committees and the legislative leaders who would determine the ultimate fate of any bill. The lobbying effort was conducted within a context of acrimonious debate between UOP and the representatives of the higher education establishment who fought to retain the clause mandating WASC accreditation.

UOP Begins Its Counterattack

At this juncture, I turned to an old political friend from my union days, former Governor Edmund G. Brown, who persuaded Assembly Member Sam Farr, a young Democratic legislator from Monterey, to carry a bill calling for a two-year moratorium before implementing the change provided for in S.B. 272. Immediately a higher education coalition formed to stop it. At this point, Murphy engaged the services of Governmental Advocates, a new lobbying partnership comprised of the former Chief Executive Officer of the California Senate, Jerry Zanelli, and Hedy Govenar, a highly effective housewife-turned-lobbyist.

Govenar bore the brunt of the UOP lobbying effort, and she would later note that had she known that the politics of higher education were so vicious, she would not have accepted UOP as a client. Her education began when she asked Dr. Teresa Hughes, an Ed.D. from the University of Southern California and Chair of the Assembly Education Committee, how she might approach the problem of S.B. 272, and was bluntly told, "Get another client."

Legislation by Slander

Govenar began to work with the University approximately five days before Farr's bill was scheduled to be heard in Mrs. Hughes' Assembly committee. On the Monday before the hearing, a column by a Sacramento Union columnist, Dan Walters, characterized the University of Phoenix as a "diploma mill," and Farr's bill as "special interest legislation" designed only to benefit the University of Phoenix. He also characterized it as a bill that would undermine California's licensure law and allow "diploma mills" to operate without state control.

Until Walters's column appeared, the members of the California Legislature knew little or nothing about either the University of Phoenix or A.B. 2048. Subsequent to the column, they still didn't know anything about the University or the content of the bill, but they knew they wanted nothing to do with a bill authorizing out-of-state diploma mills. The University had no choice but to request that Farr withdraw the legislation, and to begin plans for the next legislative session.

As a result of the Walters's column, an article appeared in the *San Francisco Examiner* on the following Sunday that repeated the falsehoods and misinformation contained in the Walters's column, as well as adding some of its own. As the result of these publications and the anti-UOP efforts of the public and private higher education lobbyists, Murphy and Govenar faced two years of suspicion and/or hostility whenever they sought to discuss UOP with members of the legislature or their staff.

The University responded immediately to the press slander by issuing written demands for retraction. The *Examiner* issued a retraction after a meeting with the University's lawyers. The lobbyists from the California Postsecondary Education Commission (CPEC), the agency charged with advising the legislature, were the source of the slander. They had also notified the Phoenix papers that UOP was trying to get a bill through the legislature that would permit diploma mills in California—*The Arizona Republic* carried a front-page story on the same Sunday.

The Arizona Republic had grown sufficiently wary of calling UOP a diploma mill, but they made the report as negative as the law of libel allowed by reporting that "intense lobbying" by UOP had helped defeat anti–diploma mill bills in Arizona. "As a result, Arizona has become a haven for diploma mills." A statement that was both false and defamatory. I responded to Pat Murphy, the editor of *The Republic,* the following day:

To the Editor

Dear Sir,

When one considers the relative newsworthiness of the University of Phoenix in the universe of local, state, national and international news worthy events, the question arises: what actions by the University of Phoenix warrant front page coverage in Arizona's largest and most influential newspaper? Perhaps, Sunday, May 1st was a slow news day with only minor riots in France. One must also assume that the editors of the Republic found Arizona's response to the publication of A Nation at Risk, a landmark study of the decline of American education by the National Commission on Excellence in Education, of less importance than a minor regulatory skirmish in the California Legislature.

In six years of writing about the University of Phoenix, neither the Republic or Gazette has ever said anything positive about the University's programs or the accomplishments of its students, nor has it ever sought an explanation for the University's growth from a student enrollment of eight students in 1977 to over 2,600 in 1983. Additionally, these papers have shown no interest in the variety of educational innovations which the University pioneered and which were subsequently adopted by hundreds of the nation's accredited colleges and universities . . .

Not only have the Republic and Gazette been uniformly negative in their coverage of the University, but they have also been uniformly obtuse in their inability to distinguish the issue of diploma mills from the larger and more important issue of government regulation of higher education and the deleterious effects of the growth of unnecessary educational bureaucracies . . .

More importantly, the Republic and Gazette should examine why higher education has become one of the most regulated industries in America and how these regulatory barriers have helped to bring about skyrocketing educational costs and the inability of these institutions to change to meet the nation's changing educational needs . . .

---

cc.

Arizona Senate President, Majority Leader, Minority Leader, Members of the Education Committee; Arizona House of Representatives Speaker of the House, Majority Leader, Minority Leader, Members of the Education Committee

The Sacramento Union and columnist Walters refused to issue a retraction, and the University sued them for a million dollars. Although the libel suit was ultimately dismissed, the discovery process—particularly the depositions—yielded a mine of information on the ways in which the educational establishment had orchestrated a campaign of disparagement against UOP both in the legislature and in the academic community.

Through discovery, the University learned that Pat Callan, the head of CPEC, and his staff had planted the story with Walters, who, until he had been contacted by CPEC, knew nothing about either the bill or the University of Phoenix. In his deposition, Walters stated candidly that he was a high school dropout, knew nothing about higher education or diploma mills, hadn't the foggiest notion of the meaning of accreditation or licensure, and that all of his information and opinions had come from the CPEC staff.

The approach CPEC employed to seduce Walters was to cast the University's efforts as behind the scenes manipulations designed only to secure "special interest" legislation. As interpreted by CPEC, Walters portrayed the University as a sophisticated player in the legislative game able to get A.B. 2048 enacted without discussion or publicity.

UOP Introduces Legislation to Quash UOP's Expulsion from California

At the beginning of the 1984 legislative session, Murphy met with Senator Joseph Montoya and, after Murphy apprised him of the machinations that led to "technical amendment," Montoya agreed to carry legislation to restore the three words that had been deleted by S.B. 272.

WASC and CPEC, with the help of Dr. Teresea Hughes, Chair of the Assembly Higher Education Committee, undertook a successful effort to kill the bill in the Assembly Education Committee, where it failed by one vote. Murphy was fairly confident when he vowed that the University of Phoenix would be back in 1985.

Victory At Last

In 1985, Senator Montoya again introduced a bill, S.B. 1036, to reinstate the three words and remove WASC's authority over out-of-state institutions. In a continuing effort to effect cooperation and a possible compromise on the issue, Murphy invited Pat Callan of CPEC to discuss the issue, but Callan remained adamantly opposed. Finally, Govenar, backed by an Attorney General's opinion that the 1981 law was inoperable, persuaded CPEC to withdraw its opposition and S.B. 1036 then passed into law. UOP's position in the California market was once again secure.

The Illinois Experience

Our experience with the licensing authorities in Illinois was a major source of the frustration that led me into ill-fated ventures. Once UOP was accredited, I immediately formed the idea of creating a national university. All that was required was to obtain a license to operate in every state. We had begun the process in California and now it was time to expand eastward.

From 1976 to 1981, IPD had operated programs under contract with two Chicago area colleges—National College in Evanston and Elmhurst College in Elmhurst. The two contracts ended in 1981 and this gave UOP an opening to move into a well-understood market, or so I thought.

In June 1982, UOP submitted an application for Illinois licensure and, thus, began a year dealing with what Dickens would have called a "circumlocution office"—no matter how carefully drafted was UOP's application, it was always insufficient. Because the criteria for licensure contained such precise words as "quality," "high quality," "high caliber," "adequate breadth and depth," it gave the staff total discretion, which they used to circumlocute the applicant.

UOP's first application was rejected for failing all of the above criteria. UOP filed a detailed rebuttal and resubmitted the following December. This time, in addition to requiring a variety of changes, the staff asked UOP to document the need for its programs in Illinois. To make that determination, the staff required UOP to notify all of the institutions of higher education in Illinois of its intention to offer programs and to host a meeting at which representatives from any institution could express an opinion on the need for such programs.

The University hosted a meeting for representatives of 29 colleges and universities at the Palmer House in Chicago on January 23, 1983. The University was required to bear all of the expenses in providing a forum in which its potential competitors could memorialize their opinions and objections. As required by the regulations, minutes of the meeting were taken by a professional stenographer (paid for by UOP) and transmitted to the Illinois Board of Higher Education.

After a presentation by the UOP Academic Vice President, comments and questions were received from the representatives of the Illinois institutions—all of them hostile. There was unanimous agreement among the assembled, that so long as a course or program with a particular title was offered in a geographical area, any other course or program of the same title would be redundant and that each institution should be the sole arbiter of the consumers' educational needs in its own market area. After reaching an unchallenged consensus that there were already too many colleges and universities in Illinois, it was moved that the assembly register its objection to granting UOP a license and the "motion was accepted without opposition."

The staff recommended, and the Board approved denial of the University's application. In a mean-spirited and egregious act, the Illinois staff informed *The Arizona Republic* that UOP had been denied licensure in Illinois and on September 5, an article appeared in *The Republic* with the headline, "Non-traditional school's standards described as 'wanting.' " The article reviewed, once more, the University's regulatory battles with the assertion that, not only could it not meet established academic standards, it was also a protector of diploma mills.

Ill-Fated Initiatives

There were four of these during the decade. I can attribute all of them to frustration/boredom/naivete. They were in order:

- Establishing UOP campuses in Kuala Lumpur, Singapore, and Manila
- Partnering with a software vendor and moving corporate headquarters to Denver
- Buying one and creating five more tech schools
- Establishing a distance education program for Hungary

My Asian venture began innocently enough when I agreed to meet with a friend of an Apollo Board member who was a consultant in international business. I was too naïve to distinguish his excitement about the Asian possibilities of education for working adults from his excitement about the consultant fees he would receive. It was, however, a learning experience and the lessons garnered from two lengthy trips to Asia highlighted by long and tedious meetings with educational bureaucrats have informed our current efforts to expand in that part of the world.

Naivete in the matter of enterprise computer systems and a liking for Denver that grew out of my three months' working on the Regis case was the motivation for a move that would surely have destroyed the Company. The idea for the move came from association with one of our overpromise, underperform software vendors whose motto was "the system is the solution."

In the euphoria occasioned by my believing that their system would be the solution to our ever-growing management information problems, I convinced myself that, in a partnership, we could sell these elegant solutions to colleges and universities across the land. The solution people could share the rent on a new headquarters in Denver and, in addition, we could attach one of our new tech schools to the whole. Oh, yes, there was an additional incentive—In 1984, downtown Denver was awash in see-through office buildings with incredible deals. The building we finally chose would pay us $500,000 to move in, with the first year's rent free. The $500,000 would pay for the move and we could begin life anew in Denver debt free and with two new businesses to build. It was a grand plan based on everything but a sound strategy.

There I was, ready to turn the management of our core business, the University of Phoenix, over to the man I was later to demote due to unsatisfactory performance to start two unrelated businesses in an unfamiliar market. And what saved me? Friable asbestos! One day, when doing a walk-through of our soon-to-be new headquarters, one of my staff noticed some gritty dust on a left-behind desk. Curious, he asked the leasing agent what it was and the answer was "friable asbestos." "What does friable mean?" I asked. The answer, "crumbling." "You mean the asbestos insulation is disintegrating and dropping through the seams in the ceiling tiles?" The answer, "Yes."

At that point, I could see liability written all over the building and, thank God, we had not yet signed the lease. One call to the EPA and one call to corporate counsel cancelled that building. The search for that building, plus the lease negotiations had consumed the better part of three months and I did not have the time to repeat the process. I put the move on hold; within weeks, my infatuation with the software vendor began to wane, and growing financial problems soon ended any thoughts of moving to Denver. Very soon I would be struggling to avoid bankruptcy.

It was the ill-fated trade school venture that occasioned the gravest financial crisis the Company has ever faced. There was a positive and negative motivation for this venture. On the positive side was my desire to assist a population more needy than that of working adults. The trade schools served the untrained, often down and out, who needed help just to get a foot onto the ladder. On the negative side was my frustration and weariness in dealing with the regulatory agencies that plagued the higher education industry coupled with having more than my fill of being head of a pariah company.

I had met several trade school executives and owners who seemed to be doing quite well and theirs was a simpler business than running a university. State licenses for trade schools were much easier to come by and trade school accrediting associations were patsies compared with the North Central Association. I soon became convinced that with my skills and the capabilities of the Apollo Group, we could soon turn trade schools into a fast-growing part of our business.

In January 1984, I hired an experienced trade school manager to write the business plan for the new venture. The plan and the projections showed a growth rate that would create a company larger than UOP in three short years. The assumptions upon which the plan was based proved to be accurate to a point—an accredited starter school could be purchased at a reasonable price, once purchased, the school could be branched, state licenses were easy to obtain, and the eligibility for student loans could be transferred from the home school to the branches.

The two assumptions that proved to be incorrect were the ones that killed me: that there would be no changes in the federal student loan program and, most important, that we had the ability to operate the schools.

Based on my assumption that a person who could manage a UOP campus could easily manage a trade school, I chose a seasoned UOP campus manager to run the schools. It simply did not work. She had only a formal knowledge of the trade school regulatory environment and no experience dealing with unemployed and often disruptive and unmotivated students, some of whom dealt drugs in the school parking lot. From a UOP campus operation, which has never had a student complaint that reached either the press or electronic media, to one in which investigative reporters arrived at the school with complainant and camera crews in tow, was unnerving to say the least.

We purchased our first school in Las Vegas in the summer of 1984. Within a year after the first purchase, we had established branches in Reno, Austin, San Antonio, Sacramento, and Tempe. It soon became apparent that we had neither the managerial or financial resources to operate them profitably. The schools absorbed an obscene amount of managerial time and they were never cash flow positive.

It soon became apparent that the operating losses would sink the Company. We couldn't just shut them down because we would have had horrendous liabilities for the outstanding federally insured student loans. Our only way out was to sell them. Fortunately, we found a greater fool. We sold the branches in Reno, Austin, San Antonio, Sacramento, and Tempe to Career Com, a company that operated some dozen schools. In only a few months after these acquisitions, Career Com filed for bankruptcy. By the time of sale, we had accumulated losses of nearly $3 million.

I turned the two remaining schools in Phoenix and Las Vegas over to my son Peter, and he managed to make them profitable for one year. The Phoenix school was not only profitable, the accrediting association considered it one of the best in the industry. At that point, we were ready to resume the branching process when regulatory disaster struck. The student loan scandal erupted, Congress intervened, the U.S. Department of Education instituted draconian student loan regulations. Any thought of profitability vanished and annual operating losses reached $550,000. We closed the schools and took a write-off of $411,000.

The loan scandal arose from the easy availability of federally insured student loans. Shady operators, some were simply criminals, realized the guaranteed loan program was a bonanza and bought into the trade school industry. Their scam was to churn the student body—recruit anyone as a student, collect the student loan, give the students shoddy educational services to induce them to drop out, and recruit more students to take their places. Most of the students had little or no understanding of the loan obligations they were incurring so, when they dropped out, they defaulted on their loans.

Had the U.S. Department of Education been diligent in uncovering abuses, there would have been no scandal. In the 15 years from 1972 to 1987, only 42 trade schools were closed down for student loan abuses. Once their bureaucratic incompetence was exposed, the Department solved the problem by raising the eligibility standards for students so high that those most in need of training could not qualify. In the five years from 1987 to 1992, 2,137 schools were closed. This drove the crooks out of the business, but it took hundreds of good schools, including the Apollo schools, out as well.

The students most impacted by the new rules were those without a high school diploma, or GED. These were called Ability to Benefit (ABT) students and they were the ones most in need of training just to get them into entry-level jobs. Between 1989 and 1992, enrollment of ABT students dropped by almost 50 percent. The annual awards of guaranteed student loans going to trade schools dropped by $500 million, and most of that drop came from the exclusion of ABT students.

In 1994, I wrote an article, "Confessions of a Trade School Owner," which all of the national journals of opinion rejected. It analyzed the trade school industry and the negative impact the "reforms" instituted by Congress and the U.S. Department of Education had on those most in need. By imposing the same financial terms for the repayment of student loans whether the student was at or below the poverty line, in the middle class, or above, the reforms took access to education from the poor and gave to affluent—all in the name of ending the scandal of education loan defaults.

By the time we closed the last trade school, our fortunes were improving and we were ready to move into a new and happier period of our history. It was a period that took us from obscurity to notoriety, to prominence, and from the status as a higher education pariah to the very model of a modern university.

10

Toward an IPO and Beyond

Preparation for and Launch of the IPO—1986 to 2000

In the five years from 1981 to 1986, I had faced bankruptcy twice, been booted out of one bank and been spurned by a half-dozen others, laid off 41 staff members in two days, paid salaries with tax monies withheld from employees, and run up accounts payable to the point of just barely being able to pay rent and utilities. Even though enrollments rose from 2,634 to 5,936 and revenues from $7.1 to $24.2 million, our financial performance was anemic and inconsistent:

Year	Profit ($000s)
1981	146
1982	29
1983	146
1984	724
1985	(114)
1986	30

By 1986, I had a good appreciation of my limitations; I was also a lot tougher. Fortunately, I began to make the decisions that were necessary to turn Apollo into a serious company.

One of my most important decisions was to bring Bill Gibbs into the Company. Gibbs came to the Company via Price-Waterhouse where he was a business advisory manager. I first met him when he helped me move the accounting function from San Jose to Phoenix. Bill was more interested in technology than accounting and did not enjoy life at P-W. As an exit strategy, he and a P-W friend, Matt Anticovich, had developed a software program for managing law offices— their ticket to a start-up, and IPO, and wealth. When I agreed to invest $125,000 in the venture and provide office space for them at Apollo, they left P-W.

The start-up failed, but by that time Bill and Matt had been woven into the fabric of Apollo, and their transition from failed entrepreneurs to Apollo employees was seamless. To make room for Gibbs, I moved Jerry Noble, the CFO, to the presidency of IPD and appointed Bill CFO and Matt CIO.

Bill was not only a great CFO, he was a steadying hand and a sound advisor in harrowing times. Once we were out of the trade school morass, I had the luxury of extending my time horizon beyond the next week and making decisions that had a strategic rationale. In September 1987, I demoted the UOP president to provost and appointed Gibbs as president of UOP. Bill also held the CFO position for a year until I brought in another P-W alumnus, Jim Hoggatt.

Naming him president of UOP really surprised Gibbs, who questioned how an accountant with only an MBA could function as president of a university. Gibbs's first managerial assignment was as head of the trade school division. He immediately perceived that it was a loser, found a greater fool, and unloaded it. I assured him that as a manager he would do a lot better than either myself or his Ph.D. predecessor. The provost and I could handle the academics; what we needed was a manager who could bring order and consistency to an academic operation.

The Last of the Original Partners Departs

Carole Crawford entered my life as a part-time secretary, then full-time, then lover, then partner. She was two standard deviations above the norm in intelligence, but her cognitive abilities were not matched by her affective ones. She applied her keen intelligence to the legal and accounting functions, but her imagination was bounded by an ideal of a mom-and-pop operation that would provide security and a good income. So long as we were a mom-and-pop operation, Carole was a dog-loyal supporter, especially in offing Ellis for whom she had an utter detestation, but a supporter only so long as I did not endanger her newly thrown rice bowl.

Once the early regulatory battles has been won, my thoughts turned to growth and glory, but she would have none of it. "Why risk a good thing; enjoy what you have created." In a memo to her of August 1984, written from San Juan, Puerto Rico, I had the following to say:

> The Company has reached a major decision point and the decisions we make will affect our futures and the futures of everyone who works for the Company. We can maintain the *status quo,* protect what we have or we can continue in the same spirit that got us to where we are and, with incentive stock options that will unleash the creative energies of the staff, grow to a $100 million company in a few short years.
>
> Obviously, I prefer the latter course for a variety of reasons. It will be more exciting, fun, and self-fulfilling even though it will be riskier . . . Growing from $14 million to $100 million in a few years will require organizational changes. We will need more professional help with different skills than are currently available with the Company. Quite apart from our need for additional professional help, I think we need a regular influx of new people with different talents and perspectives. It helps to keep us from falling in love with our own ideas and rhetoric . . .
>
> I am trying to build a management team that can take the Company to $100 million which is a hell of a task. You have chosen to oppose these efforts, to express hostility toward several of the team members and to express negative opinions as to their abilities—opinions for which I can perceive no justification. Your attitude also raises the issue of how you expect to work effectively with people for whom you have an ill concealed dislike and/or contempt. Etc., etc., etc., etc.

This memo began four years of corporate internecine warfare that intensified as the Company lurched ahead, skirted bankruptcy (but continued to grow) and didn't make revenues of $100 million in a few years as I had predicted (it took 10 years).

When Gibbs took over the UOP presidency and proceeded to professionalize the Company, Crawford's position became increasingly anomalous. At this point, she attacked me before the Board for irresponsible and unethical investments, and I chose to force her out of the Company, again with the skilled assistance of Jon Cohen. The settlement of $650,000 was based on an arm's-length valuation by Price-Waterhouse. On August 31, 1988, I became sole owner of the Apollo Group.

The Online Program

Perhaps the most important educational development during Gibbs's tenure as president of UOP was the development of the University's Online distance education program, the largest in the nation. Development of the Online campus was primarily the work of Terri Hedegaard, now Apollo's vice president for distance education.

Terri's career at Apollo illustrates the value that accrues to a company when it promotes from within. Terri came to the Company in 1981 as a part-time clerk. At the time, she was a bored, stay-at-home mom with two small children. Whatever her job, she did it superbly well and was moving up the ladder when she came to my attention. She did special projects for me, and I was so impressed with her performance that I appointed her director, and then vice president, of product development.

She was in that role when she and I visited a defunct distance education company in San Francisco that we perceived could be the foundation of a successful company—that was 1989. Terri demanded that she be given the job of creating an online campus for UOP. She moved her husband and children to the San Francisco Bay area and, as the sole support of her family, she set about a task in which no one had ever succeeded—to create a profitable electronically mediated distance education program. This was before the Internet and the World Wide Web were yet to be conceived.

Difficult though the technology was, the education was infinitely more difficult. She had to translate a classroom educational system, based on small class size with intense interaction among and between faculty and students, into a medium in which there was neither visual or verbal communication—only the written text. Not only did she have to produce a viable educational experience, she had to do it at a profit; and this required a retention rate that equaled the face-to-face classroom system. Her success can be measured by a course completion rate of 98 percent, a graduation rate of 65 percent, and a current enrollment of 8,500 students. Beyond the statistics of her success is the subjective evidence that one observes at an Online graduation. Each August, several hundred graduates travel to San Francisco with their families to attend a ceremony where they meet their classmates and instructors for the first time. The two days are filled with warmth, fellowship, and emotion as the graduates affirm friendships that are usually closer than those formed on campus.

By 1991, Gibbs had rationalized operations, and we had both timely financials and predictable performance—with an annual growth rate of nearly 30 percent. Achieving sustained growth and predictable performance was a major step in our development; the next task was to achieve acceptable profit margins. This proved to be a bigger challenge psychologically than it was operationally.

From 1986 to 1991, profit margins never rose above 1 percent. Conventional wisdom among the managers was that simply making a profit in higher education constituted a miracle. They pointed out that we could have either growth or profits, but not both. If we wished to continue 30 percent growth, I had better get used to the anemic profit margins because that was all I was ever going to get.

The reason I was agitating for a higher profit margin was my growing conviction that if Apollo was to become a major company, it would have to become a public company. I had been encouraged in this line of thought by Doug Greenwood, an Alex-Brown broker working out of Greenwich, Connecticut, who prospected for IPO candidates in Arizona. Greenwood opined that Apollo had two of the requirements for an IPO but lacked a necessary third. Apollo had revenues of nearly $70 million and a five-year compounded annual rate of growth at nearly 30 percent, but its 1 percent profit margin made it a nonstarter. Only by increasing the profit margin would it ever be possible to take Apollo public.

At this point, I turned for advice to Apollo board member Tom Weir, a banker who had brought an underperforming bank to profitability and then to an IPO. His advice was simple—give your managers the right financial incentive and you'll get the margins you need.

From the beginning of the Company, I had created and then disbanded a number of management committees. Each one I established grew too large and I would create a smaller informal committee which would slowly take over as the larger committee died a natural death. In December 1987, I established the Management Committee, which functioned well while we were still a laid-back private company, but it too had grown too large to be effective. So in December 1992, I created a new management committee, the Financial Review Committee, soon to become known as "The Serious Seven."

The Financial Review Committee's task was to focus on financial performance. The members were my direct reports—Bill Gibbs, President, and Todd Nelson, Executive Vice President of UOP; Jerry Noble, President of IPD; John Murphy, Vice President For Institutional Affairs; Jim Hoggatt, CFO; and Peter Sperling, Vice President for Administration. After 1988, I owned 100 percent of the shares of Apollo Group. As part of a tax-planning strategy, I gave Peter Sperling 40 percent and shortly after that I gave Gibbs, Noble, and Murphy each 5 percent of the ownership. Now to insure the buy-in of Hoggatt and Nelson, I gave each of them 1.5 percent. Every member of the Committee was now a shareholder, and a successful IPO would make each of them rich.

From the beginning of the Company, managerial salaries and bonuses had never been systematically determined. Salaries were pretty much based on history and what the Company could afford, whereas bonuses were based on overall profitability rather than specific performance targets. To get the desired performance, the incentives had to be a targeted mix of salaries, bonuses, and stock options.

The first necessary step was to retain a well-regarded compensation consultant to analyze managerial duties and responsibilities and determine salary ranges based on comparable positions in comparable companies in related industries. Establishing specific performance goals was much more difficult—the budget had to carve out clearly delineated functions that could be measured and over which a manager exercised control. Finally, we needed a stock option plan with vesting based on meeting growth and profit targets; most important, all options would vest with an IPO.

I brought the issue of a public offering before the Financial Review Committee in July 1992 and got approval for a management compensation study to be carried out under the direction of a to-be-formed compensation committee. I immediately appointed Tom Weir as Chair with our only other outside director a member and myself as *ex officio*—I would be the bearer of any unwelcome news to my managers. Tom understood that this was going to be a difficult task because we would be changing a strong corporate culture.

None of my managers really liked the idea of a compensation study—in their minds not only were there no comparable companies, no outsider would really understand their responsibilities or the skills needed to do their jobs. I told them to tell it to the consultant and if they could convince him, it would be fine with me. I provided the consultant with my assessment of each of my six direct reports so that he had a basis for conducting the interviews.

As could be expected, the consultant found a touchy audience, and two of them were so offended by his inability to understand the importance of their jobs, they demanded I convey their complaints to Tom Weir. By the time the consultant had produced his report, Tom and I had managed to soothe several savage breasts and the consultant's report received grudging acceptance. Now, Tom and I could address the task of constructing a performance-based incentive plan that would elicit the performance we needed.

We now directed CFO Hoggatt to develop formulas for corporate overhead allocations based on historical numbers. Next came the tedious job of defining each manager's P&L responsibility. Once we had the structure in place, Tom and I decided on our growth and profit targets. We directed Hoggatt to construct models showing low, medium, and high revenue and profit projections, which allowed us to set bonus targets. Then we quickly put together a generous plan with a five-year vesting schedule based on growth and profit targets. What made the goals we set so tantalizing was the fact that all the options would vest with an IPO.

In addition to meeting their growth and profit targets, I had convinced my managers that we had to start managing the Company as though it were a public company. That meant that we had to have a clean balance sheet, steady and predictable growth in revenues and profits with no surprises. That is what the Street would reward and that was what we had to deliver. As a result, we cleaned up our balance sheet by writing off all of my bad investments and eliminated any of the related party transactions I had entered into when I was either 85 or 100 percent owner of the Company. All of them accepted the new discipline.

Our fiscal year begins September 1st, and we installed the new compensation plan for fiscal 1993. In October 1992, we had a three-day management retreat dedicated to the changes we would have to make to reach our targets. In December, just two years before our IPO, we met with Alex-Brown bankers who requested our 1994 projections and informed us that, if we met them, we would be IPO ready by 1994.

The results were exactly what Tom had predicted. What had been absolute ceilings on profit margins evaporated like ice in an Arizona sun.

Between 1990 and 1993, we had to write off accumulated tech school losses of $3.4 million. The analysts discounted the losses and looked to Apollo's continuing operations, which were solidly profitable. Without the tech school write-offs, instead of a net income loss in 1990 and only modest profit increases in 1991, 1992, and 1993, the net income would have looked like this:

(in $000s)

1990	1991	1992	1993	1994
$1,300	$1,591	$1,132	$1,297	$4,912

In 1994, performance improved spectacularly at UOP; as a result, the Apollo net income rose 329.7 percent, and the profit margin improved 300 percent, but at 3.9 percent it was still too low. Fortunately, the underwriters based their IOP pricing on forward numbers, and 1995 showed another spectacular improvement. Revenues were up 31 percent, but profits were up 156.5 percent, with the margin up another 100 percent, to a respectable 7.7 percent.

In addition to acceptable profitability, the Apollo balance sheet was clean. All losses had been written off; there was no debt and the only liabilities were leases for space and equipment. Following are the results of nine years of taking ourselves seriously.

Apollo Group, Inc.

Year	Revenue (000)	% Increase	Net Income (000)	% Increase	% Margin
1990	52,863	—	434	—	.082
1991	68,782	30.1	713	64.3	1.0
1992	81,865	19.0	646	(9.4)	.078
1993	97,545	19.2	1,143	76.9	1.2
1994	124,720	27.9	4,912	329.7	3.9
1995	163,429	31.0	12,600	156.5	7.7
1996	214,275	31.0	21,392	69.8	10.0
1997	283,536	32.3	33,379	56.0	11.8
1998	384,877	35.7	46,297	38.7	12.0

From March to June 1992 we interviewed bankers—Alex-Brown, William Blair, Paine-Webber, Morgan-Stanley, and Smith-Barney. Each of them extolled their virtues, but our main concern was valuation. The valuations ranged from a low of $40 million to a high of $75 million—obviously investment banking is not an exact science. We had examined the few companies that we believed could be considered comparables and had concluded that Apollo was worth $100 million, based on a 1994 net income of $4.9 million that worked out to a PE ratio (price-earnings ratio) of 20 (that is, the Company was worth 20 times its 1994 net income).

All the bankers asked us what kind of dope we were smoking, but we refused to back off of our number. Finally, in early June, Alex-Brown agreed to the number. As soon as Alex-Brown agreed, Smith-Barney capitulated and then demanded to be the lead underwriter. After some soul searching, Alex-Brown agreed to take second place to the more powerful Smith-Barney.

Once we had agreed on Smith-Barney and Alex-Brown as co-managers, we set about writing the Prospectus that would set forth a description of Apollo Group, the risks involved for the investor, and the terms of the offering. The all-hands meeting was held on June 30th, and we had a final document in late August.

John Murphy and I wrote most of the narrative, Peter Sperling parsed the document for accuracy and consistency, Jim Hoggatt and Price-Waterhouse provided the financials, and Jon Cohen and the underwriters counsel hassled over every sentence. It was a tedious process that cost Apollo a couple of hundred thousand dollars and frayed everyone's nerves. However, when the Prospectus had been approved by the SEC and finally went to the printer, we found we were still pretty good friends.

However, along the way, we ran into two issues that were not settled until the very end. The first was our insistence that we would only sell nonvoting stock, and the second was the state of my health. The bankers argued that the Street would never accept nonvoting stock and insisted that we drop the demand. Apollo had been created largely to protect the accreditation status of UOP. Accreditation regulations required reaccreditation if there were any change in the ownership or control of UOP. We now argued that, if we sold voting stock, it would constitute a change of ownership of Apollo and, thus, a change of control. Ergo, we would only sell nonvoting stock. Although the Smith-Barney bankers used this issue to stage two melodramatic walkouts, the Alex-Brown bankers stayed and finally Smith-Barney capitulated. The final issue was the state of my health.

At the age of 73, I was a bit long in the tooth for a CEO, and the bankers were nervous that the Street might wonder how long I would be around. Consequently, they demanded all of my medical records and arranged conference calls with my personal physician and the surgeon who had performed the previously recounted surgeries to repair a blocked left ureter. The surgeon, who was Head of Urology at the University of Arizona Medical Center in Tucson and a nationally recognized kidney specialist, was unsuccessful in both operations and the ureter stayed blocked. The efficiency of the left kidney dropped sharply, causing a sympathetic decline in the right kidney. In addition, the left kidney produced an angeotensin enzyme that had run up my blood pressure. In the conference call, the kidney surgeon opined I was otherwise healthy, and the surgeon assured everyone that removing a kidney was not brain surgery. However, one of the Alex-Brown bankers, Malcolm Morris, demanded that the IPO that had been scheduled for September be postponed until December.

I liked all of the bankers with the exception of Malcolm Morris, a priggish Englishman who was primarily an errand boy for the senior Alex-Brown banker. Malcolm had let everyone know that he had taken a MBA at Insead and was destined for higher things. Consequently, Malcolm was not treated well in the meetings, so he seized on the issue of my health to establish the importance of his presence. The surgeon had said that the operation could easily be scheduled after the IPO, but Malcolm demanded a postponement and the other bankers finally agreed to let Malcolm have his way.

Once the IPO was postponed, I scheduled the surgery for September, which would give me plenty of time to recover before a December IPO. On the day of the surgery I was prepped for the operation and lying on a gurney ready to be rolled into the operating theater when the surgeon came by for a final chat. As he thought out loud about the pros and cons of removing the kidney, he talked himself into deciding that it was not a good idea after all. I was dressed and out of the hospital in about 10 minutes and on my way back to Phoenix. The cancelled operation gave me added reason to dislike Malcolm, and I demanded that he be removed from the banking team—none of the other bankers objected.

As a final medical note, the left kidney has atrophied and the right kidney has taken over and is doing a very good job.

The delay on the IPO allowed us ample time to prepare for the road show and to have our presentation critiqued by the bankers and the analysts.

The Road Show

Some combination of Gibbs, Hoggatt, and myself did the road show. Fortunately, we were usually accompanied by Laurie Easley, Director of Creative Services, who functioned as our den mother. As with most road shows, it was physically and emotionally exhausting. We criss-crossed the country a couple of times but finally the book was full enough to release the offering. About the only drama came when we had to price the offering. Rick Bartlett, who ran the syndicate desk at Smith-Barney, had that responsibility.

All through the preparations, we had assumed a price of $14 a share, and now Bartlett was telling us that the Street would only accept $11. That would mean a return of $10.6 million less than expected and I was furious. I assumed we were being taken and that this had been their plan all along, so I told them to pull the offering. Fortunately, Bartlett was a very nice guy and I agreed to let him try to dissuade me. Not only was he a nice guy, his analysis convinced me that $11 was the right price.

The book was not that solid and if we priced at $14, there would be little upside for the institutional buyers. Worse still, there would be little incentive for the bankers to push the stock, and without market makers, the stock would go nowhere. If, however, we priced at $11, bankers would push the stock, there would be an immediate up-tick, and the buyers would be pleased. He assured me that, in the long run, the $10 million left on the table would be returned manyfold. The fact that the stock has increased in value some 1,700 percent would seem to indicate that he had a point.

Once the euphoria of the IPO had worn off, the management team now faced the iron law of the quarter. Every quarter, the company must meet or beat analysts' expectations, or the stock tanks. Apollo had come public as a growth company, so the Street expected top and bottom line growth of 35 to 30 percent per annum, no excuses accepted.

Rather than bemoaning this new master, we turned it into a game. CFO Hoggatt was a solemn and judicious type who soon had the analysts and fund managers taking what he said as gospel. It was his job to manage analysts expectations, which, when one considers the symbiotic relationship between companies, analysts, and fund managers, was not too difficult. It was in everyone's interest to keep the stock rising at a steady pace, not too fast and not too slow. To accomplish this, analysts' projections had to be kept within the narrow range that allowed Apollo to grow smoothly at the 25 to 30 percent rate so that the quarterly numbers were never under and never more than a penny over the consensus number.

Because there are always fluctuations in a complex business like higher education, Hoggatt was a firm believer in visible revenues, so he constructed a sophisticated cash flow model that projected the next 24 months and he updated it monthly. Being thus forewarned of both shortfalls and overages, he was able to appropriately match expenditures and manage payables. As a result, Apollo has not missed a quarter since it became a public company.

These might be termed the microconditions for success with the Street. The macroconditions were not that easy. There was the unrelenting pressure to grow Apollo; each year of growth made the 25 to

30 percent harder to achieve; we knew that someday, we would finally have to face the law of large numbers. We also knew that hard work, imagination, innovation, and aggressive marketing could push that day well into the future.

We had three ways to grow: grow our established campuses and learning centers (analysts call this *same-store growth*); expand current operations through new programs and obtaining licenses in new states; and growth through acquisition, which the analysts consider inferior. Therefore we concentrated on organic growth. We had little difficulty with same-store growth; geographic expansion was another matter.

To continue the growth, we had to expand UOP into new states and between UOP and a state license stood the higher education bureaucrats, usually backed by the local higher education establishment. It was at this juncture that I had to make a major change in our political operation, and it led to the departure of my companion-in-arms, John Murphy.

The Politics of State Licensure

Not only was it essential to gain licenses to operate in other states, our relationship with the Department of Education was of increasing importance, requiring a presence in Washington, D.C. I pressured a reluctant John Murphy to hire a Washington-based assistant to deal with the U.S.D.O.E. and for him to begin the analysis of the regulatory issues we would face in the states we had targeted for expansion. He resisted. When he refused to move, I set about searching for someone to run a national lobbying operation and was fortunate to hire Charles Seigel, the press officer of the Democratic Congressional Caucus. Seigel had the experience needed to deal with the Congress and the federal bureaucracy and, surprisingly, he breathed new life into our quest for new state licenses. Hiring Seigel ended any effective collaboration with Murphy.

Once hired, Seigel quickly established our presence in Washington, after which he addressed the problem of licensure in the states we had targeted. It was not long before he had hired lobbyists in the targeted states and we were well on our way to obtaining the coveted licenses. As Charles waxed, John waned. It was not long before John's political activities were pretty much confined to California where his work and our political contributions had won him a seat on the Commission on Private Postsecondary Education. Once his term on the Commission ended, he served briefly as Academic Vice President where he did a commendable job of reorganizing the University's academic governance structure. That job completed, I appointed him Vice President for Business Development, but business innovation was not his metier, and it was soon apparent that he no longer had an important role to play.

At this juncture, John withdrew from regular communication with me or any of the members of the management team. Without asking me, or even informing me, he took a long vacation, and when he returned charged me with forcing him out of the Company. When I recounted chapter and verse of his refusal to perform the duties for which he was eminently capable, his response was surly silence. When it was clear that no meeting of the minds was possible, he resigned and from that point forward, all of our communication has been through corporate counsel. It is not possible for me to think of John without pain. I miss him every day, but I cannot dismiss our parting with "He fought well in 1917," and go on about my affairs.

His leaving brings into stark relief one of the strategies I have used in dealing with management-level employees. From the beginning, the Company has come first. I will tolerate a certain amount of inadequate performance or aberrant behavior from loyal and long-term managers; however, when a manager is no longer effective, neither friendships nor other personal ties stand in the way of his/her departure. John tested this strategy more than any other employee, but, finally, even he had to go. Inevitably, in a company that has had so many changes and has gone through so many stages of growth from start-up to maturity, every major repositioning of the Company has required a changing set of skills and attitude. My job has been to orchestrate this process by remaining emotionally aloof so that I can transfer, reassign, force out, or fire managers who have not grown with the Company. I can then hire persons with the needed skills to replace them.

Describing this strategy certainly raises the question, "Why haven't I been replaced?" Although a digression, this seems as appropriate a time as any to answer that question. I think the answer is "delegation." I came to business with no business skills or knowledge so, from the beginning, I have had to hire people to run the business. Although, under duress, I have at various times been CFO, CIO, or director of marketing, sales, or administration, I only held these positions until I could find and afford a professional to fill them.

My skills have been primarily educational and political. The educational skills have allowed me to perceive and articulate the Company's mission. The political skills have enabled me to see the ever-changing business needs of the Company and the ever-shifting relationships between and among managers as they functioned to make the business successful. I am a macromanager. I define and delegate tasks and responsibilities. I try to offer managers every possible assistance as they strive to meet their responsibilities and accomplish their assigned tasks. When it is clear that a manager has failed, then I have a fairly objective basis upon which to take action to reassign or remove them. So far, this strategy has allowed me to avoid a failure that would occasion my own resignation or firing by the Board of Directors.

Seigel joined Apollo in January 1992. I soon discovered that, while Murphy and I might be considered inspired amateurs, Charlie was a professional who brought a whole new dimension to our lobbying and political action. He also brought enthusiasm and boundless energy, two qualities common to those who are successful at Apollo. His first task was to gain advantages for Apollo in the 1992 reauthorization of the Higher Education Act which he was able to do both in the Act and in the rules and regulations.

While he continued to work in Washington he was obviously thinking about the problem of how UOP was to grow; on March 24th he sent me a long memo that pretty much set out what he would accomplish over the next six years. His primary focus was UOP, and he approached his task with a freshness that was impossible for those of us who had spent most of the previous 20 years fighting for survival.

As I have told you, I believe that Apollo has great potential and the UOP concept should be much better known and understood, both in political circles in Washington, in all the states and by the public. I was surprised to discover how little has been done in these areas in the past. I can certainly understand that during the struggles for accreditation and acceptance, these issues were of little importance. But now that UOP has grown to the extent it has, it seems to me that the Company should undertake the kind of effort I've been making here in Washington on a large scale. The more UOP and its underlying concepts are known and understood in Washington and the 46 states where we don't operate, as well as by the general public where we do operate, the better chance the Company has to grow in student body and expand into other states. . . .

I was convinced and very quickly revived the idea of creating the first national University. My mantra was, "within 10 years UOP will be within a 20 minute commute of 65 percent of the urban population of the United States."

Charlie then began the process of introducing me to political Washington. I met with Congressmen and Congresswomen, Senators, staffers, and the bureaucrats in the agencies that impact higher education, and I was both intrigued and appalled at the process. In his role as a lobbyist, Charlie was a glad-hander and a name-dropper and so were most of the politicians we met. He had an openness and friendliness that was engaging and a Jim Farley–like memory for names, places, and connections. In an amazingly short time, Apollo and UOP were better known on the Hill than all but the state universities and the nationally known private institutions. Excellent though his work was in Washington, the big payoff I got from his talents was his work in the states.

The Drive for New Licenses

Charlie wanted a real challenge and he asked that we let him try to gain a license in Michigan, a state Murphy was convinced would be a waste of our scarce resources. In the 14 years up to that time, we only had licenses in five western states and Puerto Rico (an early endeavor of mine). In the seven years since then, we added nine more.

No institution that proposed to operate as a fully configured university had ever been licensed in Michigan, but Gibbs and I decided to let Charlie try. Seigel explained that the state's Republican governor, John Engler, was making radical changes in the state, and had made very clear he wanted change in the state's education system. The approval process was daunting, but Charlie was convinced that the Engler administration's new attitude might afford an opportunity. Seigel hired a well-connected lobbyist to work with him, and Governor Engler's press secretary provided encouragement, guidance, and advice.

At first, the staff at the Department of Education, the licensing agency, reacted as one might expect—cautiously and suspiciously. Understandably, they were concerned about some for-profit university he never heard of from "Out West." It took 18 months of careful work before David Hanson, the official charged with reviewing license applications, was willing even to support the submission of an application. At that point, Hanson paid an inspection visit to the University prior to arranging a formal visit from the Committee of Scholars— once again, a committee of academics from competing institutions.

After Hanson's visit, he told us that he was extremely impressed with the University, and then came a true serendipity. Hanson indicated that there were a number of institutions in Michigan that had existed before the state first passed a law in the late 1930s requiring licensure. As a result, they were grandfathered in, and needed no license to operate in the state, though they did have to comply with state standards. Hanson mentioned that there was a school in Michigan about to close, and they were looking for someone to buy their authority. Hanson had overseen several such transfers of authority, but they were all between in-state institutions. He urged us to consider purchasing this authority, as it would assist the school that was closing, Jordan College, and expedite UOP's entry into Michigan. We were all stunned by the prospect, primarily because we would never have known of it if Hanson hadn't mentioned it; in addition, he indicated that he was willing to sign the official papers transferring the authority. The price was $500,000, and, needless to say, we were delighted to agree.

None of the private colleges in Michigan welcomed competition from UOP. They alleged that not only was there no need for UOP's services, it was an institution of inferior quality. Despite the opposition, in June 1995, Hanson approved the transfer and we were in business in Michigan. That June, Seigel had a double win, in the same week we received Michigan approval, UOP was approved for license in Louisiana.

As for the contention that Michigan did not need UOP's services, we had projected that our first campus (Detroit) would have 300 students in the first year and 750 after two years. In fact, at the end of the first year, the enrollment reached 1,000, and the second year it was over 2,000.

Exploiting the 1994 Midterm Elections

With these successes under our belt, we decided finally to think even bigger, and the midterm elections in 1994 provided us an unexpected opportunity. The Republican landslide swept into office many new governors in large states, ones who were willing to look at their states' old ways of doing things with a new eye, and that encouraged private enterprise and the opportunity to provide new models for their citizens. It wouldn't be easy for us because we'd have to work simultaneously in a number of large states, hiring and coordinating not only local consultants, but heavy-hitting Washington-based consultants who could enhance our effectiveness by exploiting any interface between national and state politics. It was complex and it would be much more expensive than anything we had done before, but we decided that it made sense—this was an opportunity we could not afford to let pass.

While many of these governors are Republicans, it should be noted that not all were. We decided to focus our efforts in a number of the large northeastern states, including New York, where Governor George Pataki had been elected the first Republican in many years; Pennsylvania, where former Republican Congressman Tom Ridge was pledging to bring a new attitude to state government; New Jersey, where Christine Todd Whitman was elected one year earlier and had already reformed the higher education licensure process; and Maryland, where a Democrat, Parris Glendening (himself a former government professor at the University of Maryland) had pledged to take a new look and open up the system. In addition, we decided to start working in Texas, where newly elected Governor George W. Bush was similarly intent on changing the way the state did business, despite a difficult and tradition-bound higher education system.

We submitted applications for licensure in New York, New Jersey, Massachusetts, Texas, and Pennsylvania. The fact that we are able to apply in Pennsylvania is a tribute to Charlie's mindful optimism and ranks with Murphy's victory over WASC in California.

Pennsylvania had a 100-year-old law that prohibited a university from being for-profit. It was the only such law in the country, and it meant we couldn't even apply for licensure until the law was changed. Beginning in 1995, Charlie worked with lobbyists, members of the legislature, and the Governor's office to effect a change in the law. He finally succeeded. In 1997, a bill rescinding the exclusion of for-profit universities passed the legislature and Governor Ridge signed it into law.

The next challenge came in Maryland. The Democratic governor, Parris Glendening, had told Charlie during his campaign in 1994 that despite his position as a faculty member at the University of Maryland, he too believed in opening up options to the state's citizens. In Maryland, our second full-time political staffer together with a duo of lobbyists (both Democrats) worked for two years to convince the Secretary of Higher Education that UOP should be licensed. Although the Secretary finally approved the application, if the applicant needed any exemptions from the state's regulations, the State Board of Higher Education also had to approve. UOP needed two exemptions from the rules: one rule required a specific proportion of full-time faculty (UOP has part-time faculty); another rule required a physical library (UOP has an online library).

Finally, on April 15, 1998, the State Board approved the license. The Maryland approval was the first foothold in the Northeast Corridor and UOP campuses were soon doing business in the urban centers clustered around Baltimore and the District of Columbia.

More recently, we had the happy experience of being welcomed with open arms by several state commissioners of higher education—Oklahoma, Texas, Massachusetts, Alabama, Illinois (surprise, surprise), and Ohio.

UOP has been inspected, tested, scrutinized, analyzed, and checked in 14 states and 2 Canadian provinces. Our accrediting body, the North Central Association, sends teams of reviewers to us on average of twice a year and we are monitored by the U.S. Department of Education. We submit quarterly disclosures to the U.S. Securities and Exchange Commission. We are undoubtedly the most scrutinized institution of higher education in the country.

In 1987, UOP accounted for 77 percent of revenue and 60 percent of profit. That's where the action was. However, the other parts of the Company made significant contributions. In 1986 when I appointed Jerry Noble as president, IPD had only six contracts with revenues of $1.6 million; today, IPD has contracts with 20 colleges and universities with revenues of $35.5 million and profits of $4.6 million. Since Noble took over, IPD has not only been a major source of revenues and profits, it has been a way for Apollo to enter markets where UOP does not have a license.

During this period, Apollo looked at dozens of potential acquisitions, but concluded only two of them: Western International University (WIU) and the College of Financial Planning (CFP). WIU was a small, Phoenix-based adult university that competed on the low end with UOP and the acquisition stopped that. CFP is the leading provider of financial planning training and education and helped to expand Apollo's range of offerings. Both were nonprofit, which we switched to for-profit.

The Cost of Politics

Today, Apollo has a substantial political operation—four full-time staffers, plus two high-level lobbyists who work in Washington and coordinate our efforts in the states where we are seeking licensure; in addition, we have 30 lobbyists working in state and provincial capitals. Even though we are licensed in 15 states, Puerto Rico, and British Columbia, Canada, we always have a lobbyist in these capitals because, in almost every year, the supporters of traditional education have bills introduced that would be detrimental to UOP's interests. Of course, we also sponsor legislation that will be advantageous to UOP.

The 1981 to 1983 attempt by WASC to have us expelled from California is an example of why we must be constantly on the alert. When I speak to investor conferences and am asked about the political dimensions of higher education, the audience is shocked to hear just how politicized higher education is and just how expensive it is to maintain a political capability.

As cynical as one can often become about politics, and regardless of the fact that politicians must spend too much of their time raising money, most of them really want to do good. Most politicians take their jobs seriously; most of the time we have been able to demonstrate to them the quality of the education we offer and convince them of the validity of our innovative method of bringing education to working adults.

Yes, we use money to get their attention—our American system of campaign finance gives us no other alternative. Sadly, it's the only way to do it when you are from out-of-state and the forces against you have money, votes, and even football tickets! In the immortal words of Jess Unruh, *"Money is the Mother's Milk of Politics."*

Apollo has had no choice but to accept the system and, like others who are able to afford it, we have benefited from it. Charlie once joked to me that he wished that "just once, a legislator would want to meet with us to talk about education, instead of raising money." However, the money treadmill runs 24 hours a day, and few politicians have time for a leisurely policy chat. Most would like to do so, and do when they can catch their breath. However, the best way to get their attention is to contribute to their campaigns so they have the time to think about what you want to talk about. Clearly, there are exceptions, especially those fortunate enough to have minor or token opposition and no need to raise huge amounts of money. These are the ones able to concern themselves more fully with policy issues. However, we learned long ago that for most legislators, a political contribution helps to ensure that a legislator can take the time to talk.

In the early years of the Company, I involved as few of the staff as possible in lobbying and fund raising. My job was to deal with the hostile world *without;* their job was to concentrate *within* on running the Company. In those years I made all of the political contributions and did all of the fund raising. By the mid-1980s, when it finally seemed that the Company was truly a going concern, I asked the executives who reported to me to assist in making political contributions. At that time, our political world was still bounded by the five states in which we did business. When Charlie came on board, our political world became the nation and the price of politics rose exponentially. If we were to be in the "game," it required contributions to members of Congress and the Senate, not to mention presidential candidates—this, on top of a growing number of state legislators and governors. Furthermore, we are absolutely nonpartisan, so many races required equal contributions to both candidates.

Until we went public, Peter Sperling and I made most of the contributions. In 1992, Seigel asked me to establish an Apollo political action committee (PAC), but it didn't seem right for an institution of higher education to have a PAC. Two years later, he asked again, and this time I reluctantly said yes. We created a PAC and I strongly suggested that the top seven people in the company should contribute to it. At the annual maximum legal contribution of $5,000 a year, we were able to raise about $70,000 in two years; shortly thereafter I persuaded the next two levels of executives to contribute. This allowed us to accumulate over $200,000. This turned out to be just the first round; within a year, Charlie had persuaded us to create three separate PACs as well. Now, Apollo itself is on the money treadmill.

I have never done a full accounting of the annual cost of maintaining the political capability that helps to ensure our survival and future growth. It would be very depressing if I did. So, I think it best to leave that task to the next Apollo CEO.

Ponderosa

Once we had settled into the routine of making our quarterly numbers, there was a certain slacking off that I found somewhat disconcerting. We were a Wall Street phenom with the stock rising to ever-new highs, so the "If it ain't broke, don't fix it" syndrome took hold. Things were going so well that some of the executives began to refer to our corporate community as Ponderosa. That did not sit well with me, but I had very little purchase in advocating anything that was not central to our core business.

I felt a little like Napoleon's mother, who reportedly enjoyed her palace and grand life but could never stop asking, "Will it last, will it last?" I was convinced that it wouldn't last unless we innovated beyond the core business. I had forced the Company into creating the University of Phoenix and the Online campus, and now I perceived that the Internet was something to be dealt with but got no takers—finally when the first browsers appeared, I managed to arouse enough interest to enable Apollo to be a part of the cyber world but not an innovator in it.

I had tried Murphy in the role of vice president for business development, but he did not work out. So, in 1997, I persuaded Jorge

Klor de Alva to leave an endowed chair at UC Berkeley and assume that position. Jorge had been an Apollo board member for six years so he had a pretty good idea of what I wanted done and he set about diligently to accomplish it. Together, we researched the K–12 space and presented a couple of possible acquisitions that were rejected out of hand. He scanned professional education and training, academic publishing, and for-profit junior colleges, and all he got for his efforts was to fall afoul of the Ponderosa.

One of the companies he turned up that was closer to our core was an English-as-a-second-language company with operations in Asia. I did a due diligence tour of Japan, Korea, Hong Kong, Kuala Lumpur, and Singapore and rejected that as well; however, it renewed my interest in an Asian venture and occasioned our investment in a venture capital fund focused on Asia.

Just before the Asian meltdown, Jorge and I made an extensive tour of China, Taiwan, Malaysia, Singapore, and Hong Kong. Mostly, we just prospected, but in Malaysia we were confident that we had put together a joint venture with a Malaysian training company that would have a lock on a huge contract to train the civil servants that would be responsible for running President Mahatir's Multi-Media Corridor—a grandiose plan to create a cyber corridor stretching 50 miles from Kuala Lumpur to a new cyber city that would become the new capitol of Malaysia.

In our last night in Asia before flying home, I was sitting in a bar on top of our Hong Kong hotel looking out over the harbor and feeling pretty pleased with myself. The Malaysian contract would be the thing that would get us off dead center and moving again, but only if I could remove the Ponderosa. But how? Gibbs was the mayor of Ponderosa and I couldn't remove Ponderosa without changing Gibbs' management style and this looked impossible. Gibbs, like Murphy, had made tremendous contributions to Apollo, and I not only owed him a considerable debt for past services, he was a good and loyal friend. To make things even more difficult, UOP was doing very well, even though Gibbs ran it on autopilot. (He didn't really run it on autopilot; what he had was a highly competent Executive VP, Todd Nelson, who ran it for him.)

Nelson was a superb manager, but I did not want to move him into the UOP presidency. UOP had become one of the nation's largest institutions of higher education by dint of good management, but now it needed an academic to give it respectability. Respectability in the proper guise would allow us to end our 20-year love-hate relationship with the North Central accrediting association and end the smothering oversight to which we had been subjected. Respectability would also greatly lessen the resistance we faced from the bureaucrats that ran the state licensing agencies.

The only solution to this dilemma was for me to step down as president of Apollo. I could then appoint Todd Nelson as president while I remained chairman. I knew that Gibbs would consider this a demotion but hoped I could persuade him to move into a role more suited to his talents. That would allow me to appoint Klor de Alva as president of UOP. Before I left the bar, I had decided to make the changes.

Once back in Arizona, I moved quickly. I first got the buy-in from the public members of the Board, then met with Nelson who concurred with my plan. With Nelson's acceptance in hand, I delivered the bad news to Gibbs who promptly resigned. I then appointed Klor de Alva as UOP president and the deed was done.

As they used to say, it has not been all beer and skittles since that fateful night in the Hong Kong bar. Shortly after Gibbs' resignation, CFO Hoggatt quit without notice, he simply phoned me and said he would be in the next day to clean out his office. Words cannot express the bitterness I felt at his abrupt and unexpected departure. He made no preparations for a transition and he obviously knew that his unannounced resignation would spook the Street. Not only would such a resignation lead to speculation about accounting irregularities, most of the analysts and fund managers considered him a brake on my tendency toward risky ventures. Hoggatt had always handled the Street and now Nelson and I were suddenly fielding 50 calls a day from buy- and sell-side analysts demanding to know what in hell was going on. Fortunately, Hoggatt had gotten almost all of his operational data from Nelson, who also had an in-depth knowledge of the financials, and was able to offer the Street some sense of security. Needless to say, the stock took a hit and that was not the last hit.

A year before Hoggatt's departure, the U.S. Department of Education began a program review of Apollo's administration of the federal financial aid programs operated by the University of Phoenix.

They had not done a review for 12 years and we thought that it would be pro forma.

UOP operates sequential courses, whereas the Department's rules are written for term-based schools, that is, semesters or quarters. By contrast, UOP has sequential courses that run for five or six weeks. Having sequential courses allows our working students the ability to stop-out when their work or home responsibilities make it impossible to attend class—for example, a new assignment, travel, the birth of a child, or illness of a dependent. Unfortunately, a stop-out that lasts for more than 60 days is considered a drop-out when term-based rules are applied, and if the student is receiving federally insured financial aid, a drop-out triggers a host of administrative and financial transactions—recalculation of schedules, refunds, reapplications, transcript evaluations, etc., etc. In short, it creates unnecessary work for the University and the students.

The USDOE team that conducted the review 12 years ago had agreed with the University in working out a set of procedures that fitted the term-based rules to the sequential courses. However, the new Review Team informed us that all of the transactions based upon the previously approved procedures were incorrect and that we would have to review and correct them. This information was released to the press and on September 17, 1998, *The Wall Street Journal*'s "Heard on the Street" column reported that the University's financial aid procedures were under review. Apollo's stock fell 30 percent in the following two days from the mid-thirties to the low twenties, where it has remained.

The fall in the price of the stock cost Apollo shareholders some $2 billion. There was some irony in this. After amending the disallowed administrative and financial transactions, which took us 18 months and over $6 million, the final financial adjustments and penalties for rule violation were $280,000.

11

Giving Back

Part I

Considering my appreciation for the novels of Fielding and Dickens, one might think that in this, the story of my life, taking Apollo Group public and securing a great fortune would be the punch line at the end of the narrative. But as you've just seen, our IPO was not even the climax of the chapter in which it was described. Taking Wall Street's money is not the end of the process but merely the beginning of a more intense process of delivering on promises and earning one's newfound riches—which is not necessarily a bad thing. Shareholder demands for rapid and consistent growth in revenues and earnings pushed us to improve our game on all fronts.

At the same time, increasing shareholder value as an ultimate goal in life, in and of itself, leaves something to be desired. As I have said repeatedly in this book, my own aims always have been centered around social change, and about increasing opportunities for those born without the middle-class entitlements that our consumer culture seems to take for granted.

At the beginning of this book I spoke of my pleasure in seeing the projects I support help people to grow in their lives and professions. The great thing about having more money than I could ever spend is the ability to increase the scope of these ventures. In other words, with a great deal of money you can do what you like. Depending on your taste, you can build more strip malls to make more money, or you can buy up sports teams or racehorses and amuse yourself losing money, or you can try to change at least a small part of the world you inhabit. I have chosen the latter with the hope that in some small way those changes will improve the lot of my fellow humans.

My post IPO efforts at social, and in one instance political, change have focused on three activities: seawater agriculture, antiaging medicine, and mounting a war against the War on Drugs. This latter effort has two chapters all to itself.

Seaphire International

One example of where money can combine with purpose is my work with Seaphire International, formerly Planetary Design Corporation (PDC). My involvement in this enterprise began quite tangentially but has grown over the years. I see in it the promise of financial returns at some point, but the ROI will be modest at best. My interest goes deeper than personal financial return; Seaphire's mission is to create wealth where none exists. If successful, it will enable small farmers in developing countries with long stretches of desert coast to irrigate their crops with seawater. If successful, Seaphire International will create a new kind of agriculture, perhaps a second green revolution.

Seaphire is an outgrowth of the University of Arizona's Environmental Research Laboratory work on saltwater-tolerant plants called *halophytes.* These are terrestrial plants, not algae, and the one Seaphire is commercializing is *salicornia,* also known as "sea asparagus" or "passe pierre." Salicornia, like its cousins the caper and the mangrove, is a halophyte, because of its unusual ability to thrive in salty water. In the wild, Salicornia grows in estuaries along the coast of France, the United Kingdom, North America, and South America, where, with the ebbing and flowing of the tide, it is covered by seawater part of every day. The French and English harvest the tips of the young plants and toss them in salad or serve them as a side vegetable. It is rumored to have been one of George Washington's favorite salad ingredients, harvested wild on the coast of Virginia.

Researchers at the University of Arizona began working with halophytes in the late 1970s as an offshoot of their work with aquaculture, growing shrimp and fish in long covered raceways. Having focused on growing animals in the salty water, they started thinking about what they might grow with the animals' wastewater. Eventually it became clear that halophytic crops could be a way to provide food and that halophyte-based agriculture would be viable in those parts of the world where freshwater supplies were limited but seawater was readily available. For the past 12 years, Seaphire has continued the research and development in both salicornia and shrimp cultivation.

Many of the poorest parts of the world are desert coastlines. In places such as Mexico, the Middle East, and Africa, there is abundant land, some of it potentially high-quality agricultural land, plenty of seawater, and a need for agriculture and jobs. Enter salicornia. Here is a plant that can be cultivated in desert coastal areas and irrigated with seawater pumped directly from the ocean. The beauty of salicornia is that it allows two underutilized resources in close proximity—seawater and desert land—to become productive.

In Egypt, for instance, 97 percent of the population lives along the Nile, the country's major source of fresh water. By greening the coast of the Red Sea, seawater agriculture would effectively give Egypt a second Nile. The same would hold true for many other impoverished, desert coastlines. Eritrea, in north Africa, is another example of a coastal country with untapped desert land and seawater that could be transformed into green food producing regions with seawater agriculture. In such places, salicornia can be the foundation for building an economy—engineering to facilitate seawater irrigation, the agriculture itself, transportation to move the produce out, living facilities for workers, manufacturing plants, and production facilities.

And there are other benefits of Seaphire cultivation. Shrimp farming is also suited to arid coastlines, but there are two main criticisms of shrimp aquaculture. First, pathogens from the shrimp wastewater that flows back into the sea can carry disease to other shrimp farms, spilling down current to another and another until it wipes out the entire region's shrimp production, together with the region's population of wild shrimp. Second, the nutrient-rich water flowing from a shrimp farm can badly damage a coastal ecosystem. The solution: Use the waste runoff as fertilizer for saltwater cultivation of salicornia. Like chicken manure used in organic farming, the shrimp waste becomes nutrients for the plants growing on salicornia farms, and microbes in the soil purify the water before it reaches the saltwater table and flows back into the sea. The synergy between these two crops can drive the growth of a local economy.

When PDC was set up in 1987, it was an assembly of like-minded scientists and citizens eager to solve environmental problems. The ecologically minded citizens invested money and other resources enabling the company to build upon and expand the initial research conducted at the University of Arizona. I first became involved in PDC through Dino DeConcini, an early investor in the organization. He introduced me to Carl Hodges, founder of PDC, and before that, founding director of the Environmental Research Lab at the University of Arizona in Tucson. I was aware of his involvement in Biosphere II, the Bass-financed, ill-starred project to create a totally contained ecosystem within a glass bubble in the Arizona desert, and I liked that kind of holistic thinking. I put some money into PDC, and I asked Carl to become a member of the board of the University of Phoenix. My first investment was in the early 1990s, and by 1994 I was serving on the board of directors.

Part of what attracted me to the company was the belief that most of the positive changes in the world occur where there is a business opportunity. The world's advancements in my lifetime are largely a result of an individual or a group deciding that a product or a service was needed by a market, usually before the market recognized the need. Whether the escalator, the personal computer, the cell phone, education for working adults, or seawater agriculture, the driving force has come from the private sector.

While PDC developed ever more productive varieties of salicornia and bred pathogen-resistant shrimp, the real potential of salicornia as a food crop and base ingredient in other products was not being developed. In early 1997 the company hired a chief operating officer (COO) with experience in a large multinational product company. His "everything has a place and everything in its place" management approach and big-company support staff expectations were poorly suited to a company with projects in several countries, a tight budget, and a whole host of unknowns. He lasted less than six months.

At this point, I realized that PDC was a great concept company but a lousy business. By 1997, the money from early investors was gone, there were no commercial products, and the Company faced bankruptcy. It was at this point that I infused new capital and took control of the Company.

Although Carl Hodges, the PDC founder and president, was a fine scientist, he, like many scientists, was not cut out for management. Fortunately, his son Roy was.

Roy had grown up around halophytes and research scientists but had pursued business and international relations, ending up as a consultant in Washington, D.C. He had grown weary of only giving recommendations and outlining strategies; as it is sometimes said, a consultant is someone who knows a thousand different ways to make love, but can't get a date. Roy wanted to put his consultant skills to a real-world test. He accepted my offer to take on the position of COO of PDC while I would assume the position of President and CEO. From that position I could mentor Roy and he could use me as a higher authority when needed.

In the ensuing two years, Roy has transformed PDC. It is now a new company with a new name (Seaphire International), new products, new ideas, and new plant and shrimp varieties but with the same basic mission. We believe that seawater agriculture will be part of the next green revolution. We believe that desert regions of the world that have never before produced food will be transformed into green farms providing people with jobs and opportunities and the world with additional food to feed its growing population.

Currently Seaphire has farms in Mexico and Eritrea, Africa. We are negotiating a joint-venture farm in India and are breaking ground on a large-scale integrated farm in Mexico, and have introduced fresh salicornia "seaphire" to the U.S. specialty produce market. It is increasingly available in the produce section of grocery stores and in gourmet restaurants. It is the nation's first vegetable crop irrigated only with seawater. The cosmetics industry is beginning to recognize the unique capability of salicornia to concentrate the nutrients and micronutrients of the sea. Salicornia extract is now a respected cosmetic ingredient.

Salicornia also produces a high-quality edible oil and even a gluten-free flour. After harvesting and pressing the seed for oil and flour, the stems of the plant are pressed into fiberboard and firelogs. In countries like Eritrea, the firelogs or briquettes are a valuable substitute for the limited firewood available for cooking and home heating.

Even the issue of global warming is impacted by seawater farming. Salicornia plants pull carbon dioxide out of the air as they grow. Carbon dioxide is one of the major greenhouse gases. Some of the carbon is stored in the roots left behind when the plant is harvested. Even more is locked up when the stems are pressed to make fiberboard, which fixes the carbon in the plant, keeping it from returning to the atmosphere until it is either burned or degraded, a process that can take up to a century or more. In this way, salicornia cultivation can make a major contribution to the problem of global warming. Most important, seawater agriculture will supplement the freshwater crops needed to feed the billions who will soon be with us.

If Seaphire can do all this and also turn a profit, the true potential of seawater agriculture and aquaculture will come to pass. If Seaphire International can make salicornia and shrimp farming profitable for small farmers, it will be possible to green the desert coasts of the developing world. Everyone at Seaphire believes this is a near-term possibility and that the millions of dollars and years spent in research and development will someday form the basis for a second green revolution.

Which brings me to the next object of my enthusiasm.

The Kronos Group

Having survived both prostate cancer and the loss of function in one kidney, I consider each day a gift, and health maintenance part of the work one must do to deserve that gift. Most everyone appreciates the benefits of longevity, but it is also true that coming into a great deal of money late in life makes one reluctant to "go gentle into that good night" just when things are getting really interesting. A combination of factors has emboldened me not to accept passively the decline of age and its sequelae that we are expected to experience.

In the mid-1990s, I met a cardiologist with a large practice in Arizona. His name is Tali Arik. We became good friends, especially through membership in the Phoenix Philosophes, a group that gets together now and then to dwell on the problems of cosmology, consciousness, and the theory of knowledge. Two years after meeting Tali, I read a *New York Times* article about the process of aging and how it might be slowed or even reversed! The article aroused my curiosity and, having experienced the physiologic and cognitive decline expected as normal for my age, I sent Tali off to do further research on the subject of aging. In December of 1997 we reviewed his research and decided it warranted a comprehensive study with a view to forming some sort of organization to promote antiaging medicine.

In March of 1998, Tali took a week in Aspen and produced a document outlining the scientific basis of antiaging and longevity medicine, along with a business plan. A month later we formed a company called The Kronos Group to explore and implement new approaches to living better longer.

A month after deciding to form Kronos, I hired the third member of the team, Jonathan Thatcher. Jonathan, still in his twenties, had founded and sold a health-related information company and had acquired a thorough knowledge of the health care industry. He had just been fired by a friend of mine who ran a small health-related company—reason: being too aggressive in advocating innovation. This group of three provided the intellectual and experiential elements critical to the early development of Kronos: scientific/medical expertise, knowledge of the industry, business experience, and strong financial backing. In addition, we articulated the vision of a new form of medicine—*the Kronos Way.*

I assigned Jonathan the task of writing a full business plan, and this required an in-depth study of the science and practice of antiaging medicine. As the plan unfolded, we found ourselves creating the Company as we planned it. Increasingly, Tali and I shared a growing admiration for Jonathan's business acumen and dedication to the task. Both of us were used to working 60- to 70-hour weeks and Jonathan was right there beside us. The plan called for a search for a CEO and this ended with the appointment of Jonathan to that position.

There are three foundations for the practice of antiaging medicine: a laboratory for conducting some 200 assays, including the assessment of oxidative stress and immune function to provide a profile of a patient's physical age; a compounding pharmacy to prepare the customized regimen of vitamins, minerals, hormones, and other pharmaceuticals indicated by the patient's profile; and a physician who can interpret the profile and counsel the patient in the theory and practice of antiaging medicine at the level of the individual patient. In order to do this, a physician must master a 10-volume protocol on the practice of medicine the Kronos Way.

In 1998, the most advanced lab for practice of antiaging medicine was Genox, located in Baltimore, Maryland. When it proved impossible to buy Genox, Jonathan hired Genox's chief scientist, Richard Cutler, a molecular gerontologist and a leader in the field, who had worked for many years at the National Institute of Aging division of the National Institutes of Health. As a molecular gerontologist, he was a leader in the field of antiaging research. Two of his theories are among the most fertile and foremost in current antiaging research and thought.

In the 1970s Cutler proposed two major hypotheses that now guide much of the international research in this field. The first of these, the Longevity Determinant Gene Hypothesis, proposes that general health maintenance and control of aging are governed by a small, and therefore potentially knowable, number of genes. In Darwinian terms, there is no reason for aging to evolve as a force in nature, because there is no selective advantage to aging and early death. We don't need a genetic mechanism to get rid of us when our time is up. In the wild, either disease or a predator or an accident takes care of that well enough.

For the human species, with its long, slow period of physical and intellectual development, there is a distinctive selective advantage to longevity. Natural selection would have operated by favoring the evolution of a longer life span. The most effective longevity therapy is to free the body to express this genetic propensity by reducing genetic damage.

Cutler's second postulate, the Dysdifferentiation Hypothesis of Aging, proposes that most age-related diseases are a result of normal by-products of development and energy metabolism. These by-products act predominantly on the genetic apparatus of a cell by changing its proper state of differentiation. In other words, as we age, cellular function blurs. Usually, at about 30, the genetic stability of individual cells begins to decline, and physiological cohesion breaks down. By the time we're 70, half our proteins may be abnormal. Even at 35, a kidney cell can become slightly less precisely a kidney cell. Neurons may start to produce hemoglobin—which is not what they are supposed to be doing. We lose receptors. Hair begins to grow in odd places, while it thins on the tops of our heads. This same loss of precise and specific function extends to the connective tissues and other organs, all of which ultimately manifests itself in the familiar signs we see in the faces and bodies of most older people.

One important function of Cutler's longevity determinant genes is to code for the defense and repair of such cellular damage. Disrepair is always taking place, in the basic process of consuming oxygen. As oxygen is consumed, electrons are given off, leaving behind *free radicals*. These are a highly reactive oxygen species that aggressively bind with "innocent bystander" atoms and molecules. Once bound, the structure of the receiving molecule is altered (the process of oxidative stress), causing damage to arteries, skin cells, retinal cells, and so on. If the molecule is part of a gene, the gene's ability to accurately replicate proteins will be compromised, leading to dysdifferentiation.

When dysdifferentiation and oxidative stress occur, neurohormonal irregularities accelerate. Joints ache; skin elasticity diminishes; lung capacity and muscle mass diminish. Cognitive decline begins. Bones weaken, cardiac output declines, and arteries stiffen. By beginning Kronos therapy in one's thirties, an individual can seriously impact and slow these changes, which have been accepted as part of normal, age-related decline. Even someone like myself, beginning in my late seventies, can see dramatic benefits. The benefits of some Kronos therapies—antioxidants to improve one's risk profile and hormone replacement to improve one's cognitive ability and physical performance—can be felt and measured in as little as a month! Indeed, life-extension benefit is conferred in as little as six months!

The second element of the needed foundation was a compounding pharmacy, and Jonathan's next coup was to negotiate the purchase of one of the nation's leading compounding pharmacies, headed by Dr. Richard Fura, whose knowledge of antiaging therapies is unsurpassed.

The third and final element was a treatment protocol and educational materials whereby we could train physicians in the Kronos Way. This task fell to Tali, who put together a team: Richard Cutler; Dr. Chris Heward, a molecular biologist (our second scientific recruit); and Dr. Charlene DeHaven, a Phoenix-based physician who already had a successful antiaging practice. In their final form, the protocol and training materials required thousands of pages in ten volumes—not only were we ready to train physicians in the Kronos Way, we were ready to create a board specialty.

When one looks at Kronos from a macro point of view, it is far more than a company that will build and operate Kronos centers. It is also a research and development organization that is dedicated to changing the practice of medicine in America. What Kronos seeks to do is to promote healthy aging, which will end the worst result of modern medicine—an old age marked by debilitating disease that consumes 65 percent of a person's total health care expenditures in the last year of life.

In premedical societies most people—infants, the young, and the old—died suddenly. There were few lingering deaths. One was either alive or dead. If the Kronos Way can enable people to age healthily, it will not only greatly improve the quality of life, it will lead to a dramatic decline in the cost of health care. It will do this by maintaining physical and mental health until one reaches one's genetically programmed life span, at which point one will die quickly.

One of the criticisms leveled at Kronos by those of an egalitarian persuasion is directed at the high fees (from $250 to $1,000 per month) Kronos must charge in order to deliver medical services the Kronos Way. Seen only as a fee for service operation, the criticism is justified. However, such criticism is blunted when Kronos is viewed from the perspective of its research and development functions. In the case of Kronos, it is the affluent members of society who are able to pay Kronos fees and, in so doing, fund its research and development. If Kronos can demonstrate the validity of its methods, then HMOs, insurance companies, and, finally, Medicare will adopt these methods, and the Kronos Way will become the norm for medical practice.

When a new patient comes to a Kronos center, he or she will spend three to four hours. The physician will take the usual history and conduct a physical exam, but the patient also will undergo a total body composition test, a DEXA scan to determine his or her ratio of fat to lean body mass and bone density, five pulmonary function tests, a test of static balance, a skin thickness test, and tests for highest audible pitch, focal point, and vibro-tactile sensitivity and a newly developed test for detecting minimal cognitive dysfunction. Patients will also have a stress test to evaluate not only their cardiovascular system but also their pulmonary capacity, lung damage, and metabolic functioning— taken together, these tests are far more comprehensive than would be the case with the usual treadmill test.

On the next visit, the physician will review the patient's oxidative stress and immune system profile, which will detect even minute amounts of toxic trace metals, and measure hormone levels and the body's capacity to deal with oxidative stress. These baseline values provide the data for the customized prescription of hormones, vitamins, minerals, and antioxidants tailored to the patient's needs.

One of the most important features of Kronos therapy is that it is physician directed. This allows the patient all the possible pharmacologic therapeutic options, which can include prescription-only products—for example, drugs known as *nootropics*, to enhance cognitive function, and antilipid agents, such as statins, which have been shown in multiple studies to decrease the risk of stroke, heart attack, and sudden death. The physician will also provide a thorough consultation on an appropriate diet and exercise regime. One month later, another profile will be prepared to better calibrate the prescription and this will be repeated until the prescription is optimized. After that, depending on the patient's response to the Kronos therapy, profiles will be prepared two, three, or four times annually.

It is the personalized specificity of the tests and the regimes offered that is the essence of the Kronos Way. These profiles tell you where you are today, where you want to be tomorrow, and whether you are getting there.

With the demographic bulge now spread across the age range from 35 to 55, we feel that we're at the birth of a new growth industry. Like Seaphire International, if successful, Kronos Group will satisfy an important human need, expand the boundaries of science, change medical practice in America, and return a profit to investors.

By the time this book is published, there will be Kronos centers in Phoenix, Los Angeles, San Francisco, and Manhattan. Kronos therapy will also be available via the Web at kronosclinic.com.

In the final chapter, I will describe how I indulge my passion for conflict even further in what may well be the most important work of my life.

12 | Giving Back

Part II
The War against the War on Drugs

I have made conventional gifts to medical research, the arts, and to my alma maters. Most important in this regard are endowed studentships for Reed College graduates to attend King's College Cambridge. However, the giving back that has most engaged me emotionally is my continued contribution to the War against the War on Drugs.

Two weeks after my IPO-induced affluence, I was in my office waiting for an appointment with my friend Dick Mahoney, a former Arizona Secretary of State who, in the previous September, had lost the Democratic Primary for the U.S. Senate. He wasn't feeling too bad since the winner was buried by John Kyl in the November Republican landslide. The appointment with Mahoney had turned my mind to politics, and it depressed me to think how Clinton and the old bulls in the Congress had managed to lose both the House and the Senate to the Republicans. When Dick arrived he was accompanied by his campaign manager, Sam Vagenas, whom I had never met. As we sat around discussing what Dick might do next, he was all for exporting management education to Mexico. "Man, it's amazing," he said. "In Mexico City you go to a good restaurant for lunch and everyone is talking on a cell phone. There's got to be lots of opportunities there." Having tried unsuccessfully for two years to export education to Mexico, I was unimpressed. I suggested instead that we brainstorm ideas for something to do politically. We didn't come up with much—term limits, welfare reform, campaign finance reform. Nothing clicked. Then I said, "Why not drug law reform?" Neither Dick nor Vagenas responded with more than a puzzled look, so I launched into a diatribe against the War on Drugs.

For the past 10 years I had been collecting articles and voluminous newspaper clippings on the Drug War and had concluded that, as public policy, it did not have one redeeming feature. It had only marginally reduced drug use, yet it had cost federal, state, and local taxpayers over $60 billion a year. It had lowered our annual balance of payments by the $100 billion we sent to the drug lords of producing countries. The eradication and interdiction programs we had forced on weak Andean governments, plus the billions U.S. users spent buying drugs, had flooded these fragile societies with narco-dollars, giving the narcos and various left and right insurgencies more power than their governments. Our Drug War had devastated these nations and was now fraying Mexico.

In the United States, the Drug War had turned many inner city streets into shooting galleries and had spawned a host of drug-related crimes. It had filled our prisons with minor offenders, creating the largest gulag since the Soviet Union. It had corrupted hundreds of Drug Enforcement Agency (DEA) and customs agents, state and local police, and even judges, and it had so weakened the Fourth Amendment that we no longer had any constitutional protection against unreasonable searches and seizures. The way I looked at it, the message the Drug War was sending to our kids was about on par with Clinton's message on abstinence.

Dick and Vagenas listened respectfully to my harangue, but the issue was foreign to them. I explained that my passion on the subject was generated primarily by the fact that the Drug War was a war against the poor, especially the minority poor. The overwhelming percentage of illegal drugs consumed in America are consumed by middle-class Whites who almost never end up in prison. The Drug War was a convenient way to keep the poor in their place, while middle-class White politicians sermonized about morality and protecting our youth, all the while ignoring the social pathologies that led to minority use and dealing in the first place.

After my diatribe, I asked Vagenas what he was going to do now that he was between engagements. He said he enjoyed the role of political consultant but, with no offense to Dick, he didn't want to deal with candidates, their personal quirks, or their groupies and hangers-on anymore. Instead, he would specialize in initiative campaigns. I immediately suggested that we might try drug law reform by initiative. Vagenas said he didn't think much of the idea, but he agreed to give it some thought. I asked him for his address and phone number and the meeting concluded.

Over the next couple of weeks I sent Vagenas some fresh clippings and asked him if I could hire him to do some research on drugs and politics. He agreed, and over the next couple of weeks of study he concluded that even the softest drug, marijuana, was the subject of antidrug hysteria, as evidenced by the series of defeats in the attempt to decriminalize or legalize it. But there were hopeful signs. In San Francisco a referendum had passed reclassifying marijuana as the lowest law enforcement priority and the California legislature had approved a medical marijuana bill.

In mid-January 1995, Vagenas (now Sam) and I met to work out details on a possible drug policy initiative. He chose the Orbit Cafe, a funky coffeehouse with a postmodern decor and colored leather couches. In that futuristic ambience, we decided to forge the broadest possible drug policy reform initiative.

Sam had determined that legalization had been proved to be a loser, so we decided to forgo labels. What we had to do was free people from prison and send the clear message: The nation's Drug War was a failure. Confirming the sheer stupidity of the Drug War could not be done by incremental education. A seismic shift was needed, a sea change in public opinion.

Deconstructing the Drug War by Stealth: A Poststructural Strategy

If we were to undertake an anti–drug war initiative, it needed to be a low-intensity campaign that only went public three weeks before an election. Ours would be what our opponents would later characterize as our "stealth campaign." We needed to keep a low profile so as not to awaken the drug warrior demons.

Given the polarization that always comes from press coverage, Sam also advised that we strike quickly and operate within a limited time frame. He pointed out that public opinion in our society is not formed over time in a linear fashion. Rather, public opinion in initiatives is formed when the voters are hit with a coherent message from a hundred perspectives—all of which must happen in a narrow window before the voters OD on the message. I agreed; in my ignorance, what choice did I have?

I will actually accept advice from those who I think know what they are talking about, and I soon found myself taking Sam's advice. In the three years I have worked with him, I have come to the conclusion that he is as close to a political genius as I am ever likely to meet. Grounded as I am in British empiricism, I find it most amazing that he and I work so well together, given that Sam is a poststructuralist grounded in Derrida and Foucault. He firmly believes that reality is pure text. I have always thought that poststructuralism is primarily a word game but it is the structure Sam used to analyze the political problem we faced and the strategy we used to address it. I still think poststructuralism is a word game but, in the mind of a political genius, it can be wonderfully powerful.

At the Orbit Cafe I set forth three short-term objectives: (1) review research on the Drug War, (2) analyze public opinion research on the issue, and (3) convene a distinguished group of Arizonans to sponsor our initiative. From this point on, Sam pretty much called the shots.

Searching for the Money Connection

I realized that we would need all of the expert help we could access and all the money I could raise. Through a friend who had taught at Princeton, I arranged a meeting with Ethan Nadelmann, head of the George Soros–funded Lindesmith Center, a drug policy think tank. I arranged to meet with him in San Francisco in late January 1995, when I laid out a sketch of our planned initiative. He had dedicated his career to debate among the elites and to education of the masses; direct political action had never entered into his thinking. I had to convince Nadelmann to provide intellectual support for our effort, because it was only through him that I could approach Soros to ask for financial support. Ultimately, Nadelmann invited me to New York to present the initiative.

Sam and I needed to convincingly demonstrate the bankruptcy of all existing approaches to the problem of drug abuse. We decided to pound home our thesis that 20 years of debate and education had reformed nothing. Despite billions spent counseling kids to "Just say no!" they had done the reverse. In just the past few years, youth drug use had doubled. Worse, ever younger kids were users.

However, the most insidious activity involved adult users. Enforcement efforts simply jacked up the cost of drugs, so addicts were forced to hustle that much more aggressively to feed their habit. A study of more than 500 Miami heroin users over a year attributed some 215,000 criminal offenses to them. The 82,000 drug sales, 25,000 shoplifts, 45,000 larcenies and frauds, 60,000 robberies and assaults, and 6,700 burglaries, resulted in an average of 375 offenses, more than one per day per user. While government promotes the notion that users commit crimes because they are on drugs, the truth is the reverse. It is the Drug War that creates the crime.

Meanwhile, incarceration of offenders had tripled the number of prison inmates. The period from 1980 to 1995 saw this number skyrocket from roughly half a million to 1,550,000. Of these, some 388,000 were jailed explicitly for drug offenses; another half a million are in prison for drug-related crimes, and Hispanics and African Americans are greatly overrepresented. The recent percentage increase in drug prisoners is four times higher among African Americans and three times higher among Hispanics than among Whites. The cost of this incarceration? Some $9 billion a year. Even worse, the deadliest aspect of the War on Drugs involves AIDS. The prohibition on drugs extends to needles, and some 25 percent of AIDS cases among homosexuals, bisexuals, heterosexuals, and their wives and children, result from addicts sharing contaminated needles.

In short, the Drug War is a multi-billion-dollar boondoggle—a welfare program for law enforcement agencies, prison developers, and bureaucrats who staff the various federal agencies that "fight" the Drug War, all supported by cynical congressional leaders who have turned drug policy into the third rail of politics. Any politician who hinted that the drug policies should be reformed immediately would be labeled a "legalizer" and a danger to the proper social order. What we now have is a criminal justice–industrial complex that is more dangerous to American liberties than Eisenhower's military-industrial complex. Unreasonable searches and seizures ordered by the Justice

Department and local criminal justice officials are routinely approved by the Supreme Court and citizens dare not protest these constitutional outrages because the loss of our liberties is a small price to pay in a war against the horrors of *drugs*.

But how did the voters feel? Sam gathered every relevant public opinion poll he could find. Analysis revealed that the public adamantly opposed legalization and overt decriminalization but preferred treatment programs (including medical marijuana) to incarceration. Voters also believed—overwhelmingly—that we were losing the War. For the first time, we spied a window, however small, for a successful drug policy reform initiative.

Our Distinguished Recruits

Sam and I began to recruit a brain trust. Sam's people were mostly ex-politicians and administrative types he had met while serving as Deputy Secretary of State; mine were from business and from the professions that provided services to the Apollo Group. In our first few meetings, membership fluctuated, but it quickly narrowed to a group of true believers who are still with us today. They crossed the political spectrum—Dr. Jeff Singer, Associate Editor of the *Arizona Medical Association Journal;* Marvin Cohen, Former Chief of the Civil Aeronautics Board; John Norton, former Deputy Secretary of Agriculture and President of the Goldwater Institute; Judge Rudy Gerber from the Arizona Court of Appeals; Richard Mahoney, attorney and former Arizona Secretary of State; Dino DeConcini, attorney, long-time Apollo Board member, and brother of former U.S. Senator Dennis DeConcini; Father David Meyers, attorney and Jesuit priest; attorney Linda Rawles, a Republican Congressional candidate; Dr. Ross Levatter, a major Cato Institute donor; and former State Senator Stan Furman, Arizona State University professor and American Civil Liberties Union (ACLU) activist.

While all of them were staunchly opposed to the Drug War, the group lacked consensus on how to resolve the issue. Libertarians sought full-blown legalization. Others were more interested in decriminalizing marijuana or in expanding treatment alternatives. After sitting in on some heated debates, Sam and I realized the only way to reach any consensus would be through a public opinion poll that would give us guidance on voter sentiment. For this, once again, we needed the buy-in of Ethan Nadelmann, our conduit to Soros financing.

In March 1995, Sam and I met in New York with Nadelmann (by now, Ethan) and other representatives of groups supporting reform, including Ira Glasser of the ACLU. Most in the gathering were interested in creating a broad initiative, but they harbored reservations. They were from think tanks or nonprofit groups with no stomach for real politics. Almost all of them believed additional public education would be necessary before we could go to the ballot box. Others warned that an early loss would set the movement back 20 years. We asked, "From where?" Ethan—really the only one who counted—knew I could finance the entire initiative alone if I had to. The ship was leaving the dock and he wanted to be a passenger. Somewhat reluctantly, Ethan agreed to help finance the focus groups and the polling. Then when he saw the results, his reservations faded.

Shaping the Initiative: Focus Groups and Polling

Campaigners customarily use the same public opinion firm for polling and for focus groups. We opted to split this function in order to reap maximum input from our experts. After all, we were venturing into uncharted waters. To lead our focus groups, we chose Celinda Lake in Washington, D.C., who had earned a fine reputation as a qualitative researcher while conducting Bill Clinton's focus groups for the 1992 campaign. To direct our polling, we selected San Francisco–based Paul Maslin, whose firm had extensive experience in shaping initiatives. The focus groups would give us an impressionist reading on public attitudes toward illegal drugs and the Drug War; polling would test these impressions and give us objective data on how voters would respond to specific language in an initiative.

Celinda wished to test some specific initiative language for the focus groups, so Sam and I developed a text for what would eventually come to be known as Proposition 200. It read as follows:

> No person shall be incarcerated for possession of a controlled substance for personal use. Those convicted of such a crime shall receive court-supervised treatment or an intermediate punishment

instead. This provision does not apply to any person who sells a controlled substance to a minor or who commits any drug offense while armed.

All persons currently incarcerated for possession of a controlled substance for personal use shall be considered for parole. This provision does not apply to any person who sells a controlled substance to a minor or who commits any drug offense while armed. This provision does not apply to offenders who are concurrently serving sentences for other crimes.

No physician prescribing, nor patient using any controlled substance for the purpose of alleviating the patient's pain and suffering, shall be charged with a criminal or professional violation or any Arizona statute, provided the physician has kept accurate records and has consulted with another physician regarding the patient's condition.

Those funds saved from not incarcerating persons convicted for non-violent personal use of a controlled substance shall be directed to treatment of drug abusers and education on the dangers of drug abuse. Such treatment shall be directed primarily to children and youth.

We conducted our focus groups in Phoenix and Tucson in April 1995. An early positive sign: When asked "Are we winning or losing the War on Drugs?," voters looked at each other and laughed. There was a near-consensus that the current program was a travesty. One woman was blunt: "I think the War on Drugs is a load of crap." Another indicator: Voters believed prison time for drug users was too harsh. Sanctions were needed, yes, but best would be a penalty somewhere between prison and nothing at all. Treatment proved most popular. Yet some voters suggested a limit be placed on the number of times offenders could qualify for mandatory treatment.

We tested buzzwords. More traditional terms—"decriminalization," "legalization"—received a resounding thumbs-down, as did the trendy "harm reduction." The term preferred by most was "medicalization." Voters tended to view the drug issue as public health problem, although they were clearly reluctant to depart wholly from drug control. Medicalization implied control and flexibility.

Most powerful in supporting our initiative was the argument that releasing nonviolent users from prison would free up vitally needed space for violent offenders. Also persuasive were the savings to be generated by alternative sentencing, savings to be invested in drug prevention for youth. As for medical use provisions, voters strongly felt that the doctor-patient relationship should enjoy protection at all costs. Most supported the medical use of marijuana despite its state and federal illegality. The specter of physicians prescribing other Schedule 1 drugs created some concern. However, the fundamental principle was that the doctor-patient relationship should be free from interference by the government. They also approved the use of a medication, if it was supported by scientific research, regardless of whether government had approved it. This view prevailed.

They were then read the text of the initiative and asked to vote. The language was approved by a margin of two to one. While focus group votes are not statistically valid, we were pleased to see how participants welcomed change. One thing was surely clear: Frustration with the current drug policies had created a huge opening for reform.

The next step was a poll. Paul Maslin, who had attended all the focus groups, prepared a survey to quantify opinion. Results of a May 1995 poll supported our earlier feedback. When voters were read the ballot language we had drafted, 63 percent voted "yes," 21 percent voted "no," and 16 percent remained undecided. When asked if we were winning or losing the War on Drugs, 91 percent said losing, and only 5 percent winning. Some 56 percent wished for more treatment and education. Only 20 percent favored more law enforcement and prisons.

Even the initiative's more controversial provisions tested well. What we feared might be liabilities—for example, that the medical use provisions could extend to other drugs—proved no problem. The provision that doctors can prescribe "marijuana and heroin" encouraged some 70 percent of voters to support us even more. Similarly, the provision calling for the immediate parole of offenders made some 70 percent of voters more likely to vote "yes."

With medicalization so popular in the focus groups, we used the term to describe the initiative and placed it beside other approaches. Results reassured: 46 percent supported medicalization, 11 percent legalization, 9 percent decriminalization. Only 22 percent backed current policy. The poll was mirroring the focus groups. Voters were seeking a middle course—some as-yet-unspecified Golden Mean between the Drug War and decriminalization/legalization. Medicalization offered a fresh approach.

After hearing arguments pro and con and hearing the ballot language again, participants voted 69 percent "yes," 21 percent "no," and 10 percent undecided. We were astounded to see ideas so controversial receiving such enthusiastic public support. We felt we might have detected a political revolt; surely it was our race to lose. We now had the basic foundation upon which to base a campaign. The Drug War had been fueled by rhetoric and billions of dollars. Two of its major linchpins were the slogan "Do Drugs, Do Time" and the belief that marijuana is demonic—a gateway drug that leads to the use of hard drugs. By severing this link between drugs and prison, and by medicalizing drugs such as marijuana, our initiative might well deconstruct the fundamental premises of the Drug War and serve as a harbinger of radical drug policy reform.

Drafting the Language

Drafting the language proved a most important, time-consuming step. Unlike legislation, an initiative cannot be amended after submission and circulation, and once the press exposes an initiative as flawed, voters grow suspicious and reluctant. The wording of the ballot can dramatically affect the outcome. We had heard of a San Francisco attorney, Barry Fadem, whose practice was limited to writing initiatives and who had a reputation for language that was both precise and astute. In June 1995, Sam and I interviewed him and came away impressed. Thereafter the three of us worked closely on the draft.

The term "medicalization," so popular among the focus groups and respondents, was hardly a household term. Yet we believed the term should be part of the title. So far, the public and press knew only the get-tough language of the drug warriors and the get-soft language of the legalizers. Second, "decriminalization" was not a popular term: We were dealing with all illegal drugs, not just marijuana. Third, we needed a novel term to save us from polarizing the debate along familiar lines. "Medicalization" was necessary to describe a totally new approach. The term would also link medical use provisions for Schedule 1 drugs to alternative sentencing for users. Physicians could prescribe medical marijuana—a public health approach focusing on treatment instead of incarceration. Although medicalization implies control, we wanted to stress that the initiative would increase funding for prevention programs through savings that would come from releasing drug users from expensive prison cells into outpatient treatment at one-tenth the cost. Our final title was "The Drug Medicalization, Prevention, and Control Act of 1996."

We now had to decide on the components of the initiative that would be submitted to the Secretary of State. Our focus groups had told us voters wanted a cap on the number of chances offenders would have before facing jail. We decided on two—what we later advertised as our own "three strikes and you're out" clause. In place of prison would be treatment or education with probation.

While drugs like methamphetamine and crack cocaine had received floods of negative press, we decided to include all illegal drugs in our sentencing provision. Exempting certain drugs would only abet our opponents' argument. And we wanted to keep a maximum number of nonviolent offenders out of prison. We also decided not to change statutory penalties from felonies to misdemeanors. We knew our foes would be sure to characterize the initiative as *legalization;* our focus on sentencing would ensure the ballot would not mention *changes in criminal penalties.* Moreover, this maneuver was consistent with the message of the campaign: There is a new way—medicalization—a midpoint alternative to the Drug War and legalization.

The medical use provisions spawned some disagreement. I was adamant that we include all Schedule 1 drugs, including LSD and heroin, instead of allowing doctors to prescribe only medical marijuana, and focus groups and polling data supported this position. However, our opposition could easily exploit such a broad inclusion. After going round and round on the issue we decided to include all Schedule 1 drugs—with the caveat that a physician support each prescription with scientific research and a second opinion. To the public, our position would thus be eminently rational, inasmuch as marijuana is currently the only Schedule 1 drug with sufficient research to support its use. We included the other Schedule 1 drugs in the event that future research might support their use.

In both our poll and focus groups we had discussed allocating money saved from not incarcerating users into treatment and prevention programs. The complex budgeting process of state government made this impossible. To generate revenue we would have to dedicate a fund. Sponsors of initiatives seek revenue sources such as the lottery or the tobacco tax for funding that is safely beyond the long reach of politicians. Already the Arizona lottery had been badly chopped up.

Recently the tobacco tax had been increased significantly. We opted for the liquor tax because most of it already went to prisons or the general fund. But we were careful not to raise the liquor tax and to earmark only $15 million per year to fund our treatment and prevention programs.

Instead of having police officers talk to children about drugs, as in the Drug Awareness Resistance Education (DARE) program, we wanted the involvement of parents. We would establish a Parents Commission on Drug Education and Prevention that would receive half of the funding generated by our share of the liquor tax. This move also had political appeal: Who could oppose parents working to reduce drug use?

Making our sentencing provisions retroactive to include some 2,000 nonviolent Arizona jailed drug violators was also tricky. We preferred to avoid any Willie Horton–like ads by our opposition. Should we free prisoners without review? have parole boards review their cases? return their cases to sentencing judges for review? Initially we chose the last alternative, but later shifted to the second due to constitutional separation-of-powers issues raised. We decided to set guidelines to inoculate our opposition from exploiting this provision. Prisoners eligible for review by the parole-handling Arizona Executive Board of Clemency would include only those serving time for drug possession and no other offense, who had not been convicted of a violent crime, and who had not been sentenced under a three-strikes-and-you're-out statute. In addition, Sam wanted anyone who sold drugs to minors or was armed while committing a drug-related offense to serve 100 percent of their sentence.

For Sam, a political operator, proposing language that was tough on violent offenders was an obvious move, but liberals in our group did not want to deprive anyone of a chance for parole. Sam pointed out that the state's truth-in-sentencing provisions already required violent offenders to serve 85 percent of their sentence. Increasing this to 100 percent would not be a significant change and, more important, it would inoculate us from appearing soft on drugs. This provision made its way into the "yes/no" ballot language.

To shape the most favorable language, we ordered the sequence of provisions carefully. The Secretary of State was inclined to follow the statutory sequence in preparing the descriptive title and yes/no language for an initiative. Either our Parents Commission or our violent-offender provision entering the yes/no language would put us in good shape.

The provisions were ordered as follows: (1) the establishment of an Arizona Parents Commission on Drug Education and Prevention, (2) the requirement that violent drug offenders serve 100 percent of their sentence, (3) the right of doctors to prescribe Schedule 1 drugs and exemption of patients from prosecution, (4) the requirement that current drug-possession inmates be eligible for parole, (5) the probation component mandating treatment instead of incarceration for those convicted of drug possession on their first two offenses, and (6) the funding mechanism, to include earmarking the liquor tax and establishing the Drug Treatment and Education Fund.

Senators DeConcini and Goldwater Sign On

During the period in which we were drafting the final form of the initiative, I made a major breakthrough. I was able to convince former U.S. Senator Dennis DeConcini to consider supporting the measure. His brother Dino and I had tried for several years to convince him that the Drug War was a failure, but it was not until he left the Senate that we were able truly to get his attention. During his time in the Senate, Dennis had earned a reputation as a drug warrior—at one time being asked by President Bush to serve as the nation's drug czar. However, he now agreed that it was better to steer users of drugs into treatment rather than prison and that the medical use of marijuana should be approved. While supportive of the international drug war, Dennis understood the pressing domestic need for a public health approach. But he would first go over the wording of any initiative very carefully before signing on.

In our many conversations with Dennis, he changed several terms in the findings-and-declarations section to ensure that voters would know we were not abandoning the criminal justice system. Two substantive issues gave him trouble: (1) that second-time offenders would stay out of jail even if they did not comply with treatment and (2) the overly broad nature of our Schedule 1 prescription provisions. We conceded the latter when we added language that gives the state Board of Medical Examiners the power to investigate any failure to comply with the medical use provisions; he conceded the former.

With Dennis's support in hand, we moved to get that of former

U.S. Senator Barry Goldwater. Our citizen group had a distinguished membership but few household names. These two endorsements would do much to inoculate us against charges that we were some far-out group seeking to legalize drugs. John Norton, President of the Goldwater Institute, was our conduit. He sent our final draft to Goldwater and then met with him and his wife Susan. After careful review, Senator Goldwater sent us an enthusiastic letter of endorsement.

Armed with the buy-in of Arizona's two best-known statesmen and a distinguished group of citizens, and with the final language politically and legally precise, we were ready to file. Our group convened, reviewed the language, gave unanimous support. On October 20, 1995, we filed the initiative and established the campaign committee of Arizonans for Drug Policy Reform, with chairman John Norton, a former Reagan official, and Treasurer Marvin Cohen, a former Carter appointee.

The Stealth Campaign Begins

Conventional wisdom holds that launching a campaign involves a huge press conference. Sam filed our initiative at 4:45 P.M. on a Friday, after the press had left the capitol building and while the bureaucrats were busy planning the weekend. Usually the filing of an initiative prompts the Secretary of State's office to notify the press. In this case, it wouldn't have mattered.

Why persist with stealth? Simple: Survey results conclusively demonstrate that voters don't decide how they will vote on initiatives until the last few weeks. Campaigns are not exercises in public education wherein one incrementally wins support for a fundamental change in public policy. Campaigns are like storms raging in the final weeks of an Arizona monsoon. Polling data showed it: We had everything to lose, nothing to gain, by raising our visibility.

There was a happy glitch in our stealth approach: Editors at the *Arizona Daily Star,* the state's second-largest newspaper, had caught wind of our initiative. On November 13, 1995, the paper endorsed us in a glowing editorial, "A Sane Drug Policy," which argued, "Again, the measure would seem a great move toward rationalizing an irrational superstructure of flawed law by targeting penalties where penalties remain essential and treatment where all the experts deem treatment in order." The item encouraged voters to sign petitions. Since this exposure was in Tucson, the item was unlikely to flash across the radar screen of potential foes up in Phoenix, the state Capital. It gave a tremendous boost to our credibility and provided the only printed literature we would hand out in our campaign. From the appearance of this editorial until we filed our signatures in July— some eight months later—not a single word had been written about the initiative in any Arizona newspaper.

Meanwhile, as is customary in initiative campaigns, we had subcontracted our signature drive to a professional firm, Lee Petition Management Inc. The drive was going well. Circulators found it remarkably easy to get signatures. They noted how the initiative offered something for everybody. Some voters liked the medical marijuana provisions; others, the stress on treatment and prevention; others, the money saved and the prison space freed for violent offenders; and still others, that violent drug offenders must serve their full sentences.

But mainly we clung to invisibility. Our campaign was run entirely out of Sam's 1,300-square-foot house. Its telephone number was a voice mailbox. Its address was a post office box. Sam had learned a valuable lesson from previous races: the less money spent on staff and overhead, the more left to spend at the end communicating with voters.

Neutralizing Potential Opponents

Our next step was neutralization. In the months following, we met with all the state's political leaders and got to them before an opposition formed and exploded the issue with standard drug-scare tactics. In all but a few of these visits we sought not support but neutrality—the best one could expect from current elected officials. After all, the politicians had created the Drug War and had made it into such an emotional issue that even those politicians who knew the Drug War was a form of popular insanity were powerless even to suggest reform. The depth of political debate was well illustrated by Speaker Newt Gingrich: "Bring drugs into the country and we'll kill you." We thought it important to let these officials know we were not political activists or legalizers but citizens who wished to change failed policies.

Members of our group of distinguished citizens met with nearly all of the state's Congressional delegation—with U.S. Representatives

Jim Kolbe, John Shadegg, Ed Pastor, and Matt Salmon. Save for the very conservative Shadegg, all said they would be unlikely to work actively against us. Pastor, an Hispanic and the only Democrat in the Arizona Congressional delegation, was sympathetic because of the impact sentencing was having on minorities. The last member of the delegation, J. D. Hayworth, was visited by one of our prominent doctors, Jeff Singer, a major Hayworth fund-raiser. Singer was able to neutralize him behind the scenes. We opted to avoid U.S. senators Jon Kyl and John McCain, since the less they knew of the issue the better.

Sam and I targeted law enforcement. Former Senator DeConcini was a friend of Maricopa County's Joe Arpaio, world-renowned as "America's Toughest Sheriff," and helped open the door. After politely heeding his spiel about pink underwear, chain gangs, and the tent-city jail, we began to inform the Sheriff of our initiative. He interrupted to tell us about several new inmate programs in the works. We knew that Arpaio was the one man who could defeat the initiative. He had two decades' experience as a DEA agent, favorability ratings topping 90 percent, and an unmatched ability to generate media attention. Dennis followed up our visit with a call and received the impression that Arpaio would remain out of the fray.

Pima County sheriff Clarence Dupnik, also a friend of Dennis's, had a personality quite different from Arpaio. During our meeting he said little. But he was sympathetic to diversion programs and liked the notion of treatment funding, and would be much more likely to support our initiative if he were not running for office again. While we saw him as an unlikely enemy, we were wrong.

Pima County Prosecutor Steve Neely liked some of our ideas but felt they would be better accomplished through legislation. Neely was more into quitting his job and moving to New Zealand to begin a new life than he was into Arizona politics. He would probably stay quiet, he told us.

Our most bizarre meeting was with Maricopa County Attorney Rick Romley—an encounter we dreaded because of his fervent antidrug crusader stance. Romley had been arrested for marijuana use as an 18-year-old and had avoided jail by enlisting in the Marine Corps. In a speech while running for County Attorney in 1988, Romley said of that incident, "Had it not been for a youth-intervention program for me, at that point in time, which was the

Marine Corps, who knows if I would have had as full and productive of a life as I have today." What that statement omits is that he was sent to Vietnam, where he lost both legs in a grenade explosion. We suspected that Romley was somewhat irrational on the subject of marijuana. Fortunately for us, he was deeply involved in another ballot measure regarding juvenile justice. Still, meeting with Romley demanded reinforcements. Sam and I took along John Norton, who knew Romley from the Goldwater Institute, and Dr. Singer, who had done medical consultation with Romley. None of this mattered. Romley began by passing out photos of babies deformed by what he claimed were marijuana-smoking mothers. From here the discussion went downhill. Romley reached the acme of Orwellian doublespeak when he explained that his program, "Do Drugs, Do Time," would make our initiative unnecessary. Romley remained volatile throughout, flashing his fetus pictures.

Our only hope was that his jihad on juvenile justice would prevent his spearheading a campaign against us. In an added effort to calm Romley down, I had one of the partners from Snell & Wilmer, our corporate counsel, assure him that I was not a drug legalizer and was only interested in reform. Anything that would delay Romley's entrance into the conflict, the better.

My next step was to arrange a lunch with Attorney General Grant Woods, set up by one of our supporters, Phoenix attorney Danny Cracchiolo. Woods agreed that the Drug War was a failure, but didn't feel our ballot measure was the proper time for such a radical step. Nonetheless, he agreed to keep a low profile, even if prodded by law enforcement to oppose us. Grant was honest: He knew and we knew that this was not going to be a stealth campaign forever.

A most revealing meeting occurred with Mike Petchel, President of the powerful Phoenix Law Enforcement Association (PLEA). During a Power Point presentation of our polling and some sample commercials showcasing former Senator DeConcini, Mike was quiet and attentive. At the end, with a near-hypnotic gaze, he uttered, "I have seen the costs of the War on Drugs in terms of corrupting law enforcement. What we're doing clearly isn't working. But, you know, it's like communism, you have to be against it." In the end, Petchel made no commitment regarding his union. What was clear is that he had experienced some kind of epiphany.

As for the state legislature, we met Senate President John Greene, Senate Minority Leader Peter Goudinoff, and House Minority Leader Art Hamilton. The meeting with Greene went well. He would remain neutral. Goudinoff was so enthused that he offered to appear in TV ads for us. Hamilton, an African American, had a brother doing time for drugs and understood at first hand the disproportionate incarceration rates for minorities. While he would not endorse, he would remain quietly supportive. We never met Speaker of the House Mark Killian. We were forewarned that the Mormon Killian was a drug warrior like Romley, and one of those was enough.

Our visits to African-American ministers and Hispanic leaders precipitated a response so positive that we hired Tio Tachias, Executive Director of the Arizona Leadership Institute, to organize an outreach effort to target minority communities. Mel Hannah formed a coalition of African-American ministers with the Arizona Urban League. In these communities we enjoyed near-universal support. Not a single African-American or Hispanic leader opposed our initiative.

Our attempts to neutralize key elected and law enforcement officials worked well. In almost every case, those who had agreed to remain neutral kept their word. Even the people who would eventually oppose us, like Sheriff Dupnik and Representative Salmon, didn't change colors until very late, and even then they remained largely mute. Ultimately, what kept these powerful leaders relatively quiet was that none of them thought our initiative had a prayer.

More Focus Groups to Shape Our Advertisements

On March 20, 1996, we conducted more focus groups. Rather than replay verbal arguments, we decided to simulate a campaign, with TV ads testing messages for and against us. With a camcorder, cheap editing, and stock footage, Sam produced 10 pro and con commercials. Helpful were the ads from Partnership for a Drug Free America—it took very little to convert them into opposition messages. We now saw much that we had seen before. Commercials citing the failure of the Drug War and speaking of a "better way" were commercials people liked. One in particular showed a victim informing us that her rapist had already been free for several years while a grandmother in

Tucson was still serving a life sentence for selling marijuana. Sam tested this ad with a friend who was a rape victim. She had agreed to appear for the focus group only, but after Sam and I had lunch with her, she agreed to do a final ad.

When we showed the opposition ads, featuring hardened criminals leaving jail and other Drug War scare tactics, they were not as effective as we had feared. Our commercials showing the endorsements of Barry Goldwater and Dennis DeConcini had provided us significant political cover. As one woman put it, "I don't like DeConcini, but he's about as tough on drugs as you can get."

An early May poll revealed that, despite our stealth, we had upped our lead, and sharply: 78 percent "yes," 10 percent "no," and 11 percent undecided. Clearly the election was framed in a way benefiting us. No need yet to depart the closet.

We finished our signature drive by late May, a month before signatures were due. The statutory number required was 112,000. Because many voters who sign petitions are not properly registered, we collected 200,000 to ensure a cushion. We audited the signatures carefully to make sure they were valid. On July 3, 1998, again in the media dead zone of 4:45 P.M., we submitted our signatures to the Secretary of State. This being the day before Independence Day made it even more unlikely we would generate attention. After the Secretary verified 212,500 signatures, the initiative was assigned its name: Proposition 200. Still, the only media activities were a few generic stories about all the 1996 ballot initiatives. Proposition 200 received hardly a paragraph.

Negotiating the Ballot Language

An early sign of our stealth campaign's success was the Secretary of State's publicity pamphlet in which citizens and groups could submit pro and con arguments for each ballot measure. The sole argument leveled against Proposition 200 was from the Arizona Libertarian Party, and they opposed the initiative for not promoting full-blown legalization. Meanwhile, pro statements were written by former U.S. Senator Dennis DeConcini; John Norton, Former U.S. Deputy Secretary of Agriculture; Marvin Cohen, Former Chairman of the Civil Aeronautics Board; Steve Mitchell, former U.S. Attorney and police officer; Court of Appeals Judge Rudy Gerber; myself; and a score of doctors.

Another sign of success was in the yes/no ballot language prepared by the Secretary of State. Our lack of viable opposition had left a huge vacuum for suggestions to make to the State Election Director, Lisa Daniels. Steve Mitchell, who joined our group in April, knew Lisa very well as a former coworker at the Office of the Attorney General. Steve made some key suggestions to Lisa about the final language. He emphasized that her office follow the lead of the legislative council that prepares summaries of ballot measures. The Legislative Counsel had placed the violent-drug-offender provision first because it was the initiative's first provision and the Counsel's summary did not mention any specific drug, since Proposition 200 makes no reference to such.

Steve's work paid off. The ballot language read:

A "Yes" vote shall have the effect of requiring the entire sentence to be served by persons who commit violent crimes while on drugs, changing sentences for persons convicted of possession or use of controlled substances, and allowing doctors to prescribe otherwise illegal substances for certain patients.

A "No" vote shall have the effect of retaining current laws on controlled substances.

This language was effective. It placed our most popular provision as the first clause of the "yes" vote and mentioned no specific drugs. The sentencing provisions did not include the most controversial plank regarding parole. Finally, the "no" language's "retaining current laws" was ideal for our message that the current system was failing and we needed a fresh, novel way.

Campaigning for the Vote

On September 10, 1996, the campaign officially began. Drug Czar Barry McCaffrey flew to Tucson to convince the Arizona law enforcement community to oppose Proposition 200. At a postmeeting press conference, he blasted the Proposition, claiming, "It is bad medicine, bad science, and it's a violation of federal law. . . . More importantly, it's a cruel hoax. . . . It has a fatal flaw that, in my judgment, is designed into it by the drug legalization group." Fortunately, no TV reporters were at the conference. The story appeared only in Tucson papers.

This was our opposition's first salvo. Had McCaffrey not become involved, there might have been no campaign against us. The damage was not the scant press coverage he had generated, but his leaning so heavily on law enforcement and drug prevention leaders to take more active part in opposition. Prominent here were Alex Romero, President of Arizonans for a Drug Free Youth and Communities Inc.; Sheriff Dupnik, who, under pressure from law enforcement peers, led the Arizona Sheriffs Association in opposition; and Jack Braddoch, a representative for liquor distributors. Romero was the garden-variety drug warrior. Despite his promise to stay neutral, Dupnik had been prodded into action by McCaffrey's control of law enforcement funding. Braddoch was involved because, even though Proposition 200 did not raise the liquor tax, the industry was concerned it might set a precedent for increases, as had occurred often with the tobacco tax.

Then we had an unexpected break—a young volunteer with Arizonans for Drug Free Youth and Communities defected to our side. He was close to Alex Romero, the president, and from that time on we had advance knowledge of all their plans. Even though the McCaffrey visit energized the organization, they got no press coverage. Their most visible activity was to picket my office, from the street. Other than the McCaffrey visit, during the entire month of September we neither saw nor heard a single media mention of Proposition 200.

By early October I had shaped the details of our funding. While Soros and I had paid the several hundred thousand dollars it took to qualify Proposition 200, we needed an additional $1,000,000 for our statewide media buy. In exchange for my contributions to the California medical marijuana initiative that was strongly supported by Ethan, Soros convened a meeting in New York with Peter Lewis and myself. We formed a consortium in which each of us contributed $335,000 to the Arizona campaign. These funds allowed us, in the final two weeks before the election, to turn our stealth campaign into a blitzkrieg.

Our mole in Romero's operation informed us that our most dangerous foe was neither law enforcement nor the antidrug community. The threat was the liquor industry—an industry highly upset by the earmarked liquor tax and an industry seriously considering spending hundreds of thousands to defeat Proposition 200. The liquor lobby had convinced the Arizona Chamber of Commerce to serve as a front and on October 11 the Chamber established a campaign committee called Citizens for a Drug Free Arizona. Tim Lawless, deputy director of the Chamber, served as Chairman and the Chamber's office was listed as the committee's address.

On October 10, Phoenix Police Chief Dennis Garrett and the heads of the state's FBI and DEA attacked Proposition 200. Ernest Howard, with the DEA, put it bluntly: "In effect, this is saying, do the crime avoid the time." We responded by pointing out these were employees of a failed drug war, motivated only by job protection. On October 16, we launched our media attack. We wanted to ensure that the liquor industry was not funneling money through the Chamber of Commerce and that as little as possible of the Chamber of Commerce's resources would be used against us. We filed a complaint with the Attorney General arguing that the Chamber was illegally providing undisclosed, in-kind contributions. While nothing came of this complaint, it clearly rocked the Citizens for a Drug Free Arizona and hampered its activities.

I sought a meeting with liquor lobbyist Michael Greene and warned him that an industry attack would spawn retaliation. After that meeting, a well-respected lobbyist and one of our supporters played one of our antiliquor TV ads for the benefit of several liquor lobbyists. The ad said: "Why are the drug legalizers and liquor lobbyists trying to defeat Prop. 200? Maybe it's because drug use is up among our youth [clips of teenagers doing drugs]? Or maybe its because alcohol use is soaring [clips of teenagers drinking]?" We could link the industry to drug legalizers because the libertarian legalizers were the only group to write a voter pamphlet statement in opposition to Proposition 200. The ad got the attention of the honchos in the liquor industry. Knowing that we had an effective retaliatory strike if liquor money were to show up late, they became minor players.

We unleashed our million-dollar radio-TV assault, on October 18. As our first tracking poll showed, we had a commanding lead—61 percent "yes," 23 percent "no," 15 percent undecided. We would start with our safest commercials to preserve our edge. The ad we led with featured former U.S. Senator DeConcini, whom our polling and focus groups had told us would be our strongest inoculating messenger. DeConcini described Proposition 200 as a new way to fight drugs that is not soft on drugs: The measure is tougher on violent drug offenders and contains its own "three strikes and you're out" clause. As with all our ads, DeConcini ended with the tag line that current policy is not working and that "Proposition 200 is a new and better way." A second ad was a montage of endorsements taken from Goldwater's letter of endorsement and supporting newspaper articles and editorials followed by comments: A former policeman makes his point about treatment over incarceration, a mother with her children speaks about the new emphasis on prevention, an elderly female caps the ad with, "Everybody knows we're losing the War on Drugs. Proposition 200 gives us a new and better way."

Meanwhile, the opposition's efforts were in such disarray that a reporter had to jump-start them. In an October 19 *Arizona Republic* item titled "Lawmen Relatively Silent on Prop. 200," County Attorney Romley complained that law enforcement had been lulled to sleep. A spokesperson for Attorney General Woods said, "He's not doing handsprings about it, but he doesn't like it." Sheriff Arpaio said he would take no position and was into other ballot measures. Ed Wrenn, a lobbyist for the Phoenix Law Enforcement Association and the Arizona Highway Patrol Association, said the groups had decided not to take a position on Proposition 200 because it had points good and bad. The *Republic* article invigorated law enforcement personnel, who looked like they were asleep at the wheel. The truth was that our strategy of neutralization was keeping every major law enforcement official out of the race until two weeks before its end.

Finally the politicians jumped in. U.S. Senator Jon Kyl and state Senator Tom Patterson, a physician, held a press conference on October 24, 1998. Kyl spoke of "one of the most misleading and dangerous drug propositions ever to be put on the Arizona ballot." A media rally the next day found U.S. Representative Salmon and former state Senator Chuck Blanchard, a "liberal" Democrat soon to become McCaffrey's chief legal aide, focused on the "thousands of dangerous felons" that would be released onto Arizona streets with the passage of Proposition 200.

A few days before these attacks we changed our commercial rotation, supplanting the DeConcini spot with an ad featuring Steve Mitchell, a former police officer and an Assistant U.S. Attorney. As Mitchell's kids play on slides, he points out how, both as a policeman and as a U.S. Attorney, he had witnessed the utter failure of our policies on the streets and in the courts. Choked with emotion, he warns, "I'm afraid that if we don't try something different my children could be the next victims." Another ad, which we rotated less frequently into the mix, showcased prison overcrowding and the millions it cost our state: Viewers beheld a jammed prison setting with an odometer tabulating the cost.

Our October 25 tracking poll showed the campaign healthy: 59 percent "yes," 26 percent "no," 15 percent undecided. As we tested our argument that Proposition 200 would be a new way of reducing drugs versus the charge that it was only a disguised effort to legalize, 55 percent supported it and only 25 percent were against it. One of the opposition's gravest errors was to harp on legalization. Though generally opposed to legalization, voters were clearly able to distinguish between legalization and drug policy reform.

On October 29, the near-statewide *Arizona Republic* railed against us in an editorial, "Proposition 200: One Toke Over the Line." While we had pocketed the endorsements of the state's three other major newspapers—the *Mesa Tribune,* the *Arizona Daily Star,* and the *Tucson Citizen*—The *Arizona Republic* was by far the most influential, and concluded, "The federal drug war is far from won, as Proposition 200's proponents correctly point out. But their strategy is tantamount to a surrender." The three papers supporting us had all reached the opposite conclusion—that Proposition 200 offered bold, new alternatives to the failed War on Drugs.

It was now time to unleash our two strongest commercials. One featured the rape victim in the focus groups, who addressed prison overcrowding and the fact that drug users serve lengthier sentences than her rapist. The other began with horrifying headlines along with photos of violent crimes committed by people under drug influence. In one case, a methamphetamine addict killed his son. The ad cited Proposition 200's requirement of full prison time for the violent offender, as throughout these words sounded: "Commit a violent drug crime, do full prison time." But the ad ended on a light, positive note: kids playing on a slide as a narrator emphasizes the prevention and treatment aspects.

The final barrage from the drug warriors came on October 30, when former Presidents Bush, Carter, and Ford released a signed letter to the media condemning our initiative and the California Proposition 215 that would legalize medical marijuana. "Both initiatives are hoaxes that seek to cloak drug legalization under the guise of compassion for the ill or strengthening drug laws," the letter warned. "Their passage would presage further increases in drug use by our children." The next day found Drug Czar McCaffrey in Phoenix with the International Association of Chiefs of Police in a rally including Attorney General Woods, Maricopa County Attorney Romley; Phoenix Police Chief Dennis Garrett, U.S. Senator Kyl, and Thomas Constantine of the Drug Enforcement Agency. Ringed by chiefs who had unanimously voted to oppose Proposition 200, McCaffrey declared: "What kind of message does this send to our children to say that heroin and methamphetamine is medicine? We see this as the legalization of all drugs."

We took hits. Yes, our tracking polls revealed it. The weekend before the November 5 election showed our support dwindling: 47 percent "yes," 28 percent "no," 21 percent undecided. Many of our soft and lean "yes" voters were moving into "undecided." Fortunately, the "no" vote still hovered under 30 percent. But the momentum appeared to be against us. It might be a long election night.

Election Night

That night found us in a suite at the Phoenix Hyatt Regency. The polls closed at 7 P.M., when our supporters began drifting in. I probed Sam's eyes, looking for a sign, but none came. With the Secretary of State purportedly in possession of on-line, up-to-date results, Sam sat at his laptop, watching the returns. Suddenly shouts erupted in the room adjoining. "Exit polls say we will win." As statewide elections lack exit polls, I was curious. Evidently this poll was linked to the Presidential race, and the ballot measures had been tacked on.

Sam, the expert, was not ready to celebrate. An hour later came the first results—some 200,000 early ballots from all over the state. We held a huge lead—two to one! At that point even Sam admitted victory. The final margin was 65.4 percent to 34.6 percent. Victory, yes. A battle won, but scarcely a war. That same night the California medical marijuana initiative passed with a margin of 56 percent to 44 percent.

Although these victories did nothing to end the Drug War, they opened up for the first time in 20 years the possibility for public criticism of the Drug War. As a front-page story in the *Los Angeles Times* declared, "Arizona Begins Revolt Against Drug War." The story noted, "No more, 'do drugs, do time' programs. No more 'zero tolerance.' No more holding jail time over the heads of offenders who balk at orders to attend rehabilitation classes." The initiatives had changed the terms of the debate over the wisdom of our drug policies, and changing the terms of a debate is halfway to winning a debate. The Drug War had been created out of the whole cloth of political rhetoric, an insidious rhetoric that traffics in fear and paranoia.

Shortly after the election, General McCaffrey declared the term "Drug War" a disaster and, together with the National Center for Drug Abuse (a command post of the drug war), called for an end to mandatory minimum sentencing, a cornerstone of the Drug War. Drug prevention service announcements, once beyond criticism, were now seen for what they are—useless scare tactics. Perhaps more important, nationally syndicated cartoonists could mock the pomposities, inanities, and lies of the Drug War propaganda. Mockery is a great corrosive for demolishing stupid public policy.

All this was a plus, but our postelection euphoria did not last long. Within days, we were once more in a battle with the drug warriors, as will be recounted in Part III of "Giving Back."

13 | Giving Back

Part III
The Second Battle
for Proposition 200

When two-thirds of the voters support a change in obviously failed policies, one would think that politicians would pay them some heed. The fact that, following the overwhelming passage of Propositions 200 and 215, an overwhelming number of elected officials at the national, state, and local levels immediately concluded that the voters were dupes provides pretty strong evidence that the political community has a deep emotional commitment to the War on Drugs.

Most of the Christian social conservative legislators equate drugs with evil, as has always been the case with "demonism": drugs are a vile thing that must be extirpated at whatever cost. When the voters reject this thinking, then the devil has led them astray and their error must be corrected. The response of social conservatives is understandable. It is the moderate legislators, the pragmatists, who are the nut cases. They are so convinced that a vote for drug reform is political suicide that they cannot see political cover even when it stares them in the face. In Arizona, their fear was so great that they were convinced that only by voting against the voters could they avoid being tagged by their next appoint as soft on drugs. Obviously, with pathological commitment to obviously failed policies so profound, reform of our drug laws is going to be a long, slow, and tedious process.

The Fallout

The victories in Arizona and California lasted only a few hours before there began a full-scale, multifront assault against Proposition 200. As the votes were being counted on election night, I was asked to conduct a television interview. Before the reporter could ask me the first question, someone shouted, "Come here quick, Governor Fife Symington is holding an emergency press conference. He says he will veto the drug measure." "Oh, shit!" I thought as the reporter, with due apologies, left to cover the Governor.

No Arizona governor had ever threatened to veto a ballot measure, and for good reason; it's not legal for them to do so. But the law had never been a problem for Fife Symington. In his private life, Symington was a high-profile developer of office complexes and had been elected mainly because he promised to bring his business acumen to the business of government. Rather than being the success he claimed, he had fraudulently held bankruptcy at bay while he campaigned for governor. Now he had been indicted for filing false financial statements and inflated appraisals on properties whose values had collapsed. Presumably he calculated that vetoing Proposition 200 would help him beat the rap, but it didn't. He would be found guilty on several of these counts although his conviction was set aside on a technicality. Fortunately, Attorney General Grant Woods was quick to the rescue, supporting the constitution and threatening to take Symington to court if he tried any sort of veto: "Our opinion is, he has no authority to veto what the people overwhelmingly favor. We expect him to follow the law, and if he chooses not to, we expect to see him in court."

Our opponents at the editorial board of *The Arizona Republic* were equally quick to defend the governor with an editorial praising the threat: "Governor, You're Correct, So Why Stop Now?" However, most of the public reaction was negative, including comments from the *Republic*'s political columnist, Kevin Willey, whose postelection column on the veto was entitled "Governor May Be Losing It." Meanwhile, a statewide poll showed that 90 percent of likely voters opposed the gubernatorial veto.

The public uproar and the Attorney General's threat caused the governor to retreat from his veto position. Within days, he said he would not veto the measures, rather he would work to undo Proposition 200 through the legislative process. He stated he would wage this legislative battle because "Proposition 200 is not something that I am sure everyone is fully aware of [because of] some of the implications that are hidden in that initiative." The attack now moved from the governor's office to the Arizona legislature and thence to the U.S. Senate and the Office of the Drug Czar, General Barry McCaffrey. We now realized that Proposition 200 had been a skirmish; the real fight was still to come.

General McCaffrey and his congressional supporters were not about to admit defeat. Even though Propositions 200 and 215 had decriminalized drugs in state law, all federal drug war statutes remained in force. In mid-November, McCaffrey's office brought state and local law enforcement officials to Washington to plot anti-Propositions 200 and 215 strategy. "What is at stake is a very cunning national strategy to legalize marijuana and other drugs," McCaffrey said. "We simply don't believe a drugged, stoned America is an outcome we're going to take lightly." McCaffrey made it clear that the voters in Arizona and California were "hoodwinked" by well-financed, deceptive advertising campaigns, so that the voter mandate did not matter. McCaffrey promised to announce his final battle plan in late December.

Meanwhile, in the U.S. Senate the effort to overturn the ballot measures was also moving with lightning speed. An emergency session of the U.S. Senate Judiciary Committee was called in early December for the sole purpose of dealing with the Arizona and California initiatives. Chairman Orrin Hatch (R-Utah) requested that George Soros and I come to defend our support of the two ballot measures; we respectfully declined. Instead, Sam persuaded Marv Cohen, the Phoenix attorney who had helped to draft Proposition 200, to testify on the pro side. Cohen had been the head of the Civil Aeronautics Board under President Jimmy Carter and had extensive experience in testifying before Congress.

On December 2, 1996, the Senate Judiciary Committee held a hearing on Propositions 200 and 215. The hearing was covered live by C-Span, and press from around the world was present. The hearing was unprecedented. The U.S. Senate had never before sought to overturn a state referendum ballot measure. The atmosphere in the room was similar to that at the McCarthy hearings, only now they were the McCaffrey hearings. Senator Orrin Hatch presided over the hearing with a sense of urgency as if the passage of Propositions 200 and 215 were hastening the end of civilization as he knew it.

Senator Hatch was flanked by Arizona's Senator Jon Kyl and their conservative brethren. The more "liberal" members of the committee did not attend the meeting. Hatch's and Kyl's message was clear: The voters of Arizona and California had been duped by money and slick media campaigns. "I must tell you I am extraordinarily embarrassed," Senator Kyl said. "I believe most [state voters] were deceived, and deliberately so, by the sponsors of this proposition." Hatch called the law "ridiculous" and stated that it would breed a new medical profession of "pothead doctors." Hatch added that the Arizona advertising was "totally deceptive" since the commercials sold Proposition 200 as a new way of fighting drugs. Maricopa Attorney Rick Romley, a welcome guest at the hearing, called the ballot measure "nightmarish."

To illustrate their point, the Senators played commercials from the Arizona and California campaigns. We were stunned when commercials that had never aired on the television were shown to the audience. The only way these commercials could have been obtained by the Senate was by some illegal conspiracy between the Judiciary Committee and the Arizona media. One Proposition 200 commercial linked the liquor lobby and the libertarian drug legalizers as opponents of the initiative. As was previously pointed out, the commercial was never meant to run, but was made only to intimidate the liquor industry and keep it from spending money against Proposition 200. How the Senate Judiciary Committee got hold of these tapes remains a mystery. However, the illegal use of these tapes only reinforced the McCarthy-like atmosphere of the hearing.

Marv Cohen, the only dissenting voice at the hearing, sketched the history of Proposition 200 and explained why the initiative was not deceptive. Proposition 200 was constructed through focus groups and polls of Arizonans, which showed that the public was convinced that the Drug War was a failure and were looking for a new way to fight drugs. He pointed out that all of our television commercials reinforced this theme and thus could hardly be considered deceptive. "What's deceptive about saying that the War on Drugs is a failure?" Cohen queried. He also pointed to our group of distinguished citizen sponsors of the initiative and took offense at some of the accusations made by Senators Kyl and Hatch: "The contention that the people of Arizona were duped is absurd. I'm not soft-headed. Former Senator Dennis DeConcini is not soft-headed. Barry Goldwater is not soft-headed."

The reaction to the hearing was not what the drug warriors anticipated. In Arizona, people found it hard to believe that the U.S. Senate was effectively saying that millions of voters were not smart enough to know what they were voting for in approving Proposition 200. On radio talk shows and in letters to the editor, hundreds of voters, both for and against Proposition 200, expressed outrage at the arrogance of the Senate, especially of Arizona Senator Jon Kyl.

Typical was Ann Gillespie's letter to *The Arizona Republic:* "The wide margin by which Proposition 200 passed was a pleasant surprise, even though we all knew it was a single round in a long uphill battle. Senator Jon Kyl showed abundant stupidity and cowardice when he ran whining to the Senate Judiciary Committee rather than staying in this state to find out why the vote went the way it did. He also showed by his actions that he cannot be trusted to represent our state in Congress. It might be worthwhile to test the waters for a possible recall campaign." And Kyl heard the voters. He submitted an apology to *The Arizona Republic* for his remarks to the Senate Judiciary Committee: "Recently I have been criticized for comments I've made after the passage of Proposition 200, the Drug Medicalization, Prevention and Control Act. Judging from that criticism, it is obvious I used the wrong words."

The U.S. Senate Judiciary hearing served only as a warm-up. Undeterred by the negative reaction to Senator Hatch's hearing, on December 30, 1996, Drug Czar Barry McCaffrey, Attorney General Janet Reno, and Secretary of Health and Human Services Donna Shalala held a joint press conference to announce that they would vigorously prosecute doctors who prescribed medical marijuana even though state law permitted them to do so.

The Repeal and the Referendum

One might think that Senator Kyl's apology for calling the voters who sent him to the Senate "dupes" when they approved Proposition 200 might have sent a message to state legislators. Wrong—we're talking about the Arizona legislature. Throughout December of 1996, the Arizona State Senate Judiciary Committee Chairman, Senator John Kaites, and House Judiciary Chairman, Mike Gardiner, worked behind the scenes on a complete repeal of Proposition 200.

The reason we had originally resorted to the initiative process is because the politicians are absolutely phobic on the drug issue. The fact that we now had the will of the voters behind us did not stop the governor from almost vetoing the measure, the U.S. Senate Judiciary Committee from denouncing Arizona voters as duped, or the federal government from threatening doctors. And the fact that 65 percent of voters approved Proposition 200 didn't stop the Arizona legislature.

In the face of the two-to-one Republican control of the legislature, we now had to put together a Republican lobbying team. Ed Wrenn, who had lobbied for law enforcement and the liquor industry, was our primary lobbyist. Our other lobbyist was the late Jeff Nelson, a Mormon with a Harvard Ph.D. and a brilliant political strategist, with many ties to socially conservative legislators. Nelson had helped us in the Proposition 200 campaign with opposition intelligence.

Senator Kaites steered the opposition. He conducted a stealth campaign by not introducing the repeal legislation until the last day the bills could be introduced. He also did not show his hand as to the scope of the so-called implementation legislation. Kaites cut up the repeal into three bills. H.B. 1190 reduced the number of prisoners eligible for parole from 1,000 to 100 by requiring that the prisoner have no prior criminal history. S.B. 1373 gutted the mandatory treatment for first- and second-time offenders and replaced it with a drug court. H.B. 2518 gutted the use and prescription of medical marijuana and other Schedule 1 drugs by making our law contingent on the approval of the federal Food and Drug Administration (FDA).

H.B. 1190 sailed through the legislature without much ado. Both Democrats and Republicans feared releasing prisoners into the street. We emphasized that these prisoners would only be eligible for a review by the Board of Executive Clemency, who could reject any prisoner deemed a danger to society, but the legislators were imagining Willie Horton commercials being run against them. Furthermore, the press was not interested in this, as they were focusing on the status of the medical marijuana law. H.B. 1190 also had an emergency clause, meaning that if it received a two-thirds majority vote in both chambers, then the bill took immediate effect and could not be stopped by a citizen referendum process. The bill received the necessary votes, thereby permanently emasculating the prison release component of Proposition 200.

We conducted our battle over H.B. 2518 and S.B. 1373 because these measures would have collectively repealed our entire initiative.

The supporters of the repeal argued that voters didn't know all the details of Proposition 200, such as the fact that it included all Schedule 1 drugs and not just marijuana. These legislators argued further that they were not repealing the ballot measure, but merely "fine-tuning" or "implementing" the ballot measure. From our intelligence sources, we had found out that County Attorney Rick Romley and McCaffrey's office were in the process of conducting a poll to show voters would vote against Proposition 200 now that it had been explained to them. We knew that the opposition was merely engaging in a phony push poll that would result in the numbers they sought. We hired our pollster, Paul Maslin, to conduct a real poll.

The dueling poll results were released on February 5. Romley's poll was a farce. Even though the ballot measure expressly excluded drug dealers, Romlely's poll, conducted by a local pollster, Bruce Merill, queried: "Do you think people who plea-bargained their sentences down from charges of dealing in drugs should be released from jail or prison?" Not surprisingly on that question, 88 percent responded "no" and 8 percent said "yes."

Maslin's survey simply read the provisions of the measure. He included in this list even the more controversial provisions such as other Schedule 1 drugs like heroin and parole for those serving drug possession sentences in prison. Even after all the hype by the Drug Czar's office and the U.S. Senate following the election, Proposition 200 still held a 20-point lead: 56 percent yes, 36 percent no, and 8 percent undecided.

Included in Maslin's poll was a further question, which would inform our strategy in the coming year:

Which of the following comes closer to your opinion (statements are rotated)?

- *The voters were duped by the sponsors of Prop. 200 and the new law will make our drug problem worse. Therefore it is important that our State Legislators and law enforcement try and repeal Proposition 200.*
- *Politicians have no right to try and repeal Prop. 200 which was passed legally by the voters. The voters made their decision and our elected officials should abide by it.*

To this question, 59 percent said that the politicians have no right to repeal, while only 28 percent supported the repeal. What became obvious is that when framed as a "will of the people" issue our support dramatically rose to the level of our 1996 two-to-one ballot victory. Henceforth, we choose not to redebate the 1996 ballot measure. Our sole argument became: "The people have spoken!"

The day after the passage of the third bill gutting Proposition 200, we introduced the son of Proposition 200: an initiative to be titled, "The Voter Protection Act," which we would place on the 1998 ballot. The initiative would make it impossible for legislators to repeal or even tinker with voter-approved ballot measures. We also created a campaign committee, "The People Have Spoken," which would allow us to target for defeat legislators who voted to undermine successful initiatives. The Voter Protection Act also ensured that our next referendum would be the Will of the People versus the legislature, rather than the question of whether doctors should be able to prescribe heroin and LSD without FDA approval. In terms of framing the issue, we achieved our desired result. A headline on the front page of *The Arizona Republic* boldly read: "PROP. 200 FUROR PROMPTS INITIATIVE: 'WILL OF THE PEOPLE IS BEING TRAMPLED'."

Fortunately, Arizona's constitutional founders have provided a remedy for citizens who disagree with the legislators. In addition to placing laws on the ballot through an initiative, citizens can stop a law from going into effect through a referendum. Within 90 days after the legislature closes, a sponsor of a referendum must collect 57,000 valid signatures to stop the law from taking effect. If the signatures are approved by the Secretary of State, at the next general election voters are asked either to vote "yes" that they agree with the legislative action or "no" that they wish to nullify the legislative action.

On April 24, The People Have Spoken filed petitions for a referendum to stay the implementation of H.B. 2518 and S.B. 1373. The signature-gathering process went fairly smoothly, considering it was conducted over a very hot summer. On July 16, 1997, we filed nearly 200,000 signatures (100,000 per initiative), nearly twice the statutory requirement. The petitions easily qualified, ensuring that Proposition 200 would remain alive and well until our rematch in November of 1998.

The National Strategy: 1998 Elections

As the Arizona Legislature was repealing Proposition 200, the Oregon Legislature was repealing the most progressive marijuana decriminalization law in the country. The law had been on the books for 24 years, but law enforcement sought changes in response to the perceived drug liberalization in Arizona and California. It was now obvious that the 1996 victories had created a national drug policy reform movement whose ripples and backlashes were being felt across America.

We decided that a national strategy was needed to focus the energy that had been unleashed by the Arizona and California initiatives. We needed a strategy to continue deconstructing the hysterical premises of the Drug War as exemplified by the slogans: "Marijuana is a Gateway Drug" and "Do Drugs, Do Time." All this to support the fraudulent claim that any drug law reform would send the wrong message to children. Presumably, putting tens of thousands of African-American fathers in prison on drug charges was sending the right message to African-American children.

Targeting additional states for medical marijuana was an inexpensive way of continuing the deconstruction of the government's demonization of marijuana. By opposing the legislative actions in Arizona and Oregon through referendums, we could also preserve the voters' mandate that treating drug users is a better way than incarcerating them.

We conducted polls in Arizona, Oregon, and seven other states. The polls showed that the referendums in Arizona and Oregon looked solid and that medical marijuana could be approved in the following states: Alaska, Washington, Oregon, Nevada, Colorado, Maine, and the District of Columbia. These states, combined with Arizona's Voter Protection Act, would give us a total of 11 ballot propositions for the 1998 election.

It was obvious from both the state and national polling that Americans believe the Drug War is a complete failure, but at the same time any vehicle for voters to express this sentiment was lacking. Politicians refused to offer alternatives, so the yearning for new drug policies remained subjugated knowledge. Arizona and California had certainly let the genie out of the bottle, but the only way to continue to promote a seismic shift in public opinion was to offer them concrete vehicles to reject the Drug War. We wanted to emulate the U.S. Term Limits strategy, which passed ballot measures in every state with the initiative process and also caused a revolution in the way Americans view politics. I talked with Peter Lewis and George Soros, who along with myself had funded 90 percent of the Arizona and California campaigns, and they agreed to put in $2 million a piece, for a total budget of $6 million to wage a national campaign.

The medical marijuana polling was solid, with each state polling "yes" at 60 percent or better. The more difficult challenges would be Arizona and Oregon, both of which had two measures on the ballot at the same time. In Arizona, the polling data was by far the closest. A poll conducted in the summer of 1998 showed that the referendums were bound to be tighter than our 65 percent to 35 percent victory. This was because the politicians had torn the two most controversial provisions of Proposition 200 from the entire package to be the subject of the votes.

A poll conducted in Arizona over the summer showed some cause for concern. When asked whether or not the FDA should approve drugs before they are prescribed in Arizona, voters responded with 50 percent approving and 45 percent disapproving. Then, voters were asked a similar question on incarcerating drug offenders in contradiction to the initiative that called for treatment: 51 percent approved and 40 percent disapproved. However, when immediately asked how they would vote on the referendums to repeal Proposition 200, the actual vote turned into a statistical dead heat with 41 percent supporting the legislature and 42 percent opposing the repeal. The message was clear; if we debated solely the content of the measures, we could lose. However, by framing the debate in terms of whether the Legislature had the right to repeal the Will of the People, we had an excellent chance of winning the campaign. As our earlier polling had shown, the message was simple. "Vote 'no' on 300, Vote 'no' on 301: Let the Will of the People Stand."

The Oregon campaign provided a similar dynamic. The difference was that voters were asked to vote "yes" on Ballot Measure 67, which legalized medical marijuana, and "no" on Measure 57, which, if approved, would recriminalize marijuana. A poll conducted in the fall showed that Measure 67 was in solid shape with 62 percent supporting medical marijuana. Measure 57 was a closer vote with 43 percent voting "yes" for the legislative repeal of marijuana decriminalization and 52 percent voting "no."

What complicated the Oregon campaign was that we could not run simply a "no-no" campaign as in Arizona. It is awkward and confusing to voters to run a synchronized "yes-no" campaign. A further problem was that we had learned from Arizona that the nonincarceration-of-drug-users message created dissonance with the medical marijuana message. It was difficult to run simultaneous advertising. Considering the 49 percent definite "yes" on medical marijuana, we decided to throw all our resources into the "no" vote on decriminalization. Medical marijuana was our race to lose and the "no" campaign on Measure 57 (recriminalizing marijuana) would provide cover by focusing the debate entirely on recriminalization. We would run a "no" advertising campaign on Measure 57 and let Measure 67 slide over the line on its own momentum.

The medical marijuana campaigns in the other states went fairly smoothly. There was no need to develop extensive local groups because the polling showed that patients and doctors were by far the most reputable spokespersons. We recruited a key doctor and patient for each state. Our main problem was signature gathering. In Maine, a winter storm made it impossible for us to gather the signatures necessary to be placed in the 1998 ballot, so we were forced to qualify Maine for November of 1999. Another problem occurred in the summer. We had simultaneous signature deadlines in Washington, Oregon, Nevada, and Colorado. The low unemployment had made it difficult to recruit the number of circulators necessary for each state. This meant that the circulators had to travel from state to state. We qualified the necessary signatures in all states, but in Colorado the Secretary of State claimed that signatures gathered by persons who were not Colorado citizens were invalid, and thus, we had not obtained the required number. As it turned out, the ruling was incorrect, so it was agreed to place our initiative on the ballot in 2000.

In all states, with the exception of Arizona, law enforcement served as the chief opponent. In Arizona, a group called Citizens Against Heroin was organized, consisting mostly of local politicians. Stan Barnes, the chairman of the group, was a talk radio host and former legislator. The opposition campaigns did little to generate visibility or to raise money. Before the final month of the campaigns, in all eight states, the opposition had held only three press conferences and spent no money on advertising. We expected very little paid advertising against us, so we waited for the last two weeks of the campaign to conduct our media campaign. Further, we did not seek out free media because we thought it would just give a soapbox to the opposition.

In Arizona, there was more activity around the Voter Protection Act than on the drug issue. Not only did the measure serve as a useful tool in framing the drug propositions, it was unexpectedly serving as something of a diversion. The Voter Protection Act in its final form required that the Legislature have a three-fourths supermajority of both houses before it could amend an initiative or referendum and these amendments could only be to further the purpose of the Act. America's toughest sheriff, Joe Arpaio, and Arizona Attorney General Grant Woods agreed to cochair the campaign committee behind the ballot measure called the Voter Protection Alliance. The measure also had strong support from various Indian tribes, who needed to preserve the integrity of the initiative process to protect their gaming projects.

Our opposition recognized the power of the Voter Protection Act and the historic consequences of its passage. The Act was polling at 75 percent "yes" and the only way the politicians could stop this train was to create their own watered-down version to confuse voters and to split the vote. The good news was that, rather than debating the drug issue, our opposition spent the first five months of 1998 in an effort to get the Legislature to approve its own version, which we labeled the "Politician's Protection Act." After a huge legislative battle, the Legislature narrowly approved the Politician's Protection Act, which allowed the politicians to amend and repeal ballot measures with a two-thirds supermajority. This would definitely complicate our efforts. We had assumed, because of the polling numbers, that there would be no need for a media campaign for the Voter Protection Act. We had also ruled out a cumbersome, united campaign that would ask for a "no-no" vote on the drug propositions and a "yes" vote on the Voter Protection Act. Now, two media campaigns would be necessary for the two related but different issues.

In July of 1998, our opposition in Arizona did find an insidious way of undermining our campaign by getting the Arizona Legislative Counsel to change its description of the ballot measure for the secretary of state's publicity pamphlet, which would ultimately affect the language voters would see on the ballot. While the original draft had mentioned only marijuana, Representative Mike Gardiner, whose wife happened to be employed by the opposition, got the Counsel to add LSD, heroin, and PCP to the description. Our attorney, Former Attorney General Jack La Sota, vigorously fought the change, but the so-called objective description remained ultimately in the hands of the legislators—the very people who had repealed our measure.

The Arizona Legislative Council language had affected our favorable ballot description in 1996, but this time it severely hurt us. Working off the counsel's description, the staff of the Arizona Secretary of State wrote the following question, which voters would see on the 1998 ballot:

A "Yes" vote shall have the effect of requiring authorization from the Federal Food and Drug Administration or the United States Congress for the medical use of marijuana before it will be lawful for doctors to prescribe Schedule 1 drugs, including heroin, LSD, marijuana and analogs of PCP to seriously or terminally ill patients in Arizona.

A "No" vote shall have the effect of retaining the provisions of state law allowing doctors to prescribe Schedule 1 drugs, including heroin, LSD, marijuana, and analogs of PCP to seriously or terminally ill patients without the authorization of the Federal Food and Drug Administration or the United States Congress.

Proposition 200 had stipulated that doctors must document scientific research before prescribing a Schedule 1 drug. The street drugs such as LSD and PCP had no scientific research to support their use. Those drugs introduced by the Legislative Counsel were listed only to scare voters away from voting "no." The language was so biased that we decided to file a lawsuit against the Arizona Legislative Counsel and the Arizona Secretary of State.

On July 31, 1998, Maricopa County Superior Court Judge Joseph Howe ruled that the language must be rewritten because the listing of street drugs on the ballot amounts to turning the official description into what appears to be an "advocacy document." This was a historic decision, since no one had ever got the Secretary of State to rewrite its ballot language. However, the victory was short-lived. The state appealed to the Arizona Supreme Court, which concluded that listing the street drugs "can be regarded as an attempt to provide appropriate and necessary information to the voting public."

By mid-October, the final stage was set in Arizona and across the country for our media blitz. In the medical marijuana states—Alaska,

Washington, Nevada, Colorado—our commercials hit the airwaves unanswered by the opposition. In the District of Columbia, we used targeted direct mail since it was a local election with very low turnout. The advertising featured doctors who had prescribed marijuana and could authoritatively say it worked and patients who could pull on the heartstrings with their emotional stories. The joint appeal to voters' rationality and feelings was a powerful message.

In Oregon, the advertising against the Legislature's attempt to recriminalize marijuana mirrored the 1996 Proposition 200 advertising. In one commercial, criminal prosecutor and State Senator Floyd Prozanski stands before a prison with barbed wire. "Our jails are so overcrowded each day we're putting dangerous criminals back on the street. Now, the Legislature's passed a foolish law. It will put people in jail for up to 30 days for possession of just one marijuana cigarette. That means we're going to have to release more and more of the dangerous criminals. . . . Vote No on 57."

The advertising in Arizona all centered around the Will of the People message. The first commercial showed people voting in 1996 to approve Proposition 200 by 65.4 percent. In the corner of the picture flashed the endorsements of former U.S. Senator Dennis DeConcini, the late Barry Goldwater, and three of the four major newspapers. Then, against a seedy image of the Legislature, a text of Proposition 200 bursts into fire as voters are told about the legislative repeal. As the announcer states, "By voting 'no' on Propositions 300 and 301, you will restore your vote . . . ," the flaming Proposition 200 text slowly morphs back into its original form. Another commercial featured a terminal cancer patient, Josh Burner. Rather than making an emotional plea for medical marijuana, the patient makes a pitch based on the Will of the People message: "Don't let the politicians take your vote away. Don't let them take my medicine away. Vote No on Propositions 300 and 301. Let the Will of the People Stand."

This message was indirectly reinforced in Arizona by our advertising campaign for the Voter Protection Act. My son Peter agreed to fund a radio campaign featuring Sheriff Joe Arpaio. The Sheriff broadened the message by noting that the Legislature had attempted to repeal many other ballot measures besides Proposition 200. Arpaio made a key distinction between the legislature's ersatz measure, The Politician Protection Act, and our measure, the Voter Protection Act. A statewide campaign of 1,000 signs also reinforced this message, which read: "Vote Yes on 105, The Voter Protection Act, and Vote No on 104, the Politician Protection Act."

The election results of November 3, 1998, proved nothing short of a national mandate for drug policy reform. We won all of our elections, going 10 for 10 with an average margin of victory of 15 points per election. Our drug policy reform effort became only the second movement (next to U.S. Term Limits) to sponsor so many victories in one election cycle. Whereas the federal government and politicians had blasted the 1996 victories before the votes had been counted, this time there was nothing but a deathly silence from our opposition, a tacit acknowledgment that the writing was on the wall for the Drug War.

The Afterglow

The ultimate success of a political movement is when objective authorities outside the movement validate its premises, and that's exactly what happened in the wake of the 1998 elections. Two reports, issued by the Institute of Medicine (IOM) and the Arizona Supreme Court, proved that what we had been saying throughout the campaigns was true.

As a response to the 1996 elections in Arizona and California, Drug Czar Barry McCaffrey had commissioned the Institute of Medicine to conduct a $1-million-dollar study to determine whether marijuana had any medical use and whether it was a gateway drug. Of course, McCaffrey had hoped that the report would simply dismiss marijuana and affirm the government's demonization of marijuana. The final IOM report released on March 17, 1999, came to quite the opposite conclusion and came close to saying that everything the government had been asserting about marijuana was wrong. The IOM report concluded:

1. Marijuana is a useful medication. The IOM report found significant evidence that marijuana relieves pain, reduces nausea, and increases appetite effects that have been especially beneficial for people with AIDS and cancer. Moreover, marijuana's sedative and antianxiety effects, the report notes, "might be desirable for certain patients."
2. Marijuana is not a gateway drug. According to the IOM, alcohol and cigarettes, not marijuana, are the first substances used by peo-

ple who progress to harder drugs. There is no biochemical basis for concluding that using marijuana "primes" individuals for the use of other drugs.

3.   Allowing marijuana's medical use will not increase recreational use. Opponents of medical marijuana fear that sanctioning medical use will increase its use in the general population. The IOM report says that "there are no convincing data to support this concern."

4.   Marijuana has insignificant addictive potential. The IOM notes that "few marijuana users develop dependence." When withdrawal symptoms appear, they are "mild and short-lived."

5.   Marijuana should be immediately provided for research and to terminally ill patients. The IOM recommends that the government's Compassion Use Program be opened up to provide marijuana to terminally ill patients and for additional research on medical marijuana.

With the government's myths to demonize marijuana definitively refuted by its own study, its "Do Drugs, Do Time" thesis would soon come under attack by the Arizona Supreme Court. Proposition 200 had called for the Supreme Court to conduct a cost-effectiveness study after the first year of implementation. On April 20, 1999, the Supreme Court issued a 32-page study proving that Proposition 200 was saving the state money and reducing crime.

The report revealed that in Fiscal Year 1998, 2,622 drug offenders were diverted into treatment instead of incarcerated under Proposition 200 (referred to here as the Drug Treatment and Education Fund [DTEF]). According to the Supreme Court, the results were outstanding:

> The outcomes reported in this DTEF Report Card are very favorable. The 98.2% matching rate between recommended and actual placement is remarkable and would not [have] occurred without DTEF funding. . . . The majority (77.5%) of urinalysis were negative for drug use, and 77.1% of those who had co-payments ordered made at least one payment. . . . For fiscal year 1998, it is estimated that the DTEF program saved at least $2,563,062. In addition, it is projected that savings for Fiscal Year 1999 will increase significantly. . . . All of these factors are resulting in safer communities and more substance abusing probationers in recovery.

Even though the Supreme Court Report on the results of Proposition 200 came out the same day as the Littleton, Colorado, shooting, it became a national news story with prominent coverage in the *New York Times,* the *Los Angeles Times,* the *Chicago Tribune, Newsday,* the *Christian Science Monitor,* and 31 other newspapers across the country. In addition, *USA Today,* the *New York Times,* the *Chicago Tribune, Newsday,* and the *Christian Science Monitor* were among the nine major editorial boards that endorsed Arizona's Proposition 200 treatment programs. The *Washington Post*'s David Broder also endorsed the programs in his nationally syndicated column.

The *New York Times* April 24, 1999, editorial, "Arizona Shows the Way on Drugs," was indicative of the national editorial support: "Arizona voters, tired of paying the exorbitant costs of imprisoning drug users and addicts who might be helped more cheaply, voted twice to provide a treatment alternative to jail. Now an Arizona Supreme Court study of the first year of probation with mandatory drug treatment instead of prison has shown the apparent wisdom of that decision. Congress and the legislatures of New York and other states should take heed . . ."

What will be the ultimate policy result of our deconstruction of the Drug War? Will it lead to decriminalization? Will it lead to a drug treatment state? Or, will it lead to drug legalization? I don't think we can answer these questions today. It is clear that popular support for the Drug War is low and getting lower. There was zero popular support for the campaign against Proposition 200. A democracy cannot fight a war forever without popular support. Each time the drug warriors put out another press release with a picture of confiscated bales of various drugs, public cynicism grows because we all know that 10 times that amount was not confiscated.

The initiative process remains our most powerful tool. However, now that our opponents are on the rhetorical defensive, maybe we can finally convince the politicians that drug reform is no longer the third rail of politics. One thing is for certain: When they write the story of the end of the Drug War, they will look back to the 1996 ballot victories in Arizona and California as the decisive turning point that was so resoundingly reaffirmed by the 10 victories of 1998. *The People Have Spoken, Will The Politicians Please Pay Heed?*

14

Epilogue

The Colloquium

As I was finishing this autobiography, I began to wonder what, if any, were the organizing principles that underlay the seemingly disparate endeavors in which I am engaged—higher education, seawater agriculture, age-management medicine, animal cloning, and finally, drug policy reform. In thinking about the matter, it was clear that a love of the new and controversial was evident in all of the activities, but that was a rather unedifying principle. Then, there was the ego-gratifying principle that all of them were dedicated to the betterment of mankind, but this left unanswered the question of just how were they benefiting mankind. To answer this, I needed the help of the people who were running these enterprises/activities, so I decided to convene a colloquium. On March 15, 1999, I sent the following memorandum:

Memorandum

To: Distribution
From: John Sperling
Date: March 15, 1999
Re: A modest proposal

A Sperling Colloquium

I realize that the title of this piece sounds egotistical but I can't think of a better beginning for what I have to propose. I would like to gather the various (some might say disparate) strands of my intellectual/entrepreneurial/political activities in one place for a colloquium among those responsible for these activities. I would hope that reports on the activities followed by discussions among the presenters might be productive of new ideas/insights/businesses. The activities are in order of their beginnings:

- Apollo Group and its subsidiaries: educational/entrepreneurial
- Seaphire International: agricultural/scientific/entrepreneurial
- Drug Law Reform: socio-political
- Genetic Savings and Clone: animal husbandry/scientific/entrepreneurial
- Kronos: medical/scientific/entrepreneurial

The persons invited to attend are:

Apollo: myself, Todd Nelson, Jorge Klor de Alva

Seaphire International: Carl Hodges, Roy Hodges, David Bush

Drug Law Reform: Sam Vagenas, Jeff Singer

Genetic Savings & Clone: Louis Hawthorne, Mark Westhusin, Duane Kraemer

Kronos: Jonathan Thatcher, Tali Arik, Richard Cutler

I have asked each participant to prepare a statement (maximum of 3 pages) explaining how the activities in which he is engaged contribute to human well-being in the present and how these activities are likely to contribute to human well-being in the coming century, especially in light of the challenges and opportunities that may be anticipated. I will forward copies of these statements to each participant.

I am proposing that we meet in Phoenix beginning with dinner at my house on a Friday evening, meet all day Saturday ending with dinner at my house on Saturday night. If there is reason for a wrap-up session, we can have a final session on Sunday morning. I will pay air fare and lodging for out-of-town participants.

All of the invitees submitted their statements, and all wrote convincingly of why their efforts were contributing to the welfare of mankind—some thought this was taking place now, but most of them thought in terms of the future.

Because of conflicting schedules, the Colloquium did not convene until the weekend of June 25–27, and it was scorching hot. Only three could not attend—Jeff Singer, David Bush, and Carl Hodges who was in Eritrea. The proceedings began with cocktails and dinner Friday night, and by the end of the evening everyone had had an opportunity to establish his philosophical position and scientific principles.

With a professor of poststructural anthropology; a Foucaultian political operative; cutting-edge plant, animal, and human biological scientists; a couple of highly skilled managers; and myself in attendance, cocktail conversation segued from Democritus and Heraclitus to Hume and Kant, to Heisenberg and Searle, to a gaggle of biological scientists I never heard of. But beyond the sometimes raucous exchanges, there was a real opportunity to take stock of what each group claimed to have accomplished, and the evening ended with shared intellectual respect.

The War against the War on Drugs

On Saturday, the formal presentations began with Sam Vagenas, my political genius who shared with us videotapes of news coverage and follow-ups to Proposition 200—the nation's first victory in the War against the War on Drugs. We sat dumbfounded as the likes of drug czar Barry McCaffrey, Arizona Senator John Kyl, and Utah Senator Orrin Hatch perpetrated hearings to address the "crisis" created by our victories in Arizona and California. At one point these drug warriors talked of trying to prosecute George Soros, Peter Lewis, and me under the RICO statutes. Each time they spoke of the devious, manipulative forces responsible for this victory, we gave Sam a rousing cheer as he sat smiling beside the television set.

Sam deconstructed the competing media campaigns video clip by video clip as he passed around a mound of clippings that ended with a *New York Times* article reporting the praise bestowed on Proposition 200 by the Arizona Supreme Court. For Sam, the hysterical rhetoric of the drug warriors was merely one more text to deconstruct.

Seaphire

Next up was Seaphire International, the saltwater agricultural company devoted to turning salicornia into a viable crop. Roy Hodges made the presentation alone since his father Carl and the other scientists were in Eritrea working on a 50/50 joint venture with the Ministry of Fisheries, the goal of which is to turn 1,200 kilometers of barren Red Sea coast into productive salicornia and shrimp farms.

In addition to plans for building farms in Mexico, Africa, India, and China, Roy reported on advances in plant breeding, growing, harvesting, and processing salicornia. He also reported on a growing collaboration between the plant breeders at Seaphire and the plant geneticists at Monsanto who were also working on salicornia—a collaboration that could cut in half the time needed to develop a viable saltwater farming industry.

Certainly, time is of the essence, because only 2.5 percent of the world's water is fresh and it is already in short supply—seawater agriculture must be a part of how we feed the billions of new inhabitants expected in this century. Salicornia is at the stage of development that traditional breeding is more effective and rapid than genetic alteration. However, if genetic alteration could double salicornia yields, one can be assured that Eritreans and other inhabitants of areas with barren coasts or salinized soils will welcome any bounty whether from traditional breeding or genetic alteration. Perhaps of more long-term importance is understanding how the genetic structure of salicornia could lead to other salt-tolerant food crops. When there is no more freshwater to expand agriculture, I would imagine that even the Europeans will be glad to eat foods from genetically altered salt-tolerant wheat, corn, and soy.

Kronos

Jonathan Thatcher, CEO, and Tali Arik, President of Kronos, aren't working to feed humanity, but rather to extend the human "health span." They described work on the August opening of the first Kronos Clinic in Phoenix and the coming on line of the Kronos state-of-the-art clinical laboratory. However, their really big news was the plan to launch kronosclinic.com in early 2000. It will be the first Internet/Web-based application to a medical specialty. It will allow Kronos to treat patients anywhere in the U.S. and then anywhere in the world where we can build a Kronos laboratory. Unfortunately, Kronos will face an even more complex regulatory environment than Apollo. Will our political skills honed at Apollo transfer to Kronos?

What Tali and Jonathan described at Kronos is the first clinically based model for managing wellness, which is an industry expected to grow by 15 percent a year over the next five years. Health care was a $155 billion industry in 1998; that will grow to a $258 billion industry in 2001. The demographics of aging alone will provide 14 percent growth. They projected 20,000 patients under care by the summer of 2000. That's why we've constructed a lab that can handle 25,000 patient profiles a month.

Dr. Richard Cutler, President of Kronos Science, gave a stunningly effective power-point presentation on the processes of aging and the role that free radicals play in those processes and the therapies designed to slow the aging processes. He concluded with an explanation of how Kronos' therapies—vitamins, minerals, hormones, nutrition, exercise, cogniceuticals, and pharmaceuticals—are designed to reduce damage and to facilitate the repair of damaged cells, mitochondria, and DNA, and in the process, improve physical and mental function. All of this provides people the best chance to grow old healthily.

Chris Heward is the head of Kronos' endocrine research unit. Ironically, his presentation was delayed until the cocktail hour, but we knew the timing was perfect when he uttered the memorable phrase, ". . . with Compound 1 you get the tan, with Compound 2 you get the tan and the erection. . . ." This was met with understandably high spirits. Chris has spent years researching melanin, the pigment responsible for darkening of the skin, and melatonin, which has remarkable antioxidant properties, a key to prolonging health. But before he began work with Kronos, he had sought a way of using melanin receptors to locate and treat tumors. That's how he happened upon Compound 1, a very potent peptide molecule that causes tanning without skin damage. He was courted by Ortho, who estimated that this could yield a $250-million-a-year product in cream form . . . if only it could penetrate the skin.

This prompted Chris to investigate ways of making the molecule water-soluble, which led to the discovery of Compound 2. With this water-soluble version, you still get the tan, but when it is injected into males, they obtain up to eight-hour erections without the usual dangers of priapism! Females experience arousal for up to 24 hours . . . AND it contributes to weight loss! Needless to say, with pharmaceutical companies spending millions to develop ever more effective lifestyle drugs (for example, Viagra for females), there is economic promise in there somewhere. In order to explore that promise, Chris has formed a company called Pepticrine, in which Kronos has a 12 percent stake.

The Mother Ships

Todd Nelson and Jorge Klor de Alva, the captains of the mother ships, the Apollo Group and the University of Phoenix (UOP), were considerably less ribald than Chris Heward, but equally upbeat as they outlined the continued growth and prosperity of the educational innovations the Apollo companies have pioneered. They described Apollo's continued national expansion, which seeks to have a University of Phoenix facility within a 20-minute commute of 75 percent of the urban population, and its first foray overseas—a campus in Rotterdam. First America, then the world.

Eighty percent of UOP students are in the newly named John Sperling School of Business, with the second greatest number in the School of Education, Health, and Human Services. University of Phoenix's MBA in Information Technology, developed in partnership with Intel, is a highly prized degree for those hoping for careers in the cyber economy of the future; e-business degrees at both the bachelor's and master's levels are ready for rollout. But the real excitement came from their discussion of distance learning. With over 10,000 distance learning students, the University has the nation's largest Internet-based program, and it has a 60 percent annual growth rate. They were loath to speculate on where the Online program might lead, but it was clear that they were acting locally but thinking globally.

GS&C

The last report came from Genetic Savings & Clone (GS&C), a company that is seeking to commercialize some of the work being done on animal reproduction at Texas A&M University. GS&C is a start-up biotechnology company that will market advanced genetic services directly to the general public over the Internet. GS&C's initial mission is to store the DNA of exceptional animals in cellular form, and eventually to provide cloning services for these exceptional animals—endangered species, guide and rescue dogs, and farm animals. A hoped-for spin-off will be a canine and feline contraceptive that will end the need to kill millions of unwanted domestic pets.

The project is headed by Louis Hawthorne, an artist-cum-apprentice entrepreneur, who reported on the work done to get GS&C's physical plant built and management hired, but the most exciting part of his presentation dealt with building the GS&C web site and his ideas for marketing its services on the Web. We all agreed that, if it works as Louis outlined it, it will be a great financial success.

The last presentations were by Mark Westhusin, a veterinary physiologist, and Duane Kraemer, a doctor of veterinary medicine and veterinary physiology, who gave power-point presentations on animal cloning. They were as stunningly engrossing as Cutler was on human aging. It was clear that animal cloning is a race to see which group can turn cloning into a financially viable business. This scientific race is not quite as noble as mapping the human genome, but to the scientists involved, it is equally compelling. When they had finished, we all understood that GS&C was just the first step in a potentially gigantic business.

As I sat looking at their final slide, a murky ultrasound of a cloned canine fetus, I realized how, truly, the best/worst was yet to come. God knows what kind of trouble I will make for myself in the years ahead, but the business synergies and the possibilities for doing some good are too engrossing to forgo, whatever the trouble that might ensue.

What Is to Be Done?

Answering the same question posed in Lenin's 1902 pamphlet, *What Is to Be Done?*, seems a good way to bring this long essay to a close. Lenin wanted a kind of socialism that has now been cast into the dustbin of history, but the question still has resonance both for societies and individuals. At 79, the question for myself might better be rephrased to "What is left to be done?" and I hope the answer is "LOTS."

Fortunately, Todd Nelson and Jorge Klor de Alva are doing quite well at running the mother ships, which gives me the time and energy to promote new ventures. Apollo International is developing according to plan, and we have completed most of the work on three Apollo Internet spin-offs. The first to be spun off is the University of Phoenix Online campus, with a current enrollment of over 12,000 students and growing at 60 percent per annum, versus a growth rate of 18 percent for the classroom-based campuses. This gives the University an overall growth rate of 20 percent and Apollo Group a market value of $1.8 billion. Within the University, the Online campus is greatly undervalued, but as a stand-alone company, it would receive full value from the market for its rapid growth. Therefore, we have created University of Phoenix Online, whose stock tracks the performance of the Online campus. This is called a *tracking stock,* and it will be offered in an IPO scheduled for early May 2000.

In addition to University of Phoenix Online, Apollo has created two additional Internet companies—e-learning.com and eduscope .com. E-learning will offer to adult learners the most complete listing of education and training courses and programs designed for the adult learner. Students will be able to enroll, apply for financial aid, receive their course materials, and so on. Each student that registers with e-learning.com will have a web site that contains a record of his/her education and training; based on that record, e-learning will provide articulation to some 200 community colleges and from community colleges to four-year institutions. E-learning.com will offer to registered students all the services the University of Phoenix now offers to its own students. In addition, it will offer a wide variety of ancillary services adult learners find desirable.

Eduscope.com has assembled a group of providers of education and training programs designed for adult learners that includes all of the Apollo Group companies augmented by a portfolio of other education and training companies that will give adult students a single source for practically any course or program they might desire. It is our intention to spin both of these companies off in IPO's.

At this writing, the Kronos Clinic in Phoenix is open and will soon be booked to capacity. More exciting is March 3, 2000; that is the date for the launch of kronosclinic.com. With a network of physicians in 50 states, kronosclinic.com will be the first company to offer medical services to people anywhere in America—and soon, in the world.

At Seaphire, the farms and shrimp ponds in Eritrea are now producing at levels above projections; Monsanto, having fled from biotechnology, has arranged for the transfer of its salicornia research operation to Seaphire. There is a new relationship with the Beijing Salicornia Development Company that could lead to a vast expansion of salicornia and shrimp cultivation on the island of Hainan. In addition, the GS&C web site is up and the first DNA specimens are safe in cryostorage. The launch of GS&C was announced in a flattering article in the March 2000 issue of *Wired* magazine, which launched dozens of TV, radio and print interviews for CEO, Louis Hawthorne.

A Millennial Strategy for the War against the War on Drugs

After winning nine anti–drug war initiatives in the 1998 elections, Peter Lewis, George Soros, and I met the following April for dinner and a chat at Soros' country house. As we discussed the future of our political action and educational efforts, it was agreed that ballot measures bring us far more bang for our buck than public education efforts. Simply put, action educates. This was well illustrated by the national press buzz that followed the successful 1996 medical marijuana initiative in California, which was followed by another buzz when the Arizona Supreme Court blessed Proposition 200, which stopped the incarceration of drug users.

Joining us at dinner were our political operatives, Bill Zimmerman and Sam Vagenas, who outlined a new set of initiatives for the 2000 election. In all the states polled, people were strongly in favor of repealing strict mandatory sentences for drug crimes, decriminalizing marijuana, and placing drug offenders in treatment rather than incarcerating them. In addition, there is a new drug war issue that certainly has electoral legs—asset forfeiture.

The citizenry is eager to end the forfeiture of a person's assets simply on the basis that some law enforcement agency has declared that the asset has been used in the commission of a crime—usually a drug-related crime. As would be expected, citizens believe that Congress, the state legislatures, and the Supreme Court have trashed the Fourth Amendment, that slender reed designed to "protect" our constitutional freedoms. Polls show overwhelming support for the constitutional principle that a citizen must be convicted of a crime before his/her assets are forfeited.

Substituting treatment for incarceration of drug offenders also received overwhelming support. Most surprisingly, the Arizona polls supported an initiative that would decriminalize small amounts of marijuana by substituting a citation and fine in place of a criminal charge plus the establishment of a legal system for distributing medical marijuana.

California will also be a major target state because it is running out of prison space due to drug convictions and the "three strikes and you're out" law. The California initiative will be modeled on Arizona Proposition 200. It will be called the Substance Abuse Treatment and Crime Prevention Act of 2000. It will make drug possession a crime for which nonviolent drug offenders must receive treatment and cannot be incarcerated. The measure also mandates diversion to treatment, instead of reincarceration, for parolees who test dirty or commit drug offenses. This initiative is projected to keep 37,000 people out of prison each year. It will also modify the state's "three strikes and you're out" law to save offenders who have gone five years without a violent crime from facing a "three strikes" sentence for felony drug possession, which now leads to a 25-year-to-life prison sentence. There will be net savings to the state of up to $200 million per year for every year the initiative is in force.

In Oregon and Utah, asset forfeiture will be on the 2000 ballot. Not only will each initiative make it more difficult to seize assets, the proceeds from the sale of forfeited assets must be transferred from law enforcement to drug treatment and prevention programs—alas, there will be no more free paramilitary paraphernalia: night goggles, assault rifles, armored personnel carriers, and battering rams.

In both Colorado and Nevada, the initiatives are sequels to the 1998 medical marijuana campaigns. In Colorado, voters were allowed to vote on a medical marijuana initiative, but the results—60 percent yes to 40 percent no—were disqualified because it was believed that the campaign had not collected the sufficient signatures. Courts later ruled that we had sufficient signatures, so the court placed a new medical marijuana initiative on the 2000 ballot. In Nevada, the state requires that a ballot measure be approved twice before it can take effect. We won 59 percent to 41 percent in 1998. Polling shows that ballot measures in Colorado and Nevada should be approved with margins similar to 1998.

Most of our victories have been in the West, so we are now seeking to expand the Arizona model to a large Eastern state to nationalize the policy of treating users rather than incarcerating them. We have chosen Massachusetts, where the initiative has two central concepts: civil asset forfeiture reform, and a diversion program for low-level drug offenders.

It is in Arizona where we will try to advance on all fronts against the serried ranks of the drug war warriors. Arizona's Drug, Medicalization, Prevention, and Control Act for 2000 seeks to clarify and expand existing law. Since the Legislature had repealed the original Act's requirement that 2,000 nonviolent drug prisoners be paroled, the initiative will reinstate this provision. The other provisions are as follows:

- Drug treatment and prevention will be paid for by those receiving treatment. Confiscated assets that have been forfeited will be placed in the Drug Treatment and Education Fund, with 75 percent of the funding designated for drug treatment and 25 percent designated for drug and gang prevention.
- There will be tougher punishments for serious drug felons, but the mandatory minimum sentences will be removed for nonviolent drug users. The mandatory minimum drug sentences will be repealed, but the maximum penalty for drug crimes—both fines and sentences—will be increased by 20 percent.
- Arizona's marijuana laws, which currently provide that someone caught with a joint could be charged with a felony and possible jail time, will be repealed. Possession for small amounts of marijuana will be changed to a violation and a fine.
- Medical marijuana provisions of the Drug Medicalization, Prevention, and Control Act of 1996 will be updated to ensure that doctors cannot be sanctioned by the federal government and that qualified patients will have access to medical marijuana through a program that will be supervised by the Arizona Attorney General.

I think I have largely answered the question, "What is left to be done?" I have lots to accomplish in what must be a relatively short life.

> The woods are lovely, dark and deep,
> But I have promises to keep . . .
> And far to go before I sleep.

Endnotes

Chapter 5

1. Newman is currently executive director of the Education Commission of the States.
2. For example, when Fr. Martin, the dean of the Graduate Division, resisted accepting the MAEd program, an exchange of letters with Fr. McInnes brought his cooperation (USF, Doc. Nos. 9 and 10).
3. USF Doc. Nos. 20–70, covering the period December 1975 through January 1977.
4. USF Doc. No. 15 Letter, Lloyd Luckmann to Noel Dyer, Pillsbury, Madison & Sutro, January 30, 1975; and USF Doc. No. 16, Letter, Noel Dyer to Lloyd Luckmann.
5. USF Doc. No. 36D, Letter, Kay Anderson to Andrew Pringle, February 20, 1976; and Doc. No. 60, Kay Anderson to Otto Butz, October 15, 1976.
6. USF Doc. No. 69A, Copy of a statement by Captain Jim Bowen, December 8, 1976. Bowen, a student in the USF Master of Arts in Public Service program, is reporting information received from VARO (a unit of the Veterans Affairs Office in Sacramento).
7. USF Doc. No. 37, Letter, Kay Anderson to Fr. McInnes, June 18, 1976.

8. USF, Doc. No. 37, Anderson to McInnes, June 18, 1976.
9. USF Doc. No. 80, Letter from Fr. Lo Schiavo to Kay Anderson, February 17, 1977, transmitting USF's response to the team's report.
10. USF Doc. No. 82, Letter, McIntyre to Sperling, June 23, 1977.
11. At the time, I was not aware of Lo Schiavo's agreement with Anderson. I only learned of it some two years later when the FBI informed me that Lo Schiavo had made a deal with Anderson to terminate the IPD contract in return for USF's accreditation.

Chapter 6

1. Letter, Kay Anderson to Brother Mel Anderson, March 29, 1977.
2. Letter, Brother Mel Anderson to Kay Anderson, March 31, 1977.
3. Letter, Kay Anderson to Don Gomolski, March 31, 1977.
4. Letter, Mel Anderson to Kay Anderson, April 1, 1977.
5. Letter, Richard Mallery to Kay Anderson, May 12, 1977.

Chapter 7

1. Transcript of portion of regular meeting (Board of Regents), November 26, 1977.
2. Letter, Sperling to Woodall, December 1, 1977.
3. Letter, Woodall to Sperling, December 8, 1977.
4. Text of Sperling's remarks before the Arizona Board of Regents, January 13, 1978.
5. North Central Association visiting team, "Report of a Visit to the University of Phoenix," June 8–10, 1978.
6. North Central Association visiting team, "Report on a Visit," August 28–29, 1978.
7. "Report and Recommendations from the North Central Association Committee on Reconsideration," October 27, 1978.
8. Letter, Sperling to Manning, November 3, 1978.
9. "University of Phoenix," Arizona House Staff Report, August 30, 1979.
10. "Accreditation of Arizona's Schools and Colleges," Arizona House Staff Report, August 1979.

Index

259